Build Your Own
Electric Motorcycle

TAB Green Guru Guides

Consulting Editor: Seth Leitman

Renewable Energies for Your Home: Real-World Solutions for Green Conversions
  by Russel Gehrke

Build Your Own Plug-In Hybrid Electric Vehicle by Seth Leitman

Build Your Own Electric Motorcycle by Carl Vogel

Build Your Own
Electric Motorcycle

Carl Vogel

New York   Chicago   San Francisco
Lisbon   London   Madrid   Mexico City
Milan   New Delhi   San Juan
Seoul   Singapore   Sydney   Toronto

The McGraw-Hill Companies

Library of Congress Cataloging-in-Publication Data

Vogel, Carl, date.
    Build your own electric motorcycle / Carl Vogel.
        p.   cm.
    Includes index.
    ISBN 978-0-07-162293-6 (alk. paper)
    1. Electric motorcycles. 2. Home-built motorcycles. I. Title.
TL448.E44V64   2009
629.28'775—dc22   2009020005

McGraw-Hill books are available at special quantity discounts to use as premiums and sales promotions, or for use in corporate training programs. To contact a representative, please e-mail us at bulksales@mcgraw-hill.com.

Build Your Own Electric Motorcycle

2 3 4 5 6 7 8 9 0 DOC/DOC 0 1 5 4 3 2 1 0

ISBN 978-0-07-162293-6
MHID   0-07-162293-4

The pages within this book were printed on acid-free paper containing 100% postconsumer fiber.

© **Mixed Sources**
Product group from well-managed forests, controlled sources and recycled wood or fiber
www.fsc.org Cert no. SCS-COC-00648
© 1996 Forest Stewardship Council
FSC

Sponsoring Editor
    Judy Bass

Editorial Supervisor
    Stephen M. Smith

Production Supervisor
    Richard C. Ruzycka

Project Manager
    Patricia Wallenburg, TypeWriting

Copy Editor
    James Madru

Proofreader
    Teresa Barensfeld

Indexer
    Judy Davis

Art Director, Cover
    Jeff Weeks

Composition
    TypeWriting

About the Author

Carl Vogel is the president of Vogelbilt Corporation, a research, engineering, and development company for alternative fuels and alternative-fueled vehicles. Vogelbilt is in the process of building renewable fueling stations in the New York City area. These stations will function on a platform of sustainability, using wind and solar energy and cogeneration to stay mostly off the grid. Some of the proposed alternative fuels that would be available at the stations are electric, E85, CNG, biodiesel, and hydrogen. Mr. Vogel is also the president of the Long Island chapter of the Electrical Automotive Association (www.LIEAA.org). Previously, he worked at Festo Corporation and Curtis Instruments, planning and designing robotic and programmable logic controller applications for computer-integrated manufacturing (CIM). While at Curtis Instruments Mr. Vogel worked on battery chargers and solid-state motor controllers for electric vehicles. He has also taught at Farmingdale State College, expanding electric vehicle and fuel cell operations R&D on campus.

Contents

Preface

Writing a book about a subject that is so dear to me has been the greatest pleasure. All the hard work and nudging from my editor to get finished have been worth it. Back in 1996, I had an idea that I had never seen before. Well, I had seen it, but not the size and style of the creation I had in mind. I wanted to build a fully electric motorcycle, and not just any motorcycle, but a full-sized motorcycle along the lines of a cruiser or large touring bike. I wanted to build a bike that had power, speed, and performance. After all, I love a good challenge, and if a motorcycle of this size had not been built before, I wanted to do it.

At the time, I came across an enormous motorcycle out on the market called the Boss Hoss. The Boss Hoss was designed in 1990 by Monte Warne, a commercial aircraft pilot. This cruiser-style motorbike was a beast, with a Chevrolet 8.2-liter V8 502-hp engine as standard power. By all means, this was not a green or fuel-efficient machine, but it was an engineering delight and a wonder to look at. This monster weighed in at over 1,300 lb (590 kg)! After seeing this bike, I came to the conclusion that if someone could design a motorcycle with a mammoth V8 Chevy engine, why couldn't I design a motorcycle to house a frame full of batteries? I came to the conclusion that I could design and build an electric bike way under 1,300 lb. From this thought came an idea and a design.

I spent a huge amount of time performing research, looking at all the electric vehicles on the market as well as resources, books, and anything I could find that had information. Unfortunately, there were very few good resources on electric vehicles, and a lot of the material was outdated. Even worse was trying to find any information on two-wheeled electric vehicles, motorcycles, or scooters. One of the best resources I came across was the book *Build Your Own Electric Vehicle* by Bob Brant, published in 1994. The second edition was published in 2009 and contains up-to-date information from authors Seth Leitmen and Bob Brant. Finding this book back in 1996 made this whole venture come together. The book contained many resources and a lot of basic information that was easy to follow and understand by the average person.

My reasons for writing the present book were many. One was to put all the resources and information in one place. I spent hours on hours trying to find information, components, parts, resources, and so much more. I thought how easy and nice it would be if I could find everything I needed in just one place. Another reason was that not everyone has the resources, capital, or time to build an electric car. It is a great project, but too much for some people. This book is a way for an average person to get his or her feet wet without falling in and drowning. I thought how great it would be if there were a book geared to a smaller electric vehicle project that more people could enjoy, build, and finish. The idea was that the reader's project did not have to be a full-out motorcycle, but perhaps a scooter, a smaller dirt bike, or just an average-sized motorcycle. Writing this book was a way to share my experience—the joys and the challenges I faced throughout building an electric motorcycle.

Carl Vogel

Acknowledgments

This book and so many things in life would not have been possible without the great support of my friends and family. Life is hard, but with great people at your side, so much is possible.

Some great sayings that I live by:

> "In order to succeed, your desire for success must be greater than your fear of failure."—Bill Cosby
>
> "Don't go where the path may lead; go instead where there is no path and leave a trail."—Ralph Waldo Emerson
>
> "An innovator needs to be a dreamer. An innovator needs to be able to see something that could happen out in time and bring that in closer by creating the environment to make an idea succeed before it would have without their unique twist. An innovator needs to be an extreme risk-taker, but also naive. If the innovator is too sensible or realistic, then he/she would not take the big chances in the first place. And these are necessary but not sufficient conditions for success. An innovator still faces Everest-sized challenges at every turn, because change is so hard—but an innovator persists despite that because his passion is even higher than that mountain."—Bill Gross, Energy Innovations

There are many people to thank: My family for their support and believing in me and my visions. My many friends who have been supportive of me for many years and have believed in my passions: David and Carol Ogden, Brian Lima,

George Froehlich, David Findley, Roger Slotkin, Tom Smith, William Froehlich, Toni Ann Deluca, William Dougherty, Rhea Courtney Bozic, Clean Fuels Consulting, Christine Zarb, Kevin Shea, Christina Howard and so many more.

I also would like to thank my great friends from the *Coolfuel Roadtrip*—Shaun, Teresa, Marty, Gus, and many more—for their support and inspiration. A congratulations to Shaun and Teresa on their first child, Matilda.

Many thanks also go out to Seth Leitmen, Judy Bass, and Patricia Wallenburg for their great help and support in writing this book. I could not have done this without them. Thank you, Seth, for all you have done. When my computer crashed and I lost most of my manuscript, Seth and Judy stepped in and made things happen. I do not know what I would have done.

Great thanks goes to my family for their support: Judy Vogel, my Mom, for her support in some of the worst of times; the late Charles Vogel, my Dad, who I wish was here today to see so many great things and the influence he had on my life; and Carol Vogel, my sister, for her ongoing support.

I also would like to thank a great teacher, Michael Duschenchuk, from my high school, who inspired me to do many great things in the future. Mike then and now is still a great friend who I see often.

A special thanks goes to all the people who have touched my life and have influenced me in some way. You are not forgotten. Thank you so much.

CHAPTER 1

Why You Need to Get an Electric Motorcycle Today!

Should anyone buy, convert, or build an electric motorcycle today? They can go as fast as 168 miles per hour! They are clean, efficient, and cost-effective. Plus, they haul! Electric motorcycles are virtually maintenance-free: They never require oil changes, new spark plugs, or any other regular repairs.

You see, electric vehicles (EVs) were designed to do whatever was needed in the past and can be designed and refined to do whatever is needed in the future. What do you need an EV to be: big, small, powerful, fast, ultraefficient? Design to meet that need. Bill Dube did it with his electric motorcycle; why can't you?

Also, think about some of the facts and statistics from the U.S. Department of Energy (DOE) and various notable sources: The DOE states that more than half the oil we use every day is imported. This level of dependence on imports (55 percent) is the highest in our history. The DOE even goes on to say that this dependence on foreign oil will increase as we use up domestic resources. Also, as a national security issue, we all should be concerned that the vast majority of the world's oil reserves are concentrated in the Middle East (65–75 percent) and controlled by the members of the OPEC oil cartel (www.fueleconomy.gov/feg/oildep.shtml).

Further, the DOE goes on to state that 133 million Americans live in areas that failed at least one National Ambient Air Quality Standard. Transportation motorcycles produce 25–75 percent of key chemicals that pollute the air, causing smog and health problems. All new motorcycles must meet federal emissions standards.

As motorcycles get older, however, the amount of pollution they produce increases. Here are some reasons why:

1. Although they are only at a relatively embryonic stage in terms of market penetration, electric motorcycles represent the most environmentally viable option because there are no emissions (www.greenconsumerguide.com/governmentll.php?CLASSIFICATION=114&PARENT=110). The energy

generated to power an EV and to move a motorcycle is 97 percent cleaner in terms of noxious pollutants.

2. Another advantage of electric motors is their ability to provide power at almost any engine speed. Whereas only about 20 percent of the chemical energy in gasoline gets converted into useful work at the wheels of an internal combustion motorcycle, 75 percent or more of the energy from a battery reaches the wheels of an EV.

3. One of the big arguments made by automobile companies against EVs is that they are powered by power plants, which are powered primarily by coal. Less than 2 percent of U.S. electricity is generated from oil, so using electricity as a transportation fuel would greatly reduce dependence on imported petroleum (www.alt-e.blogspot.com/2005/01/alternative-fuel-cars-plug-in-hybrids.html).

4. Even assuming that the electricity to power an EV is not produced from rooftop solar or natural gas (let's assume it comes 100 percent from coal), it is *still* much cleaner than gasoline produced from petroleum (www.drivingthefuture.com/97pct.html).

5. In addition, power plants are stationary sources that can be modified over time to become cleaner.[1]

The major concerns facing the electric motorcycle industry are range, top speed, and cost. Ultimately, the batteries will determine the cost and performance.

Gas car conversions have been built for years using performance-based engines and motors and currently approved frames. Why not motorcycles?

Figure 1-1 shows an example of one of many electric motorcycles, the Electric Motorsport electric GPR. The Killacycle using a blast of 1,800 amps of current can propel you a 168 mph in a little over 7 seconds (www.killacycle.com). That's fast! You can convert an electric motorcycle to go over 100 miles on a charge.

FIGURE 1-1   Electric Motorsport electric GPR. (www.electricmotorsport.com).

With lithium-ion battery technology, you can get an EV to go hundreds of miles, and the cost is still less than that of some brand-new motorcycles on the market. My point is that you can get an electric motorcycle today. You also can take any motorcycle you want and convert it to an electric motorcycle. You also can encourage the fix-it person down the street to help with the conversion so that more mechanics across the country are building electric motorcycles.

Convert That Motorcycle!

Converting a motorcycle to electric is also the easiest type of conversion. You don't need a transmission, and you don't need to deal with air conditioning, power brakes, power steering, etc. In addition, you can scale up the performance and range as you gain confidence in the technology and how to use it.

Electric motorcycles and scooters are rising in popularity because of higher gasoline prices. In addition, battery technology is gradually improving, making this form of transportation more practical (www.technologyreview.com/NanoTech/17837/?a=f). Moreover, the maintenance costs are negligible compared with the additional oil changes, tune-ups, and all the other maintenance costs of an internal combustion engine motorcycle.

Many Asian countries, especially Taiwan, suffer from heavy air pollution (Figure 1-2). Around 20 percent is contributed by motorcycles and scooters, whose emissions are worse than cars and SUVs. Unfortunately, the internal combustion

Figure 1-2 South Asia motorcycle traffic. (www.newlaunches.com/archives/motorcycles_running_on_compressed_air.php, www.newlaunches.com/entry_images/0808/16/taipei_traffic-thumb-450x298.jpg.)

engine motorcycle's legacy of destruction does not just stop with itself. The internal combustion engine is a variant of the generic combustion process. To light a match, you use oxygen (O_2) from the air to burn a carbon-based fuel (i.e., wood or cardboard matchstick), generate carbon dioxide (CO_2), emit toxic waste gases (i.e., you can see the smoke and perhaps smell the sulfur), and leave a solid waste (i.e., burnt matchstick). The volume of air around you is far greater than that consumed by the match; air currents soon dissipate the smoke and smell, and you toss the burnt matchstick.

Today's internal combustion engine is more evolved than ever. However, we still have a carbon-based combustion process that creates heat and pollution. Everything about the internal combustion engine is toxic, and it is still one of the least efficient mechanical devices on the planet. Unlike lighting a single match, the use of hundreds of millions (soon to be billions) of internal combustion engine motorcycles threatens to destroy all life on our earth.

While an internal combustion engine has hundreds of moving parts, an electric motor has only one. This is one of the main reasons why electric motorcycles are so efficient. All you need is an electric motor, batteries, and a controller. A simple diagram of an electric motorcycle looks like a simple diagram of a portable electric shaver: a battery, a motor, and a controller or switch that adjusts the flow of electricity to the motor to control its speed. That's it. Nothing comes out of your electric shaver, and nothing comes out of your electric motorcycle. Electric motorcycles are simple (and therefore highly reliable), have lifetimes measured in millions of miles, need no periodic maintenance (i.e., filters, etc.), and cost significantly less per mile to operate. They are highly flexible as well, using electrical energy readily available anywhere as input fuel.

In addition to all these benefits, if you buy, build, or convert your electric motorcycle from an internal combustion engine motorcycle chassis, as suggested in this book, you perform a double service for the environment: You remove one polluting motorcycle from the road and add one nonpolluting electric motorcycle to service.[2]

What Is an Electric Motorcycle?

An electric motorcycle consists of a battery that provides energy, an electric motor that drives the wheels, and a controller that regulates the energy flow to the motor. Figure 1-3 shows all there is to it—but don't be fooled by its simplicity. Figure 1-4 shows the basic wiring system. Scientists, engineers, and inventors down through the ages have always said, "In simplicity there is elegance." Let's find out why the electric motorcycle concept is elegant.

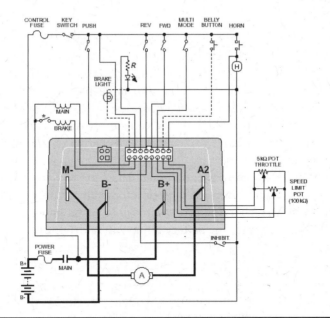

FIGURE 1-3 Electric motorcycle basic wiring system. (Courtesy of Curtis Instruments, www. curtisinst.com/index.cfm?fuseaction=cProducts.dspProductCategory&catID=10.)

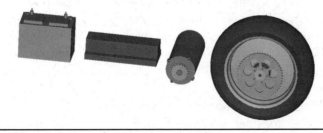

FIGURE 1-4 Simple block diagram of an electric motorcycle.

Electric Motors

Electric motors can be found in many sizes and places. Universal in application, they can be as big as a house or smaller than your fingernail, and they can be powered by any source of electricity. Each of us encounters dozens, if not hundreds, of electric motors daily without even thinking about them: alarm clocks, televisions, grinders, shavers, toothbrushes, cell phones, fans, heaters, and air conditioners.

What is the secret of the electric motor's widespread use? Reliability. This is because of its simplicity. Regardless of type, all electric motors have only two basic components: a rotor (the moving part) and a stator (the stationary part). That's right—an electric motor has only *one* moving part. If you design, manufacture, and use an electric motor correctly, it is virtually impervious to failure and indestructible in use.[3]

Batteries

No matter where you go, you cannot get away from batteries. They're in your MP3 player, portable radio, telephone, cell phone, laptop computer, portable power tool, appliance, game, flashlight, camera, and many more devices. Batteries come in two distinct flavors: rechargeable and non-rechargeable. Like motors, they come in all sorts of sizes, shapes, weights, and capacities. Unlike motors, they have no moving parts. The non-rechargeable batteries you simply dispose of when they are out of juice; rechargeable batteries you connect to a charger or source of electric power to build them up to capacity.

There are different types of batteries. There are rechargeable lead-acid, nickel–metal hydride, and lithium-ion batteries, for example, which can be used in your car to manage the recharging process invisibly via an under-the-hood generator or alternator that recharges the battery while you're driving.

Another great thing about the promise of electric cars and motorcycles is lithium-ion battery technology: It is moving so fast into the marketplace and dropping in price. Over the next few years, we can expect further drops in price, making EV conversions more affordable. Soon enough, the standard will be lithium-ion batteries in any conversion kit.

Controllers

Controllers have become much more intelligent. The same technology that reduced computers from room-sized to desk-sized allows you to exercise precise control over an electric motor. Regardless of the voltage source, current needs, or motor type, today's controllers—built with reliable solid-state electric components—can be designed to meet virtually any need and can easily be made compact to fit conveniently inside a motorcycle.

Why are electric motorcycles elegant? When you join an electric motor, battery, and controller together, you get an electric motorcycle that is both reliable and convenient.[4]

Electric Motorcycles Are Fun to Drive

Imagine turning on a motorcycle and hearing nothing! The only way you can tell that the motorcycle is on is by looking at the battery/fuel gauge. This is only the first surprise that many people get when they get on an electric motorcycle.

After I built my first electric motorcycle using the book *Build Your Own Electric Vehicle* by Bob Brant, when I went to events and held ride-and-drives, I realized that people loved the ride. Electric motorcycles are first and foremost practical—but they are also fun to own and drive. Owners say that they become downright addictive. When tooling around on a breezy electric motorcycle, you get all the pleasure of a great motorcycle ride—without the noise!

Electric Motorcycles Save Money

All this emotional stuff is nice, but let's talk out-of-pocket dollars. Ask any electric motorcycle conversion owner, and they'll tell you the bike transports them where they want to go, is very reliable, and saves them money. Let's examine the operating, purchase, and lifetime ownership costs separately and summarize the potential savings.

Operating Costs

Electric motorcycles only consume electricity. Since they are smaller than electric cars, they have fewer batteries. This means that when you charge the motorcycle, it costs less than a few pennies per mile. The gas equivalent vehicle is normally more than double the cost.

Purchase Costs

Commercially manufactured electric motorcycles are not expensive. Some cost between $8,000 and $15,000. But this book advocates the conversion alternative—*you* convert an internal combustion engine motorcycle to an electric motorcycle. You remove the internal combustion engine and all the systems that go with it and add an electric motor, controller, and batteries.

This book promotes building one yourself. As a second motorcycle choice, logic (and Parkinson's law—the demand on a resource tends to expand to match the supply of that resource) dictates that the money spent for this decision will expand to fill the budget available—regardless of whether an internal combustion engine motorcycle or electric motorcycle is chosen. So second motorcycle purchase costs for an internal combustion motorcycle or an electric motorcycle are a wash—they are identical.

Safety First

Electric motorcycles are safer for you and everyone around you. EVs are a boon for safety-minded individuals. Electric motorcycles are called *zero emission vehicles* (ZEVs) because they emit nothing, whether they are moving or not. In fact, when stopped, electric motorcycle motors are not running and use no energy at all. This is in direct contrast to internal combustion engine motorcycles, which not only consume fuel but also do their best polluting when stopped and idling in traffic.

Electric motorcycles are obviously the ideal solution for minimizing pollution and energy waste on congested stop-and-go commuting highways all over the world, but this section is about saving yourself: As an electric motorcycle owner, you are not going to be choking on your own exhaust fumes. Electric motorcycles are easily and infinitely adaptable. Want more acceleration? Put in a bigger electric motor. Want greater range? Choose a better power-to-weight design. Want more speed? Pay attention to your design's aerodynamics, weight, and power.

When you buy, convert, or build an electric motorcycle today, all these choices and more are yours to make because there are no standards and few restrictions. The primary restrictions regard safety (you want to be covered in this area anyway) and are taken care of by using an existing internal combustion engine motorcycle chassis that already has been safety qualified. Other safety standards to be used when buying, mounting, using, and servicing your electric motorcycle conversion components are discussed later in this book.

On another safety issue, though, while electric motorcycles do not emit noise pollution or any other pollution for that matter, there has been concern about their being unsafe for seeing-impaired pedestrians because the engines don't make noise. However, electric motorcycle ownership is visible proof of your commitment to help clean up the environment.

Electric Motorcycle Myths: Dispelling the Rumors

There have been four widely circulated myths or rumors about electric motorcycles that are not true. Because the reality in each case is the 180-degree opposite of the myth, you should know about them.

Myth 1: Electric Motorcycles Can't Go Fast Enough

Electric motorcycles are anything but slow. Many electric motorcycles on the market today have a top speed of 60 mph or more. The Electra Cruiser easily tops 80 mph. The beauty of building your own electric motorcycle is you determine how fast that you want your vehicle to go.

Myth 2: Electric Motorcycles Have Limited Range

Nothing could be further from the truth, but unfortunately this myth has been widely accepted. The reality is that electric motorcycles can go as far as most people need. While lithium-ion batteries will expand your range dramatically, and there are some people who are traveling across the country on electric motorcycles, the technology is not yet ready for a massive road trip.

But what is their range? The federal government reports that the average daily commuter distance for all modes of motor travel (i.e., autos, trucks, and buses) is 10 miles, and this figure hasn't changed appreciably in 20 years of data gathering. An earlier study showed that 98 percent of all trips are under 50 miles per day; most people do all their driving locally and take only a few long trips. One-hundred-mile and longer trips are only 17 percent of total miles driven. As stated in *Build Your Own Electric Vehicle*, 2nd edition, General Motors' own surveys in the early 1990s (taken from a sampling of drivers in Boston, Los Angeles, and Houston) indicated that

- Most people don't drive very far.
- More than 40 percent of all trips were under 5 miles.

- Only 8 percent of all trips were more than 25 miles.
- Nearly 85 percent of the drivers drove less than 75 miles per day.

Virtually any of today's 120-V electric motorcycle conversions will go 75 miles using readily available off-the-shelf components—if you keep the weight under 1,000 pounds. This means that an electric motorcycle can meet more than 85 percent of the average person's needs. If you're commuting to work—a place that presumably has an electric outlet available—you can nearly double your range by recharging during your working hours. In addition, if range is really important, you can optimize your electric motorcycle for it. It's that simple.

Myth 3: Electric Motorcycles Are Not Convenient

The myth that electric motorcycles are not effective as a real form of transportation or that they are not convenient is a really silly rumor. A popular question is, "Suppose that you're driving and you're not near your home to charge up or you run out of electricity. What do you do?" Well, my favorite answer is, "I would do the same thing I'd do if I ran out of gas—call AAA or a tow truck." The reality is that electric motorcycles are extremely convenient. Recharging is as convenient as your nearest electric outlet, especially for conversion motorcycles using 110-V charging outlets. Here are some other reasons:

- You can get electricity anywhere you can get gas—there are no gas stations without electricity.
- You can get electricity from many other places—there are few homes and virtually no businesses in the United States without electricity. All these are potential sources for you to recharge your electric motorcycle.
- As far as being stuck in the middle of nowhere goes, other than taking extended trips in western U.S. deserts (and even those are filling up rapidly), there are only a few places where you can drive 75 miles without seeing an electric outlet in the contiguous United States. Europe and Japan have no such places.
- Plug-in-anywhere recharging capability is an overwhelming electric motorcycle advantage. No question that it's an advantage when your electric motorcycle is parked in your own garage, carport, or driveway. If you live in an apartment and can work out a charging arrangement, it's an even better idea. Moreover, a very simple device can be rigged to signal you if anyone ever tries to steal your motorcycle.
- How much more convenient could electric motorcycles be? There are very few places you can drive in the civilized world where you can't recharge in a pinch, and your only other concern is to add water to the battery once in a while. Electricity exists virtually everywhere; you just have to figure out how to tap into it. While there are no electric outlets specifically designated

for recharging electric motorcycles conveniently located everywhere today, and although it's unquestionably easier and faster to recharge your electric motorcycle from a 110- or 220-V kiosk, the widely available 110-V electric supply does the job quite nicely if your electric motorcycle has an onboard charger, extension cord, and plug(s) available. When more infrastructure exists in the future, it will be even more convenient to recharge your batteries. In the future, you will be able to recharge quicker from multiple voltage and current options, have "quick charge" capability by dumping one battery stack into another, and maybe even have uniform battery packs that you swap and strap on at a local "battery station" in no more time than it takes to get a fill-up at a gas station today. Just as it's used in your home today, electricity is clean, quiet, safe, and stays at the outlet until you need it.

Myth 4: Electric Motorcycles Are Expensive

While this is perhaps true of electric motorcycles that are manufactured in low volume today—and partially true of professionally done conversion units—it's not true of the do-it-yourself electric motorcycle conversions this book advocates. The reality, as I mentioned earlier in this chapter, is that electric motorcycles cost the same to buy (you're not going to spend any more for one than you would have budgeted anyway for your second internal combustion engine motorcycle), the same to maintain, and far less per mile to operate. In the long term, future volume production and technology improvements will only make the cost benefits favor electric motorcycles even more.

Disadvantages

Well, there had to be a downside. If any one of the factors mentioned here is important to you, you might be better served by taking an alternate course of action. For extended trips, as already mentioned, the electric motorcycle is not your best choice at this time. This is not because you can't do it. Alternate methods are just more convenient.

As mentioned, this book advocates the use of a convert-it-yourself electric motorcycle as a *second* motorcycle. When you need to take longer trips, use your first gasoline-powered motorcycle or rent one or take an airplane, train, or bus.

Time to Purchase/Build

Regardless of your decision to buy, build, or convert an electric motorcycle, it is going to take you time to do it, but less time than a car. There is a growing network of new and used electric motorcycle dealers and conversion shops. Also it's great that the supply of the highest-grade controllers and motors is such that they do not take a long time to receive (check out Chapter 14 for sources).

Repairs

Handy electric motorcycle repair shops don't exist yet either. Although the build-it-yourself experience will enable you to rapidly diagnose any problems, and replacement parts could take only days to receive. You could just stockpile spare parts yourself. However, take time to carefully think through this or other repair alternatives before you make your electric motorcycle decision.

My Passion

The electric motorcycle was a project that became a passion for me. At the time, there were very few bikes with size and power. My goal was to build a machine that created a presence, was not wimpy, and kicked butt. It all started with an idea and lots of determination on a road few have traveled. Even in the presence of professors who said that you cannot make a bike that powerful and a consultant from a past EV company who tried to deter me from making such a powerful motorcycle (thinking I should reduce it to a scooter), I pressed on.

In 1996, the first beginnings of the then-named "Electric Hog," now named the "Electra Cruiser," grew from a crazy idea sketched on paper with a stick-figure rider (Figure 1-5) to a full-out motorcycle. With the help of the original book *Build Your Own Electric Vehicle* and a lot of work, the bike slowly came together.

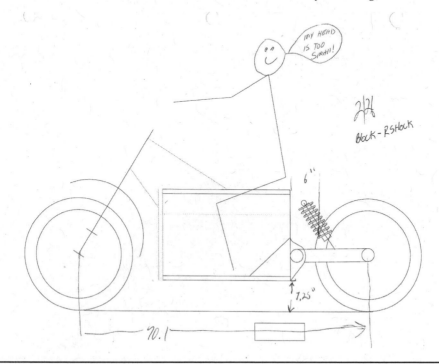

FIGURE 1-5   First drawing of the "Electric Hog."

I had made the decision back then to build my own frame to house almost 600 pounds of batteries. This shear weight caused many professionals in the engineering and EV fields to shudder and say, "No way. You can't do that." I thought differently. After all, someone put a big-block Chevy in a bike. Why couldn't I do the same with batteries? Six months later, in 1997, the design work, drawings (Figure 1-6), calculations, and most of the parts were bought. Now it was time to put it together.

Because of work and other life commitments, the project was delayed until 2000, which was no big deal. All the parts, the drawings, and everything were all laid out. I just had to find the time to bring it all together. In 2000, I jumped back into the electric motorcycle project, and within 6 months, in May of 2001, the first prototype was completed. The original archived video is still available on my Web site www.vogelbilt.com/home.html.

The bike was amazing—and more than what I ever thought it would be. I remember clearly the day it was finished. I was extremely nervous, and a few of the naysayers from the Farmingdale State College were watching, not believing that this beast of a bike would work. With the crack of the throttle, the motorcycle cruised off effortlessly to the disbelief of many. I cannot express in words the feelings I had that day with all my time and effort coming together and working so flawlessly. I will never forget just the experience of cruising quietly and smoothly; it was out of this world. Oh, and even better, seeing the faces of the disbelievers was priceless.

Coolfuel Roadtrip

After 2001, the first Electra Cruiser did well. It made its rounds at shows and EV events for two years, had a small Web site, and was just a fun experience. The motorcycle competed and was displayed in such shows as the Tour De Sol (Figure 1-7) and many other EV events.

FIGURE 1-6   Three-dimensional (3D) drawing of the first prototype produced in AutoCAD.

FIGURE 1-7   2002 Tour De Sol display Annapolis, Maryland.

In early 2003, I received an e-mail from a man named Shaun Murphy from Australia. Shaun was putting together a TV series in the United States and wanted to use my motorcycle. Shaun's concept was to use all clean, nonpolluting vehicles that were powered by only renewable resources. He wanted to travel the United States on not one drop of gasoline, a 16,000-mile journey. This was exciting news for me. Not only had I built an electric motorcycle, but now it was going to be traveling the United States and would be on national TV, Discovery Science, and worldwide TV. I will always remember the phone call at work in 2003. Shaun, a great friend of mine now, may not know this, but that phone call changed my life. It propelled me forward into renewable energy and much more. I agreed that day with Shaun to produce another motorcycle just for the TV series. In three to four months, I built a second Electra Cruiser prototype for Shaun's TV series, the *Coolfuel Roadtrip* (Figure 1-8).

FIGURE 1-8   Coolfuel crew.

For this second design, I made a bike that was lighter and had a few more features, including regenerative braking to recapture energy when stopping. What I also did for Shaun was add a sidecar for Sparky, his companion. In addition, though, the sidecar had a little something extra: a diesel generator. The sidecar actually was a range extender and a portable power unit producing 4.5 kW for charging. The beauty of the sidecar was that it ran on vegetable oil and biodiesel.

Not more than a week after completion, the second Electra Cruiser passed its running tests and was on the road from New York to Wisconsin for its 9-month trek across the United States. The motorcycle was delivered, and the crew was excited to have the Electra Cruiser as part of the program (Figure 1-9).

The Electra Cruiser went on to be filmed for 9 months on the road through all types of environments. This was a true test of an electric motorcycle. The bike got a beating and just kept going, a true testament to the abilities of the electric motorcycle in the real world. The Cruiser went through extreme temperatures, was poured on, and was dropped. You name it, the bike took it and kept going (Figures 1-10 through 1-13). I could not have asked for or paid for a better real-world test than what that bike went through. It was great, and I was like a proud parent of my child. The Cruiser was a true testament to the abilities of an electric motorcycle and an

Figure 1-9   Electra Cruiser during filming in Chicago. (Courtesy of Shaun Murphy and Gus Roxburgh, Balance Vector Productions, www.balancevector.com.)

inspiration to many people. Many thanks go out to the *Coolfuel* team; they have become great friends.

FIGURE 1-10   Cruiser during filming in New Orleans, getting dumped on by rain but still going. (Courtesy of Shaun Murphy and Gus Roxburgh, Balance Vector Productions, www.balancevector.com.)

FIGURE 1-11   Cruiser during filming in California. (Courtesy of Shaun Murphy and Gus Roxburgh, Balance Vector Productions, www.balancevector.com.)

Figure 1-12   Cruiser in Wisconsin with sidecar.

Figure 1-13   Cruiser in Chicago with the Blues Brothers theme. (Courtesy of Shaun Murphy and Gus Roxburgh, Balance Vector Productions, www.balancevector.com.)

CHAPTER 2

Electric Motorcycles Save the Environment and Energy

Besides the fact that the consumer marketplace has been consistently interested in electric motorcycles, there is at present a new interest in electric motorcycles. This is amazing because it can only mean amazing things for transportation in urban areas and developing countries. Specifically, it means zero tailpipe emissions and greater air quality. And with this comes a significant reduction in overall energy use.

Why Do Electric Motorcycles Save the Environment?

Here are some of the basic reasons why we need more electric motorcycles on the road:

1. Building your own electric motorcycle takes less time and costs less than a large undertaking such as building an electric car or a truck.
2. Electric motorcycles are fun to own or ride and are good for everyone (all races, men and women, children and adults are interested in and excited about electric motorcycles; see Figure 2-1).
3. Electric motorcycle conversions solve many problems and address many transportation concerns immediately.
4. Electric motorcycles have immediate advantages using the existing electric infrastructure taking little time to implement electric vehicles in place of fossil fuel vehicles.
5. Electric motorcycles mitigate some of the issues we face today in terms of pollution and global warming.
6. The electric motorcycle plays an important role in the world today, particularly in third world countries to reduce emissions. Making a choice to use non-polluting vehicles will have a positive impact on the environment.

FIGURE 2-1   How about 50-plus mph motorcycle? (http://visforvoltage.org/forum/motorcycles-and-large-scooters/1744.)

Environmental Benefits

Overall, from 1990 to 2007, total emissions of CO_2 increased by 1,022.8 Tg CO_2 equivalents (20.2 percent), whereas CH_4 (methane) and N_2O (nitrous oxide) emissions decreased by 38.2 percent. During the same period, aggregate weighted emissions of hydrofluorocarbons (HFCs), perfluorocarbons (PFCs), and SF_6 (Sulfur hexafluoride) rose by 59.0 percent. Despite being emitted in smaller quantities relative to the other principal greenhouse gases, emissions of HFCs, PFCs, and SF_6 are significant because many of them have extremely high GWPs (Global Warming Potentials) and, in the cases of PFCs and SF_6, long atmospheric lifetimes.[1]

Conversely, U.S. greenhouse gas emissions were partly offset by carbon sequestration in managed forests, trees in urban areas, agricultural soils, and landfilled yard trimmings, and were estimated to be 15.1 percent of total emissions in 2007.[2]

Also, as Rob Means of Electric Bikes.com says:

The environmental benefits include reduced pollution (CO_2, NO_x, and tire and brake-lining fragments) and reduced resource consumption (less material, fuel, and infrastructure). A reduction in CO_2 emissions is most important because scientific opinion is close to unanimous that global warming is already happening. The average motorcycle emits one pound of CO_2 for every motorcycle mile driven.[3]

While electric motorcycles are considered zero-emission vehicles (ZEVs), their widespread uptake will eventually cause an increase in electrical generation needs. Many power stations, particularly coal-fired and nuclear power stations, have to operate at a certain level at all times, no matter whether there is demand for the electricity or not. In Ireland (population 4 million), the ESB (Electricity Supply Board), an energy corporation in the Republic of Ireland, has stated that it could recharge 10,000 electric motorcycles each night without producing any extra power. This would probably translate to almost a million electric motorcycles in the United States. Therefore, if the power were coming from coal/gas-fired power plants, the electric motorcycle would use power that would otherwise have been wasted and still would have created CO_2 in those countries where this power was being wasted. Generating electricity and providing liquid fuels for motorcycles are different areas of the energy economy with different inefficiencies and environmental effects.

According to the Electric Vehicle Association of Canada (a nonprofit organization promoting electric vehicles that also sells electric motorcycles[4]), emissions of CO_2 and other greenhouse gases are minimal for electric motorcycles powered from sustainable forms of power (e.g., solar, wind, and geothermal) and for internal combustion engine motorcycles that are run on renewable fuels such as biodiesel.

If the aim of looking at electric motorcycles as an alternative to conventional motorcycles is to reduce CO_2 emissions, then this has to mean using the most carbon-efficient motorcycle and fuel you can buy. An electric motorcycle can be recharged from conventional grid electricity and *still* not have a significant carbon footprint compared with hybrid and diesel motorcycles.

Save the Environment and Save Some Money Too!

Because electric motorcycles use less energy than gasoline-powered motorcycles, their effect on the environment is much less. Because electric motorcycles are more efficient than petroleum-powered motorcycles, they also cost less to run.

While electric vehicles of all types will be the transportation mode of choice for years to come, electric motorcycle conversions are the next generation of electric motorcycles that the consumer marketplace can accept at this time. Since there are so many motorcycles on the road that only need to be electrified, conversions make sense and can spur our economy with jobs.

Electric motorcycle operating costs can be directly compared with the equivalent operating costs of a gasoline-powered motorcycle. To calculate the cost of the electrical equivalent of a liter or a gallon of gasoline, multiply the utility cost per kilowatt-hour by 8.9. Because internal combustion engines are only about 20 percent efficient, then at most 20 percent of the total energy in a liter of gasoline is ever put to use.

A motorcycle powered by an internal combustion engine at 20 percent efficiency, getting 8 L/100 km (30 mpg), will require (8.9 × 8) × 0.20 = 14.2 kWh/100 km. At a cost of $1/L, 8 L/100 km is $8/100 km. A battery-powered version of that same motorcycle with a charge/discharge efficiency of 81 percent, charged at a cost of $0.10/kWh, would cost (14.2/0.81) × $0.10 = $1.75/100 km or would be paying the equivalent of $0.22/L ($0.84/gallon). The Tesla car uses about 13 kWh/100 km; the electric motorcycle uses about 11kWh/100 km.[5]

Energy Efficiency

An electric motorcycle's efficiency is affected by its charging and discharging efficiencies. A typical charging cycle is about 85 percent efficient, and the discharge cycle converting electricity into mechanical power is about 95 percent efficient, resulting in 81 percent of each kilowatt-hour being put to use.[6]

The electricity-generating system in the United States loses 9.5 percent of the power transmitted between power stations and homes, and the power stations are 33 percent efficient in turning the caloric value of fuel at the power station into electric power. Overall, this results in an efficiency of 0.81 × 0.3 = 24.2 percent from fuel into the power station to power into the motor of the grid-charged electric motorcycle, which is still better than the average 20 percent efficiency of gasoline-powered motorcycles (while ignoring the energy used to pump, refine, and transport the gasoline to the gas station).

Electricity Generation: How Is It Made?

Figure 2-2 shows the U.S. energy usage by year from 1996 to 2007. To drive an electric generator or a device that converts mechanical or chemical energy to electricity, an electric utility power station uses either

- A turbine
- An engine
- A water wheel
- Or another similar machine

Steam turbines, internal combustion engines, gas combustion turbines, water turbines, and wind turbines are the most common methods to generate electricity (Figure 2-3). Most power plants are about 35 percent efficient. This means that for every 100 units of energy that go into a plant, only 35 units are converted to usable electrical energy.

Period	Coal[1]	Petroleum [2]	Natural Gas	Other Gases [3]	Nuclear	Hydroelectric Conventional [4]	Other Renewables [5]	Hydroelectric Pumped Storage[6]	Other [7]	Total
Total (All Sectors)										
1996	1,795,196	81,411	455,056	14,356	674,729	347,162	75,796	-3,088	3,571	3,444,188
1997	1,845,016	92,555	479,399	13,351	628,644	356,453	77,183	-4,040	3,612	3,492,172
1998	1,873,516	128,800	531,257	13,492	673,702	323,336	77,088	-4,467	3,571	3,620,295
1999	1,881,087	118,061	556,396	14,126	728,254	319,536	79,423	-6,097	4,024	3,694,810
2000	1,966,265	111,221	601,038	13,955	753,893	275,573	80,906	-5,539	4,794	3,802,105
2001	1,903,956	124,880	639,129	9,039	768,826	216,961	70,769	-8,823	11,906	3,736,644
2002	1,933,130	94,567	691,006	11,463	780,064	264,329	79,109	-8,743	13,527	3,858,452
2003	1,973,737	119,406	649,908	15,600	763,733	275,806	79,487	-8,535	14,045	3,883,185
2004	1,978,301 [R]	121,145 [R]	710,100 [R]	15,252 [R]	788,528	268,417	83,067[R]	-8,488	14,232 [R]	3,970,555
2005	2,012,873 [R]	122,225 [R]	760,960 [R]	13,464 [R]	781,986	270,321	87,329[R]	-6,558	12,821 [R]	4,055,423
2006	1,990,511 [R]	64,166[R]	816,441 [R]	14,177 [R]	787,219	289,246	96,525[R]	-6,558	12,974 [R]	4,064,702
2007	2,016,456	65,739	896,590	13,453	806,425	247,510	105,238	-6,896	12,231	4,156,745
Electricity Generators, Electric Utilities										
1996	1,737,453	67,346	262,730	–	674,729	331,058	7,214	-3,088	–	3,077,442
1997	1,787,806	77,753	283,625	–	628,644	341,273	7,462	-4,040	–	3,122,523
1998	1,807,480	110,158	309,222	–	673,702	308,844	7,206	-4,441	–	3,212,171
1999	1,767,679	86,929	296,381	–	725,036	299,914	3,716	-5,982	–	3,173,674
2000	1,696,619	72,180	290,715	–	705,433	253,155	2,241	-4,960	–	3,015,383
2001	1,560,146	78,908	264,434	–	534,207	197,804	1,666	-7,704	486	2,629,946
2002	1,514,670	59,125	229,639	206	507,380	242,302	3,089	-7,434	480	2,549,457
2003	1,500,281	69,930	186,967	243	458,829	249,622	3,421	-7,532	519	2,462,281
2004	1,513,641	73,694	199,662	374	475,682	245,546	3,692	-7,526	467	2,505,231
2005	1,484,855	69,722	238,204	10	436,296	245,553	4,945	-5,383	643	2,474,846
2006	1,471,421	40,903	282,088	30	425,341	261,864	6,588	-5,281	700	2,483,656
2007	1,490,985	40,719	313,785	141	427,555	226,734	8,953	-5,328	586	2,504,131

Figure 2-2   Energy usage by year, 1996–2007.

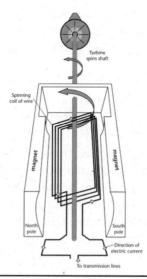

Figure 2-3   Turbine generator. (www.eia.doe.gov/kids/energyfacts/sources/electricity.html.)

Steam Turbines Are the Leader

Most of the electricity in the United States is produced by steam turbines. A turbine converts the kinetic energy of a moving fluid (liquid or gas) to mechanical energy. Steam turbines have blades on a shaft through which steam is forced, thus rotating the shaft, which is connected to a generator. In a fossil-fuel-fired steam turbine, the fuel is burned in a furnace to heat water in a boiler to produce steam.

The predominant fuels used are coal, petroleum (oil), and natural gas. They are burned in large furnaces to heat water that makes steam, which, in turn, pushes on the blades of the turbine.

Did you know that most electricity generated in the United State comes from burning coal? In 2006, nearly half the country's 4.1 trillion kilowatt-hours of electricity used coal as its source of energy.

Natural Gas

Natural gas, in addition to being burned to heat water for steam, also can be burned to produce hot combustion gases that pass directly through a turbine, spinning the blades to generate electricity. Gas turbines are used commonly when electricity usage is in high demand. According to the U.S. Department of Energy (DOE), in 2006, 20 percent of the nation's electricity was fueled by natural gas.

Petroleum

Petroleum also can be used to make steam to turn a turbine. Residual fuel oil, a product refined from crude oil, is often the petroleum product used in electric plants that use petroleum to make steam. Petroleum was used to generate about 2 percent of all electricity generated in U.S. power plants in 2006.

Nuclear Power

Nuclear power generation is a method in which steam is produced by heating water through a process called *nuclear fission*. In a nuclear power plant, a reactor contains a core of nuclear fuel, primarily enriched uranium. When atoms of the uranium fuel are hit by neutrons, they split (fission), releasing heat and more neutrons. Under controlled conditions, these other neutrons can strike more uranium atoms, splitting more atoms, and so on. At some point, continuous fission takes place, called a *chain reaction*, releasing heat. The heat is used to turn water into steam, which, in turn, spins a turbine that generates electricity. Nuclear power was used to generate 19 percent of all the country's electricity in 2006.

Hydropower

Hydropower, the source of almost 7 percent of U.S. electricity generation in 2006, is a process in which flowing water is used to spin a turbine connected to a generator.

There are two basic types of hydroelectric systems that produce electricity. In the first system, flowing water accumulates in reservoirs created by dams. The water falls through a pipe called a *penstock* and applies pressure against the turbine blades to drive the generator to produce electricity. In the second system, called *run-of-river*, the force of the river current (rather than falling water) applies pressure to the turbine blades to produce electricity.

Geothermal Power

Geothermal power comes from heat energy buried beneath the surface of the earth. In some areas of the country, enough heat rises close to the surface of the earth to heat underground water into steam, which can be tapped for use at steam turbine plants. This energy source generated less than 1 percent of the electricity in the country in 2006.

Solar Power

Solar power is derived from the energy of the sun. However, the sun's energy is not available full time, and it is widely scattered. The processes used to produce electricity using the sun's energy historically have been more expensive than using conventional fossil fuels. Photovoltaic conversion generates electric power directly from the light of the sun in a photovoltaic (solar) cell. Solar-thermal electric generators use the radiant energy from the sun to produce steam to drive turbines. In 2006, less than 1 percent of the nation's electricity was based on solar power.

Wind Power

Wind power is derived from the conversion of the energy contained in wind into electricity. Wind power, producing less than 1 percent of the nation's electricity in 2006, is a rapidly growing source of electricity. A wind turbine is similar to a typical windmill.

Biomass

Biomass includes wood, municipal solid waste (garbage), and agricultural waste such as corn cobs and wheat straw. These are some of the biologic energy sources used for producing electricity. These sources replace fossil fuels in a boiler. The combustion of wood and waste creates steam that is typically used in conventional steam electric plants. Biomass accounts for about 1 percent of the electricity generated in the United States.[7]

Efficiencies of Power Plants

Overall average efficiency from U.S. power plants (33 percent efficient) to point of use (transmission loss is 9.5 percent) is 29.87 percent.[8] Accepting 80 percent efficiency for an electric motorcycle gives a figure of only 23.9 percent overall efficiency when the motorcycle is recharged from fossil-fuel-fired electricity. This is still higher than the efficiency of an internal combustion engine running at variable load. The efficiency of a gasoline engine is about 16 percent, and for a diesel engine, efficiency is about 20 percent.

An electric motor does not suffer from such a rapid decrease in efficiency when running at variable load, and this accounts for the increased efficiency of hybrid motorcycles. Using fossil-fuel-based grid electricity entirely negates the motorcycle efficiency advantages of electric motorcycles. The major potential benefit of electric motorcycles is to allow diverse renewable electricity sources to fuel them.

U.S. Transportation Depends on Oil

Although small amounts of natural gas and electricity are used, the U.S. transportation sector is almost entirely dependent on oil. A brief look at a few charts will demonstrate the facts. It doesn't take a brain surgeon to think that this situation is both a strategic and an economic problem for us all. Figure 2-4 shows how transportation drives U.S. oil consumption and pollution, and Figure 2-5 illustrates that oil is not going to be here forever.

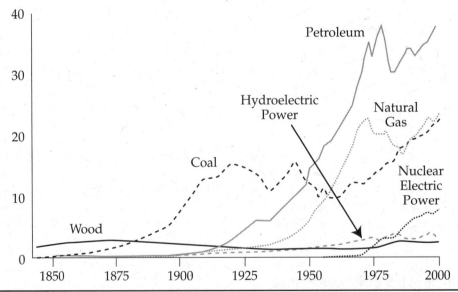

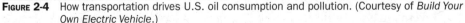

FIGURE 2-4   How transportation drives U.S. oil consumption and pollution. (Courtesy of *Build Your Own Electric Vehicle*.)

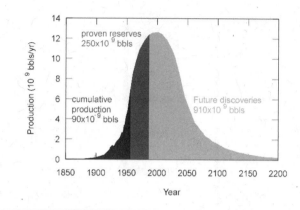

Emission Facts

Gas-powered cars are the primary source of air pollution in the United States. In addition to their effect on our health, exhaust gases and particles from cars do extensive damage to crops, vegetation, and wildlife. In particular, motor vehicles are a significant source of water pollution. Oil, antifreeze, and small tire particles accumulate on roads and highways; during the rainy season, they are washed into our streams and waterways, causing damage to aquatic life. One of the leading sources of metallic pollution in bays is copper from automobile brake pads. An average automobile annually produces

- 3.42 pounds of hydrocarbons
- 25.28 pounds of carbon monoxide
- 1.77 pounds of nitrogen oxides

Finally, noise pollution from automotive traffic additionally stresses our lives.

Calculating emissions is an inherently tricky business. There are so many variables that there are no exact numbers in this game. The numbers here were calculated by David Swain, an engineer at the U.S. Environmental Protection Agency's Ann Arbor Mobile Emissions Laboratory. An alternative emission factor, listed as the "EPA Mobile 4.1 Model," cites carbon monoxide levels emitted by the average car as 65.3 g/mi. Using this number, the CO savings after 500 miles with an electric motorcycle would be approximately 70 pounds! Figure 2-6 shows a model of balanced future energy usage made possible by working from the desired future goal back to today.

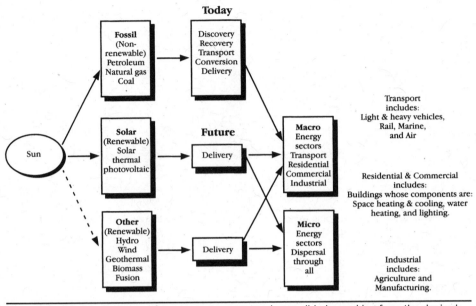

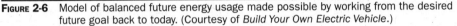

FIGURE 2-6   Model of balanced future energy usage made possible by working from the desired future goal back to today. (Courtesy of *Build Your Own Electric Vehicle*.)

Further Economic and Competitive Matters

Your investment in an electric motorcycle can pay dividends beyond U.S. borders. Your purchase supports the growth of an industry that could make a big difference in developing countries. For example, as its economy prospers, China is in the unique position to skip the polluting gas moped and scooter phase altogether and leapfrog directly from human-powered bikes to clean electric motorcycles. The pollution savings are staggering, far beyond what the United States could achieve alone.

Short trips account for most of the motorcycles on the road and most of our air pollution. Therefore, for the health of the planet, leave your gas-powered motorcycle at home, and ride your electric motorcycle.[9]

Economic Benefits

The economic benefits of electric motorcycles are better, in terms of quick payback, than insulating your home.[10] Substituting electric motorcycle trips for gas-powered motorcycle trips saves on purchase price, insurance, and registration fees. Beyond the purchase price, motorcycles cost about $0.10/mi in fuel and parts. Some families will use an electric motorcycle to augment their gas-powered motorcycle use, whereas others will find tremendous savings by living with one less motorcycle. For some folks, there's no comparison because they don't have a license to drive and don't need a license for an electric bike.[11] Check with local laws in your area: this varies with size and speed of the electric vehicle.

To most of us, automobiles represent a cheap, fast way to get where we're going. Many automobile expenses, however, are hidden and do not express the true costs of a fossil fuel vehicle. When included, they make the true cost of driving much higher than we realize. Those are direct costs. Indirectly, through many types of taxes, you also pay for the land, roads, freeways, bridges, and tunnels. Through government, you also pay to provide cleaning, landscaping, irrigation, signs, signals, reflectors, and police and emergency services. According to the American Automobile Association, a new car costs $6,720 a year to operate. Electric bicycles, for errands and short commutes, offer an alternative to the high costs of driving. Obviously, maintenance and fueling costs are minimal. Thus every mile you ride an electric bike instead of driving *saves you money*. Fuel, for example, costs about 0.20 cents/mile. You also may be able to save on bridge tolls, parking lot fees, and tickets. Here are the numbers:

- The charger plugs into a standard 110-V ac electrical socket and charges in 3 hours or less. Charger output is 6 A.
- Charging for 3 hours produces 18 Ah, more than enough to fully charge a 17-Ah battery, and costs about 5 cents.
- The charger uses 1.3 A at 120 V ac, or 156 W.
- Three hours of charging uses 468 Wh, or 0.468 kWh.
- At a cost of 11 cents/kWh, that's about 5 cents per charge or 0.3 cents/ mile.

Some people, however, can realize much larger savings. For example, a household with several cars might work out a way to live with one less car. That would free up insurance, registration, and smog-check costs. Another family might find that their car qualifies for a reduced insurance rate because it is used less or in a certain way.

In addition to the personal benefits you'll receive, society at large also realizes economic benefits. Increased electric motorcycle use means cleaner air, which reduces the incidence of respiratory diseases and their associated health care costs. Widespread use also could reduce pressure for more roads and road maintenance.[12]

Summary

In summary,

- Forty percent of our energy comes from petroleum.
- Twenty-three percent comes from coal.
- Twenty-three percent comes from natural gas.

- The remaining 14 percent comes from nuclear, hydroelectric, and renewable-resource power.

To simplify, Bob Brant once stated, "Our entire economy is obviously dependent on oil." Furthermore, the United States consumes 20.8 million barrels of petroleum a day, as well as 9 million barrels of gas. Automobiles are the single largest consumer of oil, consuming 40 percent, and they are also the source of 20 percent of the nation's greenhouse gas emissions.[13]

Electric motorcycle ownership is the best first step you can take to help save the planet. Electric motorcycles are used regularly in China, as seen in Figure 2-7, and can have a *real* difference in abating pollution and greenhouse gases.

As Seth Leitman and Bob Brant stated, however, there is still more you can do. Do your homework. Write your senator or congressperson. Voice your opinion. Get involved with the issues. But don't settle for an answer that says we'll study it and get back to you. Settle only for action: Who is going to do what by when and why. I leave you with a restatement of the problem, a possible framework for a solution, and some additional food for thought.

FIGURE 2-7   Electric motorcycles in China. Why not everywhere?

EPA Testing Procedures for Electric Motorcycles

To underscore the fuel efficiencies, let's look no further than the EPA.[14]

Example 1

According to an EPA rule change, an electric motorcycle is tested in accordance with EPA procedures and is found to have an Urban Dynamometer Driving Schedule energy consumption value of 265 Wh/mi and a Highway Fuel Economy Driving Schedule energy consumption value of 220 Wh/mi. The motorcycle is not equipped with any petroleum-powered accessories. The combined electrical energy consumption value is determined by averaging the Urban Dynamometer Driving Schedule energy consumption value and the Highway Fuel Economy Driving Schedule energy consumption value using weighting factors of 55 percent urban and 45 percent highway. Thus

$$\text{Combined electrical energy consumption value} =$$
$$(0.55 \times \text{urban}) + (0.45 \times \text{highway}) = (0.55 \times 265) + (0.45 \times 220) = 244.75 \text{ Wh/mi}$$

Since the motorcycle does not have any petroleum-powered accessories, the value of the petroleum equivalency factor is 82,049 Wh/gal, and the petroleum-equivalent fuel economy is

$$82{,}049 \text{ Wh/gal} \times 244.75 \text{ Wh/mi} = 335.24 \text{ mi/gal}$$

Example 2

If the motorcycle from Example 1 is equipped with an optional diesel-fired heater in an extreme case: For the purposes of this example, it is assumed that the electrical efficiency of the motorcycle is unaffected.

Since the motorcycle has a petroleum-powered accessory, the value of the petroleum equivalency factor is 73,844 Wh/gal, and the petroleum-equivalent fuel economy is

$$73{,}844 \text{ Wh/gal} \times 244.75 \text{ Wh/mi} = 301.71 \text{ mi/gal}$$

Enough said!

CHAPTER 3

History of the Electric Motorcycle

The history of the electric motorcycle is not as energizing as what is happening today (sorry for the pun, but I thought I had to go there). The earliest references to electric motorcycles in the patent history occur in the late 1860s. One Web site I saw had some cool historical pictures that show just how far we've come in this world in terms of looks, yet the technology is pretty much the same. (http://www. totalmotorcycle.com/future.htm#1800s)

Steam First!

Before the electric motorcycle came the steam motorcycle.

Copeland Steam Motorcycle

In 1884, Arizona engineer Lucius Day Copeland combined a high-wheeled bicycle driven by levers with a small steam engine. The result was a steam-powered motorcycle. The steam engine developed about ¼ horsepower and had the boiler and gasoline heater built around the steering column. A flat leather belt drove the large rear wheel. The machine could go about 15 mph and carried enough fuel and water for an hour of operation. The bicycle Copeland started with appears to be like the one patented by Lorenz (see Figures 3-1 and 3-2).

Copeland didn't get any financial backing for the steam bicycle, so he built it tricycle form, which is shown in his 1887 patent (Figure 3-3).

Writer Allan Girdler tells about Sylvester Roper, born in 1823 in New Hampshire. During the Civil War, Roper worked at the Springfield Armory, where his interest turned to steam power. In 1869, Roper built a steam-powered motorcycle (Figure 3-4).

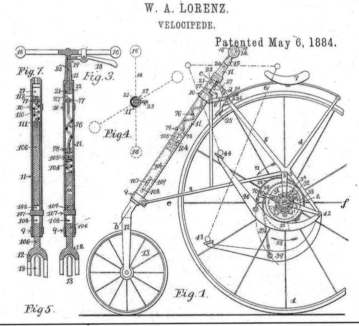

FIGURE 3-1   Lucius D. Copeland's steam bicycle, 1884. (http://patentpending.blogs.com/photos/
uncategorized/early_tricycle_1.jpg.)

FIGURE 3-2   Another view of Lucius D. Copeland and his steam bicycle. (http://patentpending.
blogs.com/photos/uncategorized/early_tricycle_1.jpg.)

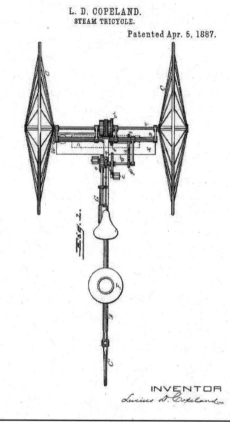

L. D. COPELAND.
STEAM TRICYCLE.

Patented Apr. 5, 1887.

INVENTOR
Lucius D. Copeland

FIGURE 3-3   Inventor's drawings from Copeland's 1887 tricycle patent. (http://patentpending. blogs.com/photos/uncategorized/early_tricycle_1.jpg.)

FIGURE 3-4   Roper's original 1869 motorcycle. (Courtesy of the Smithsonian Institution.) (http:// www.motorcyclemuseum.org/classics/bike.asp?id=3 and http://home.ama-cycle.org/ membersonly/museum/images/b3/classic_600.jpg.)

Roper's machine was remarkable by any standard. It looked a lot like the new bicycles of the day, but with a small vertical steam boiler under the seat, which also served as a small water tank. The boiler supplied steam to move two small pistons that powered a crank drive on the back wheel. The machine was very neat and compact, but there is more: Roper controlled the steam throttle by twisting the bike's straight handlebar. Twist-grip control was reinvented in 1902 by the early pilot Glen Curtiss. It was reinvented yet again around 1908 at the Indian Motorcycle Company.

Roper went on to build more motorcycles and several steam-powered automobiles. He probably built his first automobile during the Civil War. He was far ahead of his time with all his inventions. The Stanleys, who built Stanley Steamers, said that they'd learned from Roper.

Roper reached the age of 73 in 1896. That June, he showed up at a bicycle track near Harvard with a modified steam motorcycle. They clocked him at a remarkable 40 mph. Then the machine wobbled, and Roper fell off. He was dead when they found him. The autopsy showed he'd died, not from the fall, but from a heart attack.[1]

I am grateful to Keith Hollingsworth, from the University of Hawaii Mechanical Engineering Department, for calling my attention to Roper's motorcycle. For more on Daimler's motorcycle, see and listen to Episode 921 at the Web site (www.uh.edu/engines/epi921.htm).

Two illustrations from the 1897 *Encyclopaedia Britannica* show early motor-powered vehicles (Figures 3-5 and 3-6). The tricycle style four-wheeler on the left in Figure 3-5 was built by Richard Trevithick, inventor of the first successful railroad, in 1802. On the right in Figure 3-5 is an 1885 motor-powered tricycle.

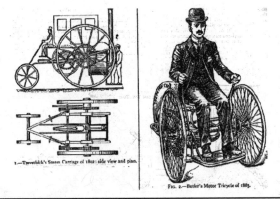

1.—Trevithick's Steam Carriage of 1802: side view and plan.

FIG. 2.—Butler's Motor Tricycle of 1885.

FIGURE 3-5   Illustration of Richard Trevithick's steam-powered four-wheeler from the 1897 Encyclopaedia Britannica. (http://books.google.com/books?id=ET7ExPBvMwC&pg=PA6&lpg=PA6&dq=trouve+electric+tricycle&source=bl&ots=LL59NIrmL&sig=2PKF_bcl_js4rjzoYRWnKtca0Mg&hl=en&sa=X&oi=book_result&resnum=1&ct=result#PPA4,M1.)

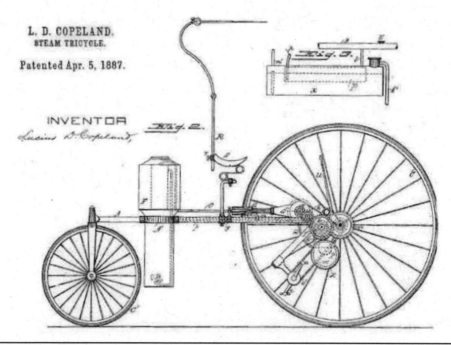

FIGURE 3-6   Illustration of an early steam-powered tricycle from 1897 Patent Pending Blog. (http://patentpending.blogs.com/patent_pending_blog/motorcycle_technology.)

In 1881, French inventor Gustave Trouvé demonstrated a working three-wheeled automobile, and France and Great Britain were the first nations to support the widespread development of electric vehicles in November at the International Exhibition of Electricity in Paris.[2]

Early 1900s

By 1911, electric motorcycles were available, according to an early *Popular Mechanics'* article, and by the 1920s, Ransomes, a current maker of forklifts, explored the use of an electric-powered motorcycle. This and other developments helped to pave the way for the company to use electric mining cars and lorries.[3]

In addition, the Automatic Electric Transmission Company of Buffalo, New York, built a vehicle called the Automatic Electric in 1921. This was a small two-seater with top speed of 18 mph and a range of 60 miles per charge. It had a 65-in wheelbase and weighed 900 lb. It sold for $1,200. In 1927, the company was bought by the Walker Electric Company.[4]

The Early 1940s

In 1941, fuel rationing in occupied Europe encouraged the Austrian company Socovel to create a small electric motorcycle. Approximately 400 were manufactured.[5]

1970s–1990s

In 1973, Mike Corbin set the first electric motorcycle land speed record of 101 mph. By 1974, Corbin-Gentry, Inc., began the sale of street-legal electric motorcycles.

Professor Charles E. MacArthur made the first electric vehicle ascent on Mt. Washington, in New Hampshire, using a Corbin electric motorcycle. The event evolved into an annual rally called the Mt. Washington Alternative Vehicle Regatta.

Late 1990s

In the late 1990s, Scott Cronk and EMB created the EMB Lectra VR24 electric motorbike. This machine pioneered the use of variable-reluctance motors (hence the VR) and was marketed as street legal.[6]

Vogelbilt Corporation's Electra Cruiser Was in *Coolfuel Roadtrip*

In 2001, Vogelbilt Corporation produced the first prototype of the Electra Cruiser (Figure 3-7). Table 3-1 lists the Vogelbilt specifications. The Electra Cruiser will be appearing in the *Coolfuel Roadtrip* TV series (Figure 3-8). The show's focus will be a search for sustainable, natural, organic, renewable, eco-innovations across the United States.

FIGURE 3-7   The first Electra Cruiser.

FIGURE 3-8 The Electra Cruiser coming out for the show.

TABLE 3-1 The Electra Cruiser Prototype 1 Specifications

Performance
> Top speed over 80 MPH
>
> Acceleration 0–60 MPH in 6–8 seconds

Batteries
> 10 Trojan 12 V Deep Cycle TMH 27

Motor Controller
> Zapi 120 V dc at 500 amps with regenerative braking

Transmission
> 5 speed Baker Right Side Drive with hydraulic clutch
>
> Belt Drives LTD. Primary 3" belt drive
>
> Reverse achieved by switching direction of dc Motor

Electric Motor
> Advanced dc series wound 120 V dc 78HP
>
> dc-to-dc Converter
>
> Vicor 120 V dc input 12 V dc output @ 200W

Suspension
> Rear swing arm—dual coil over shocks
>
> Front—Harley style wide glide front end

Cooling System
> Custom made centrifuge pump located on tail shaft of dc motor
>
> Used for cooling of optional high amperage motor controllers
>
> Future use for managing battery temperature

Frame
> Custom designed frame built to contain the 10 batteries within

The goal of the Eco-Trekker Tour and the TV series is to provide ecological knowledge through entertainment. We're happy to be a part of it.

Latest News

The prototype Electra Cruiser was delivered to Wisconsin for the *Coolfuel Roadtrip* TV series, hosted by one of my great friends, Shaun Murphy. Shaun loves the new bike and is riding across the country with it. Sparky the dog is also having a blast.

We've posted a few pictures from out west on www.vogelbilt.com/video/.

The national daytime TV show *Living It Up! With Ali & Jack* invited Shaun to be a guest on the show while he was in New York with the Electra Cruiser in November of 2003. The show was a hit, and Sparky had a ball in the audience.

In addition, I was interviewed by writer Paul Garson, representing a number of different publications that wanted to do a story on the bike. The Electra Cruiser will be mentioned in *V-Twin* magazine, Walneck's *Classic Cycle Trader*, the *Robb Report*, and several other publications.

Lastly, during the recent blackout in New York, the bike and the biodiesel generator in the sidecar were used to power my house, running on pure B100 (essentially vegetable oil).

The Idea

The Electra Cruiser (formerly the "Electric Hog") was an idea that became reality through many years of hard work and determination. It was my belief that a one-of-a-kind vehicle could be built using simple and innovative designs. The result is a unique, rugged, retro-looking design that is well balanced, comfortable, and fun to ride. And most of all, it is a *zero-emissions vehicle* (ZEV) using only batteries as its source of power.

The Prototype

On May 15, 2001, the finished prototype rolled out under its own power. This was a marvelous sight, 3 years of work and engineering finally coming together. The project was a remarkable challenge because there was nothing to compare the vehicle with except for its gasoline counterparts (Figures 3-9 through 3-11).

FIGURE 3-9   Electra Cruiser during filming of *Cow Power* in Wisconsin.

FIGURE 3-10   Electra Cruiser on display during the New York leg of trip.

Figure 3-11 Electra Cruiser in California during final filming of the USA journey for camera adjustments.

Future Plans

- Implementation of advanced battery technology for improved range, performance, and charging
- Reduction in weight, replacing steel components with aluminum and other lightweight alloys
- Regenerative braking coupled with improved motor controller technology
- Future designs to include sidecar with low-emission turbine generator (biodiesel) or fuel-cell technology

The KillaCycle—Bill Dube Breaks NEDRA Records

The KillaCycle changed the entire game in 2000. This time record for Bill Dube's KillaCycle says it all:

ET: 9.450 seconds
Event: Woodburn Drags 2000
Track: Woodburn, Oregon
Driver/owner: Bill Dube/Scotty Pollacheck
Hometown: Denver, Colorado
Sponsor: Boulder Technologies

Class/voltage division: MT/A

Specs: 312 V, Boulder Technologies 624 thin-film, lead-acid cells, Zilla 1400-A controller, twin Advanced DC 6.7-in motors modified for racing

The KillaCycle made a record run of 152 mph (245 km/h) at 9.4-s quarter-mile (400-m) time at Woodburn Drags in 2000, in Woodland, Oregon.

E-mail from Bill Dube

Monday, June 7, 1999

I brought the KillaCycle to Bandimere last Saturday for its shakedown tests and even with the controller set at 120 hp (less than half of what the machine can produce), I managed to set a new world record for an electric motorcycle in the 1/4 mile.

The bike ran 13.995 right out off the trailer. I backed that up with a 14.050 run to seal the NEDRA record. This beats Don Crabtree's record (set on May 22) by more than 2 seconds. The bike gave me zero trouble, so I will check all the connections, snug up the nuts and bolts, tighten the chain, and turn up the controller for the next race.

I plan to race again on Friday, June 25 at Bandimere Speedway. This next time the controller will be set for 250 hp.[7]

Figures 3-12 through 3-15 show Bill Dube and the A123 Li-ion cell–powered KillaCycle setting a new quarter-mile (400-m) record of 7.824 seconds and 168 mph (270 km/h) in Phoenix, Arizona, at All Harley Drag Racing Association (AHDRA) 2007.

FIGURE 3-12   KillaCycle performing burnout formally called pass to increase traction. (http://www. killacycle.com/2007/11/11/7824-168-mph-at-pomona-ahdra-nov-10th.)

FIGURE 3-13   KillaCycle owner Bill Dube speaking with Scotty Pollacheck, rider. (http://www. killacycle.com/2007/11/11/7824-168-mph-at-pomona-ahdra-nov-10th.)

FIGURE 3-14   KillaCycle owner Bill Dube during interview. (http://www.killacycle. com/2007/11/11/7824-168-mph-at-pomona-ahdra-nov-10th.)

Figure 3-15   KillaCycle pit stop and interview with Bill Dube. (http://www.killacycle. com/2007/11/11/7824-168-mph-at-pomona-ahdra-nov-10th.)

New World Record at Bandimere—7.89 Seconds (Also 174 mph!)

The KillaCycle made drag racing history *again* at Bandimere Speedway on October 23, 2008—7.89 seconds at 168 mph is a new official National Electric Drag Racing Association (NEDRA) record and makes KillaCycle the world's quickest electric vehicle of any kind in the quarter mile![8]

Lightning struck twice on the mountain as the KillaCycle set a new mark for top speed in an earlier run that afternoon—7.955 seconds at 174.05 mph. The M&H Racemaster tire really gripped the awesome track prep provided by Larry Crispe and the crew at Bandimere Speedway. The current was 1850 A per motor, which nobody had done before, and, well, the rest is history!

Jim Husted at Hi-Torque Electric brought electric motors that took more revolutions per minute, current, and voltage "from any other [battery] pack the group ever thought possible." The A123 Systems nanophosphate batteries are an amazing technological leap for the electric transportation industry as a whole. We'll get into that discussion in Chapter 7.[9]

Ducati Project

Just a few blocks away from the headquarters of Tesla Motors in San Carlos, California, is a nondescript industrial building on American Street. Parked in front is a large blue and gold trailer, the kind you see in the pit areas of many racing venues. Down a hallway, past a pair of cluttered offices, is a warren of shops dedicated to building the fastest racing motorcycles on the circuit. One room is a veritable museum of national and international champions, custom-built cycles that garnered fame for their drivers and the little family-run businesses that built them.

Back in one of the shops stands a Ducati motorcycle, stripped to its frame. It too has lofty aspirations. Come this June, it hopes to be the first electric motorcycle to win the Time Trials Extreme Grand Prix (TTXGP) on the Isle of Man in the Irish Sea. A demanding 38-mile course that rises from sea level to 400 m and twists and turns its way along the coast, this race has long tested the skill and mettle of the best gas-bike racers in the world.

If the highly modified Ducati wins or even places well in the competition, it will be the catalyst that owner Richard Hatfield and his investors are looking for to launch his new venture, a trio of high-performance electric two-wheelers. The first will be a supercycle clone of the skeleton bike shown standing on the frame in San Carlos. The second will be a bit tamer, a more consumer-tailored version that's a step down from the superbike, and the third will be an electric scooter that Hatfield dubs the "45-45-45." "It'll do 45 mph for 45 miles and cost $4,500," he explained as he led Russell Frost, a fellow journalist, and me on a tour of the racing cycle center.

"I got the proverbial late-night call," Richard Hatfield explained with a smile. That motor and the A123 lithium nanophosphate batteries will power the supercycle and make that ghost of the Ducati a serious competitor in the zero-carbon race around Man.

As you might expect, Bill Dube, the owner of the record-busting KillaCycle, is an active participant in the Ducati project, as is A123 Systems, whose batteries power the KillaCycle. Where Dube's machine is about acceleration, Hatfield's is about endurance. Both are also very much about speed. You won't trek out to Sturges for the annual Harley convention on them, but the average, off-the-shelf Milwaukee thrashing machines that will give Hatfield's supercycle any serious competition will be few and far between. That's the plan, at least.

As Hatfield's machine gradually morphs from Ducati to Manx with the skilled guidance of A&A Racing's Ray Abrams and Bill Dube, his little Chinese scooter demonstrates the potential of a supercycle heart and lung transplant, although it should be noted that both the batteries, the 250-A hub motor, and the custom-designed controller all are made in China. Hatfield and his Mandarin-speaking fiancée have spent months scouring the country vetting manufacturers.

When I asked Hatfield how powerful the motor was, I thought he said 250 W, which would make it a sluggard performance-wise. A sluggard it is not. With the ability to handle up to 250 A of power, the blue prototype is a big-time performer, even with two big adults astride. Scuff marks on the plastic fairings bear witness to the fact that the mild-mannered-looking machine has caught more than one person unaware. Hatfield cautions everyone to wear a helmet and keep your wrist low on the throttle.

I got to take the first run on the scooter up the street between rows of blue-collar businesses—repair shops, car customizers, glass fitters. The acceleration is everything a sane person could want and more. The speedometer goes to 60 km/h. You can easily peg it well beyond that. Hatfield claims that it'll do 50 mph, and I believe him—and it doesn't take all that long to get there, either.

Steadily, a crowd started to form, drawn by the speedy but strangely quiet and smokeless machine. In short order, a professional motorcycle racer took his turn and returned with the now-famous EV-grin. He was amazed. If this is a foretaste of what the Manx machine can do, he wants to be on the list for the commercial version. Another onlooker was prepared to buy five of them right then and there after riding it.

Okay, it does great on the flat, but what about San Francisco's notorious hills? Hatfield reports that it'll handle them easily. After two adults rode the machine around the block, I reached down to check the temperature of the motor and controller. They were barely warm.

Hatfield hopes to begin production some time this summer. Assuming that we begin to see a return to $3/gal gasoline and people again start looking for more efficient, less costly ways to commute, his 12-cents-a-day scooter will make a tantalizing choice, especially with this kind of performance.[10]

Vectrix Corporation

Vectrix Corporation was formed in 1996 to develop and commercialize ZEV platform technologies focused on two-wheel applications. The single focus of Vectrix has been to provide clean, efficient, reliable, and affordable urban transportation. Vectrix's two-wheeled ZEVs are currently being marketed to consumers and government fleets. Vectrix has headquarters in Middletown, Rhode Island; engineering and test facilities in New Bedford, Massachusetts; sales offices in London and Rome; and production facilities in Wroclaw, Poland.[11]

The Vectrix VX-1

The 2009 VX-1 is a redesigned version of the Vectrix Personal Electric Vehicle (PEV). It is a powerful all-electric, all-highway-capable PEV that goes 62 mph, has a range of 35–55 miles, and does it all for about a penny a mile. *Motorcyclist Magazine* said:

> "It's smooth, it's quiet, it's clean and it's all-electric. It's also fully alternative," said Mike Boyle, Vectrix CEO. "In many ways this has been the perfect storm—the transformation of the two-wheel industry, the rise in gas prices, the economic pressures, and the increased awareness in the environment."

In response to rising gas prices, the two-wheel industry is up 65 percent (Motorcycle Industry Council) this year and is the fastest growing segment of the transportation industry. The all-electric Vectrix is extremely economical, operating at just pennies per mile and the equivalent of 357 miles per gallon, compared with 14 mpg for a leading SUV and 46 mpg for a leading hybrid car. Leading gas-powered motorcycles and scooters range from 52 to 87 mpg.

An increased focus on environmental issues also has consumers looking to lower their carbon footprint. Tests conducted by the Southwest Research Institute in San Antonio, Texas, on behalf of Vectrix Corporation reveal that two-wheel electric vehicles are three times cleaner than gas-powered motorcycles and scooters and 10 times cleaner than gas-powered cars:

- Based on 15,000 miles a year, an average car emits 3.17 tons of CO_2 a year, a motorcycle emits an average of 0.9 tons, and a Vectrix just 0.33 ton.
- By replacing one car 70 percent of the time with a Vectrix, a household can reduce CO_2 emission by 5 tons a year.
- Engineered to provide an eco-friendly, powerful alternative for commuting and recreational needs, Vectrix:
  - Reaches a top speed of 62 mph and offers acceleration from 0–50 mph in 6.8 seconds.
  - Has an average range of 30–55 miles on a single charge.
  - Offers minimal maintenance, simple operation, and low noise.
  - Weighs 515 pounds, has a 60-inch wheelbase and 30-inch seat height, seats two comfortably, and is highway legal.

Compared to traditional gasoline scooters that can produce up to 10 times the pollution of an average automobile, Vectrix is totally emissions free. It is virtually silent and highly efficient—a patented regenerative braking system redirects energy back into the Vectrix battery pack, which helps to extend its range by up to 12 percent.

Vectrix is more cost effective than gas or hybrid vehicles, since electricity is now one-tenth the cost of gasoline. The Vectrix nickel metal hydride (NiMH) battery pack has an estimated life of up to 10 years based on 5,000 miles per year. An onboard charger plugs in to any standard 110/220-V electrical outlet to charge the battery pack in just 2–3 hours.

Sophisticated design efficiencies of the smart, sleek Vectrix include a high-efficiency gearbox and drive train, aluminum construction for weight reduction, and aerodynamic styling to reduce drag. A low center of gravity, stiff frame, and even weight distribution provide superior handling.

For consumers with urban commutes, Vectrix is both convenient and cost effective. The driver can stop and go with one hand by simply twisting the throttle back for acceleration and twisting it forward to slow down smoothly and safely. Fast acceleration and handling make it easy and safe to zip in and out of traffic.

Summary

We have seen some great electric motorcycles over the years. Chapter 4 will show you more bikes for the taking if you do not want to convert to an electric vehicle from an existing chassis.

CHAPTER 4

Current Electric Motorcycles on the Market

Electric Motorcycles: Cool *and* Green

This chapter will describe some of the coolest electric motorcycles on the market today. Descriptions will include diagrams and pictures showing the different classes and styles. Electric vehicles (EVs) are fun to own and ride, and this chapter also will describe how everyone (all races, men and women, children and adults) is interested in and excited about EVs.

There's nothing wrong with cool, and I have to admit that few vehicles are cooler than motorcycles (at least in theory, although not all of us would ride one). You're basically sitting on an engine with wheels. It can't get much simpler than that. Motorcycles are not always practical, but the people who love their bikes really love them.

This chapter also will include a discussion of the advantages and disadvantages of EVs and address current trends in the EV industry. In addition, I will provide a brief description of the Electra Cruiser I built and its road to fame on television and the Discovery Channel. The Electra Cruiser's trip across the United States proved that EVs are viable and dependable.

But cool is not enough. The vast majority of motorcycles are still running on fossil fuels, and that's a problem. As battery technology improves, we're starting to see more electric motorcycles.[1] Some are available commercially; many are do-it-yourself (DIY) custom jobs. Here we look at some of the coolest ones.

Eva Håkansson's Electrocat Electric Motorcycle

Figure 4-1 shows Eva Håkansson astride her Electrocat motorcycle. I'm starting with her because she is a true pioneer in the world of electric motorcycles (she describes herself as a "hardcore EV geek with a green heart and passion for power and speed").

FIGURE 4-1   Eva Håkansson and her Electrocat electric motorcycle. (www.evahakansson.se.)

Eva built the Electrocat with her father, Sven Håkansson, and it is probably the first street-legal electric motorcycle in Sweden. It is based on a Cagiva Freccia C12R, model year 1990, but the insides are pure electric goodness.

Figure 4-2 shows the Electrocat's Thunder Sky litihum-iron-phosphate cells and the original Briggs & Stratton Etek motor. The blue box is the Alltrax AXE7245 controller. Charging takes half an hour on a powerful garage charger (longer with the smaller onboard charger—about 7 hours), and the range is 80 km (50 miles) per charge at 70 km/h (44 mph).[2]

KillaCycle and KillaCycle LSR Electric Motorcycles

I'm not finished with Eva Håkansson yet. She's part of the team that created the KillaCycle, an insanely powerful electric dragbike that set a new world record on October 23, 2008—"7.89 seconds at 168 mph is a new official National Electric Drag Racing Association (NEDRA) record and makes the KillaCycle the world's quickest

FIGURE 4-2   Electrocat batteries and electric motor. (evahakansson.se.)

Figure 4-3 Eva Hakansson with the KillaCycle. (www.evahakansson.se.)

electric vehicle of any kind in the quarter mile!" (Figure 4-3). Congrats to Scotty Pollacheck for having the guts to do that run.

How fast does the KillaCycle accelerate from 0–60 mph? *Less than a second* (0.97 second to be exact). The batteries are 1210 lithium-iron-nanophosphate cells from A123 Systems. We are building a brand new motorcycle optimized for high speed—the KillaCycle LSR. (However, the original KillaCycle dragbike will continue pushing the envelope on the dragstrip.) The warm-up target for KillaCycle LSR is to reach 200 mph (322 km/h) in the beginning of the 2009 season. The next target, later in the season, will be to reach 300 mph (482 km/h) and, hopefully, take the overall electric record of 314 mph (505 km/h) toward the end of the year. The ultimate goal is to break the overall motorcycle record of 354 mph (570 km/h).[3]

An EV conversion solves so many problems and transportation concerns immediately. It just needs to happen.

Zero Motorcycles

Zero Motorcycles recently revealed its new high-performance electric street motorcycle, the Zero S. This highly anticipated launch marked Zero Motorcycles' official entry into the street-legal category. The company's new flagship motorcycle uses Zero's proprietary Z-Force power pack and aircraft-grade alloy frame to make the Zero S the quickest production electric motorcycle in its class. Zero Motorcycles has already booked substantial pre-orders for the Zero S without sharing details or images and now anticipates a soaring demand. The Zero S will begin shipping to customers soon (Figure 4-4).

Said Neal Saiki, inventor and founder of Zero Motorcycles:

Our goal from the beginning was to engineer a high-performance electric urban street motorcycle that would change the face of the industry. The Zero S is a revolutionary motorcycle that is designed to tackle any city street, hill, or obstacle. . . . The innovation behind the Zero S is what separates it from the competition. The Zero S is a high-performance motorcycle that also happens

Figure 4-4 Zero S motorcycle. (www.zeromotorcycles.com.)

to be fully electric and green. The fact that it's electric means not having to get gas and reduced maintenance.

Developed to aggressively take on urban environments and encourage the occasional detour, the Zero S integrates revolutionary technology with innovative motorcycle design. Instant acceleration and a lightweight design combine to form an industry-leading power-to-weight ratio that increases the motorcycle's range and handling abilities. At only 225 lb, the Zero S has a range of up to 60 miles and a top speed of 60 mph. With 31 peak horsepower and 62.5 ft · lb of torque, the Zero S is designed for optimal performance off the line, in sharp turns, and while navigating obstacles.

In addition to its performance and maneuverability, the Zero S uses a completely nontoxic lithium-ion array, and most of the motorcycle is fully recyclable. The landfill-approved power pack recharges in less than 4 hours while plugged into a standard 110- or 220-V outlet. Eco-friendly with zero emissions, the Zero S is also economy-friendly, with an operating cost of less than 1 cent per mile or kilometer.

At $9,950, the Zero S is priced competitively and also qualifies for the recently approved 10 percent federal plug-in vehicle tax credit, a sales tax deduction, and other state-based incentives. This effectively reduces the final cost of purchase by a minimum of almost a $1,000. The Zero S was developed to comply with all street and highway motorcycle standards and can be licensed for the road in most countries. It is available for purchase through Zero Motorcycles' Web site at www.zeromotorcycles.com.

The Zero X electric motorcycle gets 40 miles per charge from its proprietary patent-pending lithium-ion array and charges in 2 hours. The third generation of the Zero X is priced at $7,750, with an introductory price of $7,450 through December 31, 2008.[4]

Zero Motorcycles is the next step in motorcycle evolution and represents the ultimate electric motorcycle technology. Unencumbered by conventional thinking about how to design, manufacture, and sell high-performance electric motorcycles, Zero Motorcycles is on a mission to turn heads and revolutionize the industry by combining the best aspects of a traditional motorcycle with today's most advanced technology. The result is an electric motorcycle line that's insanely fast and environmentally friendly.

Zero Motorcycles first entered the motorcycle category with the launch of the 2008 Zero X electric dirtbike. Exceeding all expectations, the Zero X sold out in late 2008 and blazed the path for the long-awaited launch of the Zero S Supermoto motorcycle (Figure 4-5). You can find out more about the Zero S Supermoto motorcycle and Zero Motorcycles in general at the Web site www.zeromotorcycles.com.

Figure 4-5   Look at that motorcycle go! (Courtesy of Zero Motorcycles, www.zeromotorcycles.com.)

Brammo Motorsports

Brammo Motorsports (www.brammo.com) based in Oregon, released an electric motorcycle called the Enertia Bike for sale in the United States in early 2008. It has a top speed of 50 mph and a range of 45 miles, and it can fully recharge via a standard plug in 3 hours. It weighs just 275 lb and uses a direct chain drive for power. You can see a video of the bike in action at the Enertia Web site. The power is stored in six Valence Technology lithium-phosphate batteries that are mounted above and below the frame. The motorcycle is driven by a "pancake type" high-output direct-current (dc) motor.

Brammon initially offered a limited-edition carbon model for $14,995, and it could be ordered online for a delivery in the first quarter of 2009. You also could reserve a standard model at $11,995, which was available by the end of 2008.[5]

With a low moment of inertia and an agressive rake angle, this motorcycle handles like a dream and has an affinity for changing direction. Couple this with the smooth, efficient power delivery from the electric drivetrain, and you've got a recipe for excitement. With 100 percent of its torque available from 0 rpm, the Enertia is certainly no slouch off the line. At its quickest setting, the Enertia will sprint from 0–30 mph in 3.8 seconds.

Beyond the obvious goal of empowering customers to enjoy guilt-free transportation, Brammo wants to empower customers to set their own performance limits on the Enertia (Figure 4-6). If you're a beginner or would like to achieve maximum range on every ride, perhaps you should start at a lower power setting than someone with either a very short commute or an ambitious right wrist. The company's Momentum software will enable you to download information about your driving habits and customize your bike to the performance setting that fits you and your environment best.

Figure 4-6   Side view of the Enertia motorcycle. (enertiabike.com.)

At its quickest setting, the 13-kW, 18-hp electric dc motor will propel the Enertia from 0–30 mph in 3.8 seconds. The cost is about $14,999 if you want the first batch of bikes or $11,995 if you can wait until later. Around 100,000 people have already expressed interest via Brammo's Web site. Figure 4-7 presents a rendering of the insides. Figure 4-8 shows the bike. It looks surprisingly clean compared to what we're used to seeing with gas motorcycles.

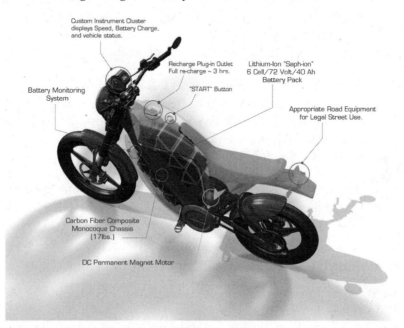

FIGURE 4-7 Specifications of the Enertia bike. (enertiabike.com.)

FIGURE 4-8 The Enertia motorcycle. (enertiabike.com.)

Voltzilla: DIY Electric Motorcycle by Russ Gries

Some people just can't wait for a commercially made electric motorcycle, so they take matters in their own hands. Russ Gries is a DIY kind of guy, and when he was given a free electric forklift, he decided to turn it into an electric motorcycle.

He used the carcass of a 1976 Honda CB550 that he got for $50 as a frame, and then he removed the gas engine to install an electric motor and batteries. After about 120 hours and a net cost of $15.61 (that's right, he got money for recycling the rest of the forklift), the result is Voltzilla. It's a bit different from most electric conversions in good part because of its forklift ancestry:

- It runs on 24 V; most others are 48 V and up.
- The transmission was retained because Gries wanted the flexibility of variable gearing for the hills where he lives (most other converted bikes are direct drive from the motor to the rear sprocket).
- It has a reverse, just like the forklift.
- The four batteries are from golf carts. They are used 6-V, 220-A models. Most other conversions use smaller batteries with less capacity.
- Its current top speed is around 35 mph (56 km/h), but after a drive-pulley swap, Gries should be able to get 60–65 mph (100 km/h)

Electric Motorcycle Conversions: Easier Than You Think

An electric motorcycle conversion is easier than an electric car conversion because you don't have to worry about the transmission and clutch, power steering, vacuum pumps, heaters, air conditioners, and the weight and size of everything that gets moved around.[6] An El Ninja–type conversion is even easier than most motorcycle conversions because the battery and motor mounting are so straightforward and provide configuration flexibility. After a thorough description of technology, performance, and maintenance, this book will describe the design tradeoffs in converting a gas motorcycle to an electric motorcycle. It then will walk you through the building process, using step-by-step build descriptions, CAD drawings, CAD mockups, and photographs of the conversion process.

KTM "Race Ready" Enduro Electric Motorcycle

Now, if we turn our gaze to the future, Austrian motorcycle maker KTM has announced that within two years it will make a 100 percent electric enduro "race ready" motorcycle. According to *Hell for Leather* magazine:

> The Austrian company is releasing very few details of the Zero Emissions Motorcycle, but has revealed that it develops 29.5 ft · lb of torque and carries lithium-ion batteries capable of lasting 40 minutes under "race conditions" and that it can be fully recharged in just 1 hour. . . . KTM's battery pack and

electric motor together weigh 17 kg (for a total machine weight of 90 kg, or 198 lb—that's 7 kg lighter than a KTM 125 EXC), but some of this weight will be offset by the elimination of the clutch, exhaust pipes and canisters, fuel tank, and other necessities of internal combustion. The company expects that the Zero Emissions Motorcycle will carry a small price premium over a KTM Enduro of similar performance.

Honda and Yamaha to Make Electric Motorcycles in 2010–2011

All eyes are currently on hybrids (such as Honda's upcoming all-new Insight) and electric cars, but electric motorcycles also deserve some attention (if only because they are less noisy). We've featured a few DIY models, like the Voltzilla and the electric Kawasaki, but so far, few big players have made them, which has allowed newcomers like Vectrix to get a toehold. But that's about to change.

On the horizon, though with fewer details, Yamaha and Honda have both announced that they will be making electric motorcycles in 2010–2011. "Both firms hope to bring to market electric motorcycles that perform on a par with bikes with 50-cc engine displacements. The vehicles will be powered by high-performance lithium-ion batteries."[7]

EVT America

2009 Z-30 versus the 2007 Z-20b

EVT America's 2009 Z-30 (Figure 4-9) is almost identical to the 2007 Z-20b in body style, which I find to be far more suitable than the very attractive but less functional

FIGURE 4-9   The EVT Z-30 electric scooter. (evtamerica.com.)

2007 Z-20a. However, technically, there are significant differences and improvements. Here is a list of what is new and better:

- The Z-30 has a 3,000-W three-phase 60-V brushless hub motor built on a 10-in rim and sports 10 × 3.5 in six-ply Deparment of Transportation (DOT) tires.
- The new motor is capable of reaching speeds of approximately 45 mph (72 km/h) but with superior torque and climbing ability. It has been kicked up from 2,500 to 3,000 W.
- To make it easier and less expensive to replace plastic parts, the 2009 Z-30 (as well as the R-30) is available in only two colors: metallic red or metallic blue.
- The body and frame of the Z-30 are sturdier and better fit with 99 percent stainless steel nuts, bolts, washers, and screws.
- The floorboard will have a thick rug included as a fashion accessory.
- The range of the bike remains roughly the same, but it is reduced indistinctly if the motorcycle is used at full speed at all times because of the more powerful motor. Nonetheless, it still should exceed a 30-mile range at normal cruising speeds when used with fully charged good working batteries.*
- The new controller is a Kelly controller specifically and expressly designed and modified for the Z-30. It also has a built-in overheat preventer that reduces the amperage under extreme conditions. Note: The Kelly controller for the R-30 or Z-30 retails for $350 plus shipping and handling and can be purchased directly from EVT America separately.
- The Z-30 will no longer have an alarm or a kickstand on-and-off relay that proved to be unreliable in the first production and became a common problem because of shipping. The top priority is most definitely *reliability*. The kill switch will remain as a safety feature. The alarm is replaced with a stainless steel disc brake lock included with purchase.
- A windshield assembly kit and a trunk assembly kit are offered as options and are priced separately. The trunk comes in only one color: black.
- The 2009 Z-30 has superior heavy-duty rear air shock absorbers that provide a smoother ride.
- The front and rear coated disc brakes are of much better quality and fit; they are also Department of Transportation (DOT)–compliant.

---

* Range will vary depending on the weight of the rider(s), terrain, wind resistance, and road conditions. For example, a run on a relatively flat road with few stops and a 160-lb rider will get much better range than a run on a hilly road with multiple stops and a 280-lb rider. Range is in direct proportion to energy consumption. The slower you drive, the farther you will go. Stop and go with full acceleration after each stop may cut the range by as much as 50 percent. Just as cars have better mileage on the highway and less in city driving, the same happens with an EV. It's all about energy consumption.

- The new models have graduated to an advanced dc-to-dc converter (60–12 V) with an inline fuse for added safety and the ability to handle higher peak current.
- The new extra tough harness is made to European standards, shielded for ultrasound frequencies, simplified for functionality, and better color-coded to ensure continuity and easier maintenance.
- The dash now contains a speedometer/odometer with both mph and km/h with European standards of accuracy and a fiberoptics glowing needle.
- The Z-30 comes with the much-awaited SmartSpark battery equalizer (made in the United State) for 60 V with LED lights, which maintains the batteries precisely balanced during both charging and discharging, thereby increasing the life of the batteries significantly. It is also able to monitor the condition of each battery and detect if one is not functioning properly. Note: The SmartSpark equalizer for a 60-V vehicle retails for $219 plus shipping and handling, and it can be purchased separately from EVT America.
- The rest of the Z-30 will be much the same in appearance, although it now has more clearance under the frame and battery box owing to the new shocks. The Z-30 still has the 5 × 12-V, 35-Ah sealed lead-acid battery pack as well as DOT lights throughout.
- The company is equipping all the 2009 models with an improved Soneil International, Ltd., of Canada automatic 60-V charger. Note: The Soneil charger (60V/5A LAB Charger Model No. 6010SR) for any R or Z models retails for $248 plus shipping and handling and can be purchased separately from EVT America.
- The Z Range and Speed have been tested with a 160-lb (73-kg) driver. Ideal conditions met; flat paved road; 2.0 mph (3.2 kp/h) frontal wind; 78°F (25.5°C) temperature; new fully charged batteries. Multiple test results average plus or minus tolerance of 10%.
- Climbing capacity has been tested with a 160-lb (73-kg) driver. The Z30 has excellent climbing ability but at a cost of much higher energy consumption.

2009 R-30 versus the 2007 R-20

Not wanting to change in any way or alter the classic retro style of the R models, the company's 2009 R-30 looks almost identical to the 2007 R-20 (Figure 4-10). However, technically, there are significant differences and improvements. Here is a list of what is new and better:

- The R-30 has a 3,000-W three-phase 60-V brushless hub motor built on a 10-in rim and sports 10 × 3.5 in six-ply DOT tires.

FIGURE 4-10   The EVT America R20. (evtamerica.com.)

- The new motor is capable of reaching a maximum speed of approximately 45 mph (72 km/h) but with superior torque and climbing ability. It has been kicked up from 2,500 to 3,000 W.
- To make it easier and less expensive to replace plastic parts, the 2009 R-30 (as well as the Z-30) is only available in two colors: metallic red or metallic blue.
- The body and frame of the R-30 are sturdier and better fit with 99 percent stainless steel nuts, bolts, washers, and screws.
- The floorboard is an aluminum-plated cover over the area where the feet go, and a thick floor rug is included.
- The range of the bike remains roughly the same but will be reduced indistinctly if the motorcycle is used at full speed at all times because of the more powerful motor. Nonetheless, it still should exceed a 30-mile range at normal cruising speeds when used with fully charged good working batteries.*
- The new controller is a Kelly controller specifically and expressly designed and modified for the R-30, and it has a built-in overheat preventer that reduces the amperage under extreme conditions. Note: The Kelly controller for the R-30 or Z-30 retails for $350 plus shipping and handling and can be purchased separately directly from EVT America.

_____

* Range will vary depending on the weight of the rider(s), terrain, wind resistance, and road conditions. For example, a run on a relatively flat road with few stops and a 180-lb rider will get much better range than a run on a hilly road with multiple stops and a 280-lb rider. Range is in direct proportion to energy consumption. The slower you drive, the further you will go. Stop and go with full acceleration after each stop may cut the range by as much as 50 percent. Just as cars have better mileage on the highway and less in city driving, the same happens with an EV. It's all about energy consumption.

- The R-30 will no longer have an alarm or a kickstand on-and-off relay that proved to be unreliable in the first production and became a common problem because of shipping. The top priority is *reliability*. The kill switch will remain as a safety feature. The alarm is replaced with a stainless steel disc brake lock included with the purchase.
- A windshield assembly kit ($75) and a trunk assembly kit ($125) are optional and must be ordered separately. The trunk comes in only one color: black.
- The 2009 R-30 model has superior heavy-duty rear air shock absorbers and significantly stronger front shock absorbers that provide a smoother ride.
- The front and rear coated disc brakes are of much better quality and fit; they are also DOT-compliant.
- The bike has graduated to an advanced dc-to-dc converter (60–12 V) with an inline fuse for added safety and the ability to handle higher peak current.
- The new extra tough harness is made to European standards, shielded for ultrasound frequencies, simplified for functionality, and better color-coded to ensure continuity and easier maintenance.
- The dash now contains a speedometer/odometer with both mph and km/h with European standards of accuracy and a fiberoptics glowing needle.
- The R-30 comes with the much-awaited SmartSpark battery equalizer (made in the United States) for 60 V with LED lights, which maintains the batteries precisely balanced during both charging and discharging, thereby significantly increasing the life of the batteries. It is also able to monitor the condition of each battery and detect if one is not functioning properly.
- The rest of the R-30 is much the same in appearance, although it now has more clearance under the frame and battery box owing to the new shocks. The R-30 still has the 5 × 12-V, 35-Ah sealed lead-acid battery pack as well as DOT lights throughout.
- The company is equipping all the 2009 models with an improved Soneil International, Ltd., of Canada automatic 60-V charger.

Summary

There are many types of electric motorcycles on the market today. However, conversion is the best alternative because it costs less than either buying ready-made or building from scratch, takes only a little more time than buying ready-made, and is technically within everyone's reach (certainly with the help of a local mechanic and absolutely with the help of an EV conversion shop).

Conversion is also easiest from the labor standpoint. You buy the existing internal combustion vehicle chassis you like (certain chassis types are easier and better to convert than others), install an electric motor, and save a bundle. It's really quite simple. Chapter 10 covers the steps in detail.

To do a smart motorcycle conversion, the first step is to buy a clean, straight, used internal combustion vehicle chassis. A used model is also to your advantage (as you'll read in Chapter 6) because its already-broken-in parts are smooth, and the friction losses are minimized. A vehicle from a salvage yard or a vehicle with a bad engine may not be the best choice because you do not know if the transmission, brakes, or other components and systems are satisfactory. Once you select the vehicle, then you add well-priced electrical parts or a whole kit from a vendor you trust and do as much of the simple labor as possible, farming out the tough jobs (machining, bracket making, etc.).

Whether you do the work yourself and just subcontract a few jobs or elect to have someone handle the entire conversion for you, you can convert to an EV for a very attractive price compared with buying a new motorcycle.[8]

CHAPTER 5

Geometry: A Basic Lesson on Rake, Trail, and Suspension

For your conversion and motorcycle build, you might want to alter or design extreme effects into your motorcycle. Maybe you want to have a really cool front fork, raked out chopper, or other radical design (see Figure 5-1). This is great, but be aware of the positive and negative affects of rake, trail, and fork angle. This is another subject most people do not touch on or talk about, and frankly, there is insufficient information on this when you research the topic. In this chapter I will explain more about rake, trail, and fork angle so that you have a better understanding of how they affect the handing and safety of your motorcycle. This is just a general overview, and more geometry and calculations are needed if you really want to get specific. This is just enough to give you a basic knowledge.

I discovered a great book containing all this information in one place if you really need to dig into the design and specifics. In Chapter 14, listed under "Books," you will find more information on the book entitled, *Motorcycle Handling and Chassis Design*. Also, I want to send a thank-you to Chris Longhurst (www.carbibles.com) for his great photos and input into this chapter.

There are many aspects of a motorcycle's shape that affect its behavior. The one that is most easily identifiable is the geometry of the fork. The relationship between the frame and front wheel is governed by a number of factors that I will cover in the following pages. Because the front wheel is the steering wheel of a motorcycle, the handling of the bike is radically affected by its design. The three main terms I will discuss are *rake, trail,* and *fork angle*. I will provide a little information on the *rear swingarm* too.

Rake

Rake all starts off at the headstock of the frame. The *headstock* is the point where the front fork joins the frame, with bearings at the top and bottom, and through which passes the fork's steering head. The angle of this tube to the vertical, when the bike

FIGURE 5-1   The all too well-known 1969 movie *Easyrider* gave rise to raked-out bikes and custom rides. (http://image.guardian.co.uk/sys-images/Arts/Arts_/Pictures/2007/07/27/easyrider460.jpg.)

is fully trimmed, is referred to as the *rake* (Figure 5-2). In all but specific custom applications, the angle of this tube, the steering head, is the same angle as the pivot point of the fork. Normal angles range from 28–35 degrees depending on the type of bike and application, but this is not set in stone.

The rake is *not* the angle of the fork. In most cases, the two angles happen to be the same, but don't assume that they are. Fork angle can change a few degrees in the negative or positive direction depending on design and needs.

Small differences in rake angle of half a degree or so can be explained by any change in the height of the back end off the ground compared with the front. If the back end is lower and the front end higher, the whole bike's natural horizontal line slopes up at the front, thereby making the natural vertical line lean backwards, affecting the rake. This also applies to any change in the height of the front end of

FIGURE 5-2   Picture of bike front headstock angle in relation to ground. (Courtesy of Chris Longhurst, www.carbibles.com/suspension_bible_bikes.html.)

the motorcycle. This could occur easily with a change in loaded weight, change in tire diameter, or change in spring loading in the suspension. Any change can have a slight effect, which is okay; radical changes can have a dramatic effect (Figures 5-3 and 5-4).

FIGURE 5-3   Rolling frame with reference to height and ground.

FIGURE 5-4   Rolling frame with reference lines drawn showing trail.

Some aftermarket frames or other custom applications have a larger than normal headstock and provide the ability to change the angle of the steering head. This is accomplished by a set of eccentric bearing housings offset a few degrees, resulting in the ability to change the angle of the fork in relation to the rake. This is

FIGURE 5-5   Offset bearing for neck.

a simple and easy solution if you have the need to change the rake (Figure 5-5). Angle changes become more important as you look more closely at the relationship of rake and trail.

A few other simple factors or changes can alter your rake and trail. These are as easy as changing rear suspension height, tire diameter, and length of the front fork. All these changes may have a positive or a negative effect on the handling of your motorcycle. You will need to determine what is right for you.

The rake of the frame is a contributing factor that determines steering performance and handling. It correlates directly with the speed of the response of the steering. A steep angle, meaning less angle, equals quick-responding steering; a laid-back rake, meaning more angle, equals slow steering. An angle that is too steep at low speed is light; the machine will handle with unbelievable ease at low speeds but will be completely out of balance at high speeds. It will easily develop a fatal high-speed wobble. A rake with a lot of angle will cause the bike to handle sluggishly at high speeds. It will seem almost too steady. You will have trouble balancing the bike at lower speeds or on winding roads. It will feel generally sluggish and clumsy. All this has a direct relation to trail, which I will explain next.

Trail

This is the second part of the equation in relation to rake. *Trail* is determined by the distance at ground level between a vertical line intersecting the wheel spindle perpendicular to the ground and a line that passes through the headstock hitting the ground at some distance away from the vertical line through the spindle (Figure 5-6).

The trail should be between 4 and 6.5 inches so that the bike handles easily at both high and low speeds. The length of trail affects the ease with which the bike steers. The longer the distance of trail, the more stable the bike is, but the heavier the steering will be, and the harder the bike will be to steer. The shorter the distance, the lighter and more twitchy is the steering. Cruisers generally have a longer trail; sports bikes usually have a shorter trail. The best solution is a compromise between the two, shooting for an average length in trail with predictable handling.

If you are still having trouble understanding trail, we can use the typical castor used on a shopping cart as an example (Figure 5-7). We all know that when the cart

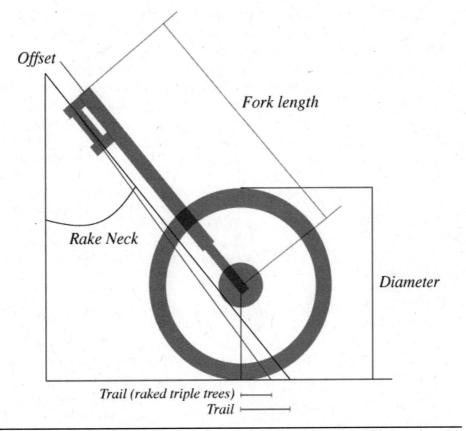

Offset

Fork length

Rake Neck

Diameter

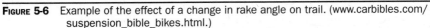

Trail (raked triple trees)

Trail

FIGURE 5-6   Example of the effect of a change in rake angle on trail. (www.carbibles.com/suspension_bible_bikes.html.)

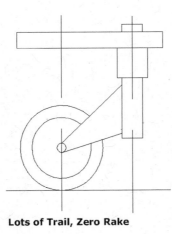

Lots of Trail, Zero Rake

FIGURE 5-7   The castor on a shopping cart in relation to trail and rake.

is pushed forward, the castor wants to go straight. The distance between the pivot point and the spindle, where the wheel rotates, is essentially the trail. Imagine pushing this cart being pushed and trying to physically change the direction of the castor as you are moving. You cannot do it, or it is very hard to change the direction. Try it. If you lengthen the distance even more, the resistance to turning increases. We can apply this same example to trail. A bike with a lot of trail will be hard to turn and corner but goes straight nicely.

Fork Angle

The angle of the fork is not necessarily the rake angle. Be aware of this. Some manufacturers and certain aftermarket forks offer an extra rake angle worked right into them. This is accomplished with the triple trees or the headstock bearings. This could be to your advantage as a simple way to modify and change the rake angle and trail if want without changing the rake of the actual frame (Figure 5-8).

Fork Length

Another way to change the angle of rake without modifying the frame is to change the fork length. Forks come in various lengths and are offered by many aftermarket manufactures. You will find thousands of aftermarket parts offered for Harley-Davidson-style motorcycles. By lengthening the front end, you change the geometry and raise the height a little. This will have a direct effect on your rake angle and trail. In most cases, it will increase your trail length (Figures 5-9 through 5-11).

FIGURE 5-8   Raked triple-tree example. (Courtesy of Custom Chrome, www.customchrome.com.)

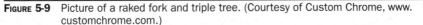

FIGURE 5-9   Picture of a raked fork and triple tree. (Courtesy of Custom Chrome, www. customchrome.com.)

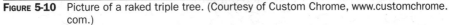

FIGURE 5-10   Picture of a raked triple tree. (Courtesy of Custom Chrome, www.customchrome. com.)

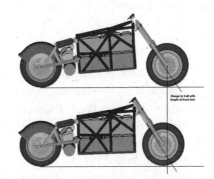

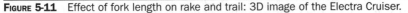

FIGURE 5-11   Effect of fork length on rake and trail: 3D image of the Electra Cruiser.

Fork Dive

Since we are learning about fork length and angle and their relation to rake and trail, it is only fitting to touch on *fork dive*, also known as *brake dive*. When you apply the brakes of a moving motorcycle, the weight transfers to the front wheel, thus compressing the suspension. When stopping, a motorcycle equipped with telescopic forks adds weight to the front wheel, transmitted through the fork. This transfer of weight to the front wheel compresses the fork, changing its length. This shortening of the fork causes the front end of the bike to move lower, and this is called *fork dive* or *brake dive*.

Fork dive can be disconcerting to the rider, who may feel like he or she is about to be thrown over the front of the motorcycle. If the bike dives so far as to bottom out the front fork, it also can cause handling and braking problems. One of the purposes of the suspension is to help maintain contact between the tire and the road. If the suspension has bottomed out, it is no longer moving as it should and is no longer helping to maintain contact. This is an important concern in your conversion to an electric vehicle (EV). Batteries and electrical components added to the bike may change the total weight of the motorcycle, either making it lighter or heavier than the stock vehicle. Also, take into consideration as you compress the front fork that you change the length, thus changing the rake and trail. Under severe stopping forces, if your bike is not set up properly, you can dramatically change the rake and trail. If this happens, your front end can become squirrelly and difficult to control. If you look at Figure 5-11 and imagine the reverse effect of compressing the fork, rake and trail will decrease.

Brake dive with telescopic forks can be reduced in the following ways:

- Increasing the spring rate of the fork springs
- Increasing the compression damping of the forks

See following sections on travel and spring rate.

Travel

The total travel of a suspension system is the distance the suspension travels between total compression and total extension. The travel distance on off-road and dual-purpose bikes tends to be very high; the rear suspension travel on cruisers tends to be relatively little. This value is usually listed in the motorcycle's manual or is available online.

Adjusting the suspension based on the travel is the easiest place to start in modifying the suspension for load and rider. Ideally, the suspension should sag under the weight of the rider by 30 percent of the total travel.

Start by measuring the distance between two points along the suspension's travel with the bike upright but without the rider's weight on the bike. For example, measure the distance from the front axle to where the fork enters the bottom of the triple tree. On the rear, measure from the rear axle to a point on the frame directly above it.

Next, the rider should put as much of his or her weight on the bike and any other load the bike normally will carry while holding it upright. Measure between the same two points, and find the difference of the two measurements. This should be approximately 30 percent of the total travel of the suspension.

Increase the preload to reduce the sag; decrease the preload to increase the sag. On rear suspension, most coil-over shocks have an adjustment with a ramp that, when rotated, will increase or decrease preload. For the front fork, in most cases, you need to take the suspension apart and increase or decrease tension via shims or

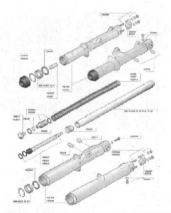

FIGURE 5-12   Typical Harley-style front fork assembly with spring. (Courtesy of Custom Chrome, www.customechrome.com.)

spacers on the spring (Figure 5-12). In the worst case, you even may have to replace the springs with ones with a different spring rate (see "Spring Rate" below).

Here's an interesting story from when I was building the second Electra Cruiser concerning a lesson I learned regarding the preload and springs on the front fork. During the initial build, the bike was assembled, and the rear suspension and fork looked great. The bike sat high on the suspension, as expected, because the batteries were not loaded in the frame. All seemed normal. The day came to load the full battery pack, all 560 lb, in the frame and test the loaded suspension. The frame, now fully loaded with batteries, was slowly lowered to the ground to support its own weight, all 560 lb of lead and 150 lb of transmission and electric motor. To my surprise, the front fork bottomed out solid! The bike was not even fully loaded or even moving, and it bottomed out. I soon found out that the wrong fork was sent to me. I replaced it with a new one with heavy-duty springs and modified the spacers on the springs to create more preload. With heavy-duty springs and more preload, the front fork supported the added weight perfectly.

Spring Rate

A spring's *rate* is a measure of how much force is require to compress the spring a given distance. The higher the rate, the more force it takes to compress the spring a given distance, and the less it compresses under a given force. If the sag of a motorcycle's suspension for a given rider and weight cannot be set properly using preload adjustments, typically the spring must be replaced with one with a different rate. In the case of the rear suspension, the entire coil-over shock assembly may need replacement. If the sag is too great, a higher-rate spring must be used, and vice versa. Even when the sag is set correctly, sometimes the springs have to be replaced. This depends on the weight of the rider. If the rider is too light for the design of the springs, the ride will be harsh, even when sag is correct.

FIGURE 5-13   A bike with a raked fork.

If the rider is too heavy, the ride may be mushy, brake dive may be excessive, and so on.

In most telescopic forks, the springs can be replaced in a straightforward manner. The coil-over springs on the rear shocks can be another matter. Not only can they be of a unique design, but the shock itself may be incompatible with a different-rate spring if it lacks sufficient damping adjustment.

Progressive-rate springs are springs whose rates change as the spring is compressed. As the spring is compressed, the rate increases. Springs can be progressive either by having the coils at one end of the spring wound differently than at the other end or by actually being two separate springs with different rates held together by a spacer. For most modern sports bikes, progressive-rate springs are not recommended unless fitted at the factory.

Progressive-rate springs are intended to give the best of both worlds: a smooth ride, yet response handling over rough surfaces. For maximum suspension performance, however, straight-rate springs are usually recommended.

Rear Suspension

The rear suspension of your motorcycle plays an important role in many aspects of your EV's performance. It is another part of the equation that you can modify to improve the ride and change the geometry of your motorcycle conversion. You will find that a few slight changes can improve the ride and handling greatly. Of course, on the other hand, some drastic changes also can prove dangerous. I will not get into great detail on it here, but only to touch base with some basic knowledge. Figure 5-14 shows the early prototype Electra Cruiser with the suspension loaded with the weight of the batteries, verifying rake, trail, suspension loading, and ride height.

Rear Suspension Styles

For your conversion, you have a few choices of the rear suspension style. Your selection depends greatly on the type of drive train you chose for your build or

FIGURE 5-14   Prototype of Electra Cruiser loaded with 560 lb (254 kg) of batteries.

conversion. The most popular and classic style is the twin-shock regular swingarm (Figure 5-15). This design is very popular and has been used since the early days of motorcycles. The next is a monoshock, which is an older style used on a similar regular modified swingarm. This style is a little more compact than the twin-shock swingarm (Figure 5-16). Both styles primarily use a standard chain- or belt-drive system. Figures 5-17 and 5-18 show a hybrid version of rear suspension I designed, patented, and built for the first-generation Electra Cruiser. It combined the swingarm version and the monoshock version. This design created a swingarm with more rigidity than a standard twin-shock swingarm. Figure 5-19 shows the monolever suspension system, which houses the driveshaft and ultimately the rear drive all in one unit. This type of system eliminates the need for a chain- or drive-belt for the transmission.

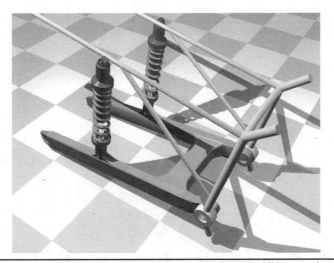

FIGURE 5-15   Twin-shock regular swingarm rear suspension. (www.carbibles.com/suspension_ bible_bikes.html.)

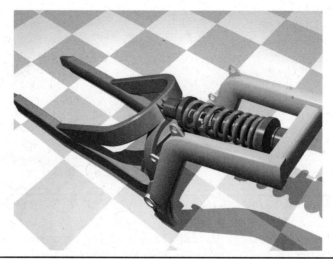

FIGURE 5-16   Monoshock H-style swingarm rear suspension. (www.carbibles.com/suspension_bible_bikes.html.)

FIGURE 5-17   3D drawing of the Hybrid swingarm design: First-generation Electra Cruiser.

FIGURE 5-18   Hybrid swingarm design: First-generation Electra Cruiser.

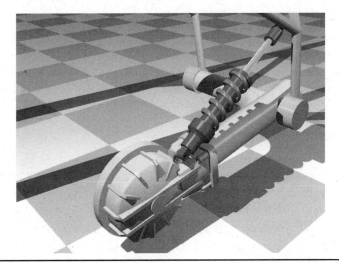

FIGURE 5-19   Monolever rear suspension system. (www.carbibles.com/suspension_bible_bikes. html.)

Twin-Shock Regular H Swingarm

This is the classic motorcycle suspension system used on most early-style bikes (see Figure 5-15). It uses an H-shaped swingarm pivoted at the front to the frame. On either side there are basic coil-over shock absorbers that provide the suspension. This is about as basic as you can get on a motorbike and has been around for as long as the motorbike itself. This style of suspension became less popular nearing the 1980s because of weight considerations and the availability of newer, stronger materials. Under extreme riding conditions, bending and flexibility became an issue.

Monoshock Regular H Swingarm

The monoshock system appeared in 1977 for niche markets and racers (see Figure 5-16). This design in one form or the other has been around since the 1930s, but it was only in the early 1980s that monoshocks started to appear on production bikes. The premise was that manufacturers could save some weight by redesigning the rear suspension and removing one of the coil-over units. In addition, the design added more strength to the swingarm.

Hybrid Twin-Shock H Swingarm

This Vogelbilt design is a hybrid of the twin-shock H swingarm (see Figures 5-17 and 5-18). This variation proved to work very well, providing improved strength and rigidity to the rear suspension. The design allowed us to use wasted space under the seat for the twin-shock design and added strength to the swingarm. For this particular bike, a 750-A controller at 120 V dc powered the electric motor. With this type of amperage, the motor was generating an enormous amount of torque at startup. Couple this with a 12:1 final gear ratio in first gear, and this bike was belting out over 2,000 foot-pounds of torque to the rear wheel. The rear swingarm had to be strong because the transmission and motor would have ripped it apart and bent a normal suspension system. In testimony to this power, the bike broke two sets of heavy-duty steel Harley-Davidson-style chains.

Monolever Suspension

The monolever suspension system was introduced in 1980 by BMW on its R80GS big dirt bike (see Figure 5-19). This style of rear suspension houses a shaft drive within the monolever geared to the rear wheel, eliminating the need for chains and belts. A single shock/strut unit is mounted to one side of the bike rather than in the center, as with other monoshock suspensions. The tension or loading of the shock is normally adjustable if needed. This design is very simple and rugged. Best of all, changing the rear wheel is a snap. This drive train will allow you to couple the electric motor to a driveshaft, eliminating the need for a chain or drive belt.

With your conversion, be aware that any changes in the rear suspension can change the geometry of the bike. Pay careful attention to the sprung and unsprung heights. Changes in the rear suspension height will change the rake angle and the trial length. A few measures or changes can easily rectify a situation. On most motorcycles, an adjustment can be made to the preload on the springs to change tension and height (Figure 5-20). With this adjustment, you can add or remove

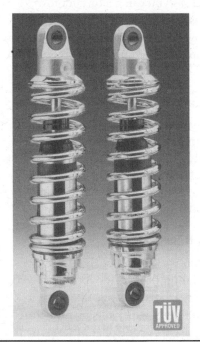

FIGURE 5-20   Shock/spring preload. (Courtesy of Custom Chrome, www.customchrome.com.)

tension on the springs to compensate for load and adjust the ride height. If this is not an option, aftermarket springs are available for different loads or have adjusters on them. From aftermarket suppliers, you can find adjustable shocks, lowering kits, and heavy-duty springs. If a change in the loading of the rear suspension does not fix the problem, you can increase or decrease the diameter of the tire to alter the angle of the rake. By doing so, you can raise or lower the rear of the bike, thus changing the rake angle and trail.

Conclusion

In the process of your custom build or changes from a stock vehicle, pay particular attention to any changes in the geometry and ride height. You can use these changes to your advantage by combining fork rake and length, ride height, and tire size to your advantage. These are just the basics so that you have a good understanding of bike geometry. To explain everything would take a complete book on the subject. Simple changes may have little effect, but any radical changes can have drastic or dangerous effects. During your build, try to keep the weight of your components as low as possible to control the center of gravity.

CHAPTER 6

Frame and Design

Back when the idea to build an electric motorcycle first came to me, I had to do a lot of work and research in terms of concept and design. The first bike I built was more like art. It was a beast, but it was my work and my design—it was so many things. The book *Build Your Own Electric Vehicle* was my bible for resources, calculations, and many other aspects of the bike. The book pointed me in the right direction to find the answers I needed. Chapter 5 in *Build Your Own Electric Vehicle* was about chassis and design and contained a lot of information, calculations, and formulas that are very close to what is contained herein. In the interest of not messing with something that worked well, it was my decision, with the help of Seth Leitman, author of *Build Your Own Electric Vehicle*, to follow a similar format. This chapter is written with an electric motorcycle in mind and is geared for smaller electric vehicles (EVs). Most of the calculations are the same; some just need to be scaled back to account for a lighter vehicle and two fewer wheels.

Choosing a Frame and Planning Your Design

The frame is the foundation of your EV conversion. While you might decide to build your own chassis from scratch, there are fundamental principles that can help you with any EV conversion or purchase—things that never come up when you are dealing with an internal combustion engine vehicle—such as the influence of weight, aerodynamic drag, rolling resistance, and drivetrains. This chapter will step you through the process of optimizing, designing, and buying or building your own EV. You will become familiar with some of the tradeoffs involved in optimizing your EV conversion. Then you will design your EV conversion knowing that the components you have selected will accomplish what you want them to do. When you have figured out what is important to you and have verified that your design will do what you want, you will look at the process of buying a frame, an existing motorcycle, or maybe a rolling frame.

Knowledge of all these steps will help you immediately and assist you as you read other chapters in this book on crucial components. I will try to guide you through every pitfall that I encountered. After reading Chapter 5, you should have a good knowledge of the frame geometry and what to do and not to do. The principles in this book are universal, and you can apply them whether buying, building, or converting. Choose the best frame or complete bike for your EV conversion. Stick with something that is simple yet easy to work with as the foundation for your EV.

I have found it better to try to work with what is available and off the shelf rather than to try to make everything from scratch. In some cases, it takes a little thinking and ingenuity, but you will figure it out. The biggest selection and most available parts are for Harley-Davidson motorcycles. However, you literally can pick up a book from five different aftermarket companies such as Custom Chrome, and in each book you will find over 1,000 pages of parts and accessories to choose from. Your build will take on a life of its own, and there are many choices you can make.

You are likely to be converting a vehicle, but that could be almost like building from scratch. There is not much to a motorcycle once you take out the engine. Even after you select the frame or bike conversion, there is so much you can do that you are not limited. The secret is to plan ahead and be clear (or just have a very good idea) about what you want to accomplish before you make your selection.

Keep in mind, though, that at any point during you calculations or design, something can happen to change things, so be prepared. Unlike converting a car or truck, a motorcycle or smaller vehicle has less room for error or just less room. One simple design error can hit you like a domino effect. Keep in mind the added weight you may have to carry when choosing your frame and suspension. From Chapter 5 you should have a good idea of your suspension options and how to beef your suspension up if necessary.

You can forget about aerodynamics unless you are building a sleek "crotch rocket." In addition, your frame must be big enough and strong enough to carry you and the additional weight, along with the motor, drivetrain/controller, and batteries. Moreover, if you want to drive your bike on the highway, federal and state laws require it be roadworthy and adhere to certain safety standards.

The first step is to know your options. Your EV should be as light as possible; streamlined, with its body providing minimum drag, and optimized for minimum rolling resistance from its tires and brakes and minimum drivetrain losses. The motor-drivetrain-battery combination must work in conjunction with the space available and the size of the vehicle you select. It also must be capable of accomplishing the task most important to you: high speed, long range, or something midway between the two. Therefore, step two is to design for the capability that you want. Your EV's weight, motor and battery placement, rolling resistance, handling, gearing, and safety features also must meet your needs. You now have a plan.

Step three is to execute your plan—to buy the frame or bike that meets your needs. At its heart, this is a process that is no different from any other vehicle purchase you've ever made, except that the best solution for your needs might be a vehicle that the owner can't wait to get rid of. The tables are completely turned from a normal buying situation. Used is usually the least expensive, but with a motorcycle, you can just start with a frame and work your way from there. Figure 6-1 gives you the quick basic picture (see page 82). The rest of this chapter covers the details.

Selecting a Frame Dos and Don'ts

During your building phase, whether you are building your motorcycle or other vehicle from scratch or converting an existing vehicle, there are certain guidelines established by your state department of motor vehicles (DMV) that you must follow. In saying this, I am assuming that your vehicle will be a highway-use vehicle with two or three wheels. The equipment guidelines I have listed are the requirements set forth by the State of New York DMV (nysdmv.com). From my knowledge, New York has some of the strictest requirements in comparison with other states. To find out more information and the exact requirements of your state, locate your state DMV Web site or call for more information. You will need to access the division of safety services.

Given that the New York guidelines probably are the strictest, I would go with these guidelines as you start. Do not assume that these are all the requirements or that I am 100 percent correct; requirements may change. Make sure that you follow up with your state DMV. Again, I strongly stress this point: Follow the guidelines, if not for the sake of following the law, then for your own safety! What would be truly uncool would be if, after you complete an exceptionally built vehicle, you fail the requirements and the inspection. This could mean anything from a simple fix to an expensive design change that you could have avoided from the start.

Whether you decide to build from scratch or from an existing motorcycle, I will supply you with some priceless advice and knowledge. First off, I highly recommend converting an existing vehicle. If this is going to be an on-road vehicle you are converting, make 100 percent sure that you have all the papers, title, and vehicle identification number (VIN) for this vehicle. I cannot stress this enough. I don't care if it was free or your buddy got you a great deal, it is not worth it without the proper paperwork. Don't do it! Unless you are willing to waste months of time tracking down paperwork, keeping records, holding receipts and serial numbers on all parts, scheduling daylong treks to the DMV field investigation unit, and paying hundreds of dollars in fees, don't do it.

Additionally, with all that stated, you will need to have the vehicle weighed on a certified scale with an official receipt. You will need to verify and supply the state department of transportation (DOT) with numbers from your tires, windshield (if

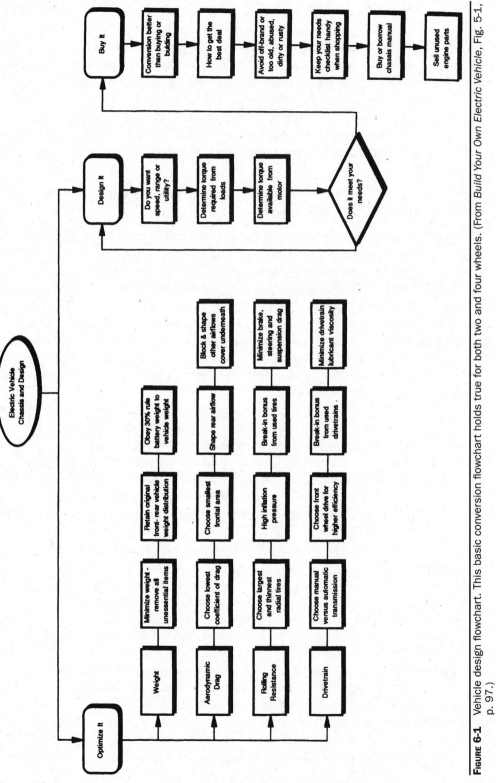

FIGURE 6-1 Vehicle design flowchart. This basic conversion flowchart holds true for both two and four wheels. (From *Build Your Own Electric Vehicle*, Fig. 5-1, p. 97.)

you have one), all lights and turn signals, and other equipment. I think you get the picture. Unfortunately, this was my experience, I built a motorcycle from scratch with no VIN or anything. It took me well over 3–5 months to get my VIN, and I kept on top of it and pushed the DMV hard to get it done. This is not counting all the time I spent on paperwork and much more. To say the least, it was a learning experience that I do not want to experience again. My experience is yours to gain from.

Optimize Your EV

Optimizing is always step number one. Even if you go out to buy your EV ready-made, you still should know a little bit about the vehicle so that you can decide if you're getting the best model for you. In all other cases, you'll be doing the optimizing—either by the choices you make up front in vehicle and component selection or by your decisions later on. In this section you will learn how to calculate the following factors:

- Weight, climbing, and acceleration
- Aerodynamic drag and wind drag
- Rolling resistance
- Drivetrain system

We will look at equations that define each of these factors and construct a table of real values for a 300- to 1,000-lb vehicle with nine specific vehicle speeds. These values should be handy regardless of what you do later. If your design changes a little, you will have your notes to fall back on. When you calculate the real vehicle's torque requirements, you will see if the torque available from the electric motor to the drivetrain is sufficient for your needs and performance requirements. This design process can be infinitely adapted and applied to any EV you have.

Standard Measurements and Formulas

For calculations, we will use the U.S. vehicle standard of miles, miles per hour, feet per second, pounds, pound feet, foot pounds, etc. rather than the kilometers, newton-meters, etc. in common use overseas. Regarding formulas, you will find the following 13 useful; they have been grouped in one section for your convenience:

1. Power $[(lb \cdot ft)/s]$ = torque $(ft \cdot lb)$ × speed (rad/s) = force in feet per second (force times velocity, or FV)
2. $1\ hp = 550\ (ft \cdot lb)/s$
   Applying this to Equation 1 gives you

3. $1 \text{ hp} = FV/550$
   where V is velocity (speed) expressed in feet per second
4. $88 \text{ ft/s} = 60 \text{ mph}$
   Multiply feet per second by $(60 \times 60)/5{,}280$ to get mph
5. $1 \text{ hp} = FV/375$
   where V is velocity (speed) expressed in mph and F is force in pounds
6. Horsepower (hp) = (torque $\times$ rev/min)/5,252 = $\pi/60 \times FV/550$
7. Wheel rev/min (rpm) = (mph $\times$ rev/mi)/60
8. Power (kW) = $0.7457 \times$ hp (1 hp = 746 watts)
9. The standard gravitational constant g = 32.16 ft/s^2 or almost 22 mph/s
10. Weight W = mass M $\times$ g/32.16
    (For the rest of this book, we will refer to a vehicle's mass as its weight.)
11. Torque = $[F(5{,}280/2\pi)]/(\text{rev/mi}) = 840.38 \times F/(\text{rev/mi})$
    Revolutions per mile (rev/mi) refers to how many times a tire rotates per mile.
12. $\text{Torque}_{wheel} = \text{torque}_{motor} \times$ (overall gear ratio $\times$ overall drivetrain efficiency)
13. $\text{Speed}_{vehicle}$ (in mph) = $(\text{rpm}_{motor} \times 60)/$(overall gear ratio $\times$ rev/mi)

EV Weight

In your EV conversion, weight is the most important thing, and we need to reduce it as much as possible. However, in a motorcycle, you will be somewhat limited as to how much you can reduce the weight. Try to cut as much as you can in a safe manner. Also consider maximizing the strength of the vehicle and its frame. In this section you will take a closer look at various items in terms of weight.

Remove All Unessential Weight

You do not want to carry around any unnecessary weight. This means that you need to go over everything carefully with regard to its weight versus its value. Your biggest weight issues involve the internal combustion motor, fuel tank, and transmission.

During Conversion

As you remove the internal combustion engine parts, you will have a clean canvas with which to work. As you plan your conversion, keep in mind all the things you might add to the vehicle, and always consider how to reduce weight or not add any unnecessary weight. The reason for all your work is simple—weight affects every aspect of an EV's performance—acceleration, climbing, speed, and range. Try to plan ahead.

Weight and Acceleration

Let's see exactly how weight affects acceleration. The heavier something is, the more force is required to move it. This is one of the basic relationships of nature. It is known as Sir Issac Newton's second law:

$$F = Ma$$

or force F equals mass M times acceleration a. For EV purposes, this can be rewritten as

$$F_a = C_i Wa$$

where F_a is acceleration force in pounds, W is vehicle mass in pounds, a is acceleration in mph/s, g is standard gravity (which is 21.94 mph/s), and C_i is a unit conversion factor that also accounts for the added inertia of the vehicle's rotating parts. The force required to get the vehicle going varies directly with the vehicle's weight. Twice the weight means that twice as much force is required.

C_i, the mass factor that represents the inertia of the vehicle's rotating masses (i.e., wheels, drivetrain, flywheel, clutch, motor armature, and other rotating parts), is given by

$$C_i = I + 0.04 + 0.0025(N_c)^2$$

where N_c represents the combined ratio of the transmission and final drive. The mass factor depends on the gear in which you are operating. For internal combustion engine vehicles, typically the mass factor for high gear is 1.1; third gear, 1.2; second gear, 1.5; and first gear, 2.4. For EVs, from which a portion of the drivetrain and weight typically has been removed or lightened, the mass factor typically is 1.06 to 1.2.

Table 6-1 shows the acceleration force F_a for three different values of C_i for 10 different values of acceleration a and for a vehicle weight of 1,000 lb. The factor a' is the acceleration expressed in ft/s^2 rather than in mph/s = 21.95 = 32.2 × (3600/5280)—used only in the formula (because acceleration as expressed in mph/s is a much more convenient and familiar figure to work with). Notice that an acceleration of 10 mph/s, an amount that takes you from 0–60 mph in 6 seconds nominally requires extra force of 500 lb; 5 mph/s, moving from 0–50 mph in 10 seconds, requires 250 lb.

To use Table 6-1 with your EV, multiply by the ratio of your vehicle weight, and use the "$C_i - 1.06$" column for lighter vehicles such as your motorcycle. The "$C_i = 1.1$ or Greater" column will not be used unless you are building a beast of a bike or maybe a three-wheel machine in which there will be more weight. For example, the 1,100-lb Electra Cruiser would require 5 mph/s = 1.1 × 241.4 = 265.5 lb.

Weight and Climbing

When you go hill climbing, you add another force:

$$F_h = W \sin \Phi$$

TABLE 6-1   Acceleration Force F_a (in pounds) for Different Values of C_i

a (in mph/sec)	a'= a/21.95	F_a (in pounds) C_i = 1.06	F_a (in pounds) C_i = 1.1	F_a (in pounds) C_i = 1.2
1	0.046	48.3	50.1	54.7
2	0.091	96.6	100.2	109.3
3	0.137	144.8	150.3	164.0
4	0.182	193.1	200.4	218.6
5	0.228	241.4	250.5	273.3
6	0.273	289.7	300.6	328.0
7	0.319	338.0	350.7	382.6
8	0.364	386.3	400.8	437.3
9	0.410	434.5	450.9	491.9
10	0.455	482.8	501.0	546.6

From *Build Your Own Electric Vehicle*, Table 5-1, p. 100.

where F_h is hill-climbing force, W is vehicle weight in pounds, and Φ is the angle of incline, as shown in Figure 6-2. The degree of incline—the way hills or inclines are commonly referred to—is different from the angle of incline, but the figure should clear up any confusion for you. Notice that sin Φ varies from 0 at no incline (no effect) to 1 at a 90-degree incline (straight up); in other words, the full weight of the vehicle is trying to pull it back down. Again, weight is involved directly, acted on this time by the steepness of the hill.

$$\text{Degree of incline} = 1\% = 1 \text{ ft}/100 \text{ ft} = \text{rise/run}$$

Angle of incline Φ = arctan rise/run $\cong$ arctan 0.01 $\cong$ about 0 degrees, 34 minutes

Table 6-2 shows the hill-climbing force F_h for 15 different incline values for a vehicle weight of 1,000 lb. Notice that the tractive force required for acceleration of 1 mph/s equals that required for climbing a 5 percent incline, 2 mph/s for a 10 percent incline, etc. on up through a 30 percent incline. This handy relationship will be used later in the design section.

To use Table 6-2 with your EV, multiply by the ratio of your vehicle weight. For example, a 1,100-lb motorcycle such as the Electra Cruiser going up a 10 percent incline would require 1.0 × 99.6 = 109.6 lb.

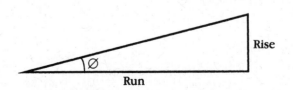

FIGURE 6-2   Angle of incline defined. From *Build Your Own Electric Vehicle*, Figure 5-2, p. 100.

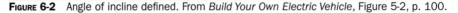

TABLE 6-2   Hill-Climbing Force F_h for 15 Different Values of Incline

Degree of incline	Incline angle O	sin O	F_h (in pounds)	a (in mph/sec)
1%	0° 34'	0.00989	9.9	
2%	1° 9'	0.02007	20.1	
3%	1° 43'	0.02996	29.6	
4%	2° 17'	0.04013	40.1	
5%	2° 52'	0.05001	50.0	1
6%	3° 26'	0.05989	59.9	
8%	4° 34'	0.07062	79.6	
10%	5° 43'	0.09961	99.6	2
15%	8° 32'	0.14838	148.4	3
20%	11° 19'	0.19623	196.2	4
25%	14° 2'	0.24249	242.5	5
30%	16° 42'	0.28736	287.4	6
35%	19° 17'	0.33024	330.2	
40%	21° 48'	0.37137	371.4	
45%	24° 14'	0.41045	410.5	

From *Build Your Own Electric Vehicle*, Table 5-1, p. 101.

Weight Affects Speed

Although speed also involves other factors, it is definitely related to weight. Also, horsepower and torque are related to speed per Equation 3:

$$hp = FV/550$$

where hp is motor horsepower, F is force in pounds, and V is speed in feet per second. Armed with this information, Newton's second law equation can be rearranged as

$$a = (1/M) \times F$$

and because $M = W/g$ (Eq. 10) and $F = (550 \times hp)/V$, they can be substituted to yield

$$a = 550(g/V)(hp/W)$$

Finally, a and V can be interchanged to give

$$V = 550(g/a)(hp/W)$$

where V is the vehicle speed in feet per second, W is the vehicle weight in pounds, g is the gravitational constant (32.2 ft/s²), and the other factors you've already met. For any given acceleration, as weight goes up, speed goes down because they are inversely proportional.

Weight Affects Range

Distance is simply speed multiplied by time:

$$D = Vt$$

Therefore,

$$D = 550(g/a)(\text{hp}/W)t$$

So weight again enters the picture. For any fixed amount of energy you are carrying on your vehicle, you will go farther if you take longer (drive at a slower speed) or carry less weight.

Besides reducing any unnecessary weight, there are two other important weight-related factors to keep in mind when doing EV conversion weight distribution.

Remove the Weight But Keep Your Balance

One of the key factors that you always want to be aware of on your motorcycle is the center of gravity. Simply said, during your planning and build, try to keep all components, particularly the heavy ones, as low on the frame as possible. One heavy component we do lose in a conversion besides the engine is the fuel tank. Depending on the size of the fuel tank removed from the vehicle, you reduced the weight by 40–70 lb. Not only did you reduce the weight, but you also removed weight that was high up on your vehicle that you no longer have to wrestle with when the bike leans. In essence, you changed the center of gravity of your bike (see Figure 6-3).

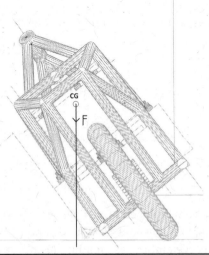

Figure 6-3   Bike center of gravity.

Remember the 30 Percent Rule

The "30 percent or greater" rule of thumb (battery weight should be at least 30 percent of gross vehicle weight when using lead-acid batteries) is a very useful target to shoot for in a motorcycle conversion. Your batteries are essentially your fuel tank; the more batteries you have, the larger is your "tank." This theory is good to a point, but it is also true that the more energy you can store, the more range you can achieve. When using advanced batteries (see Chapter 7) you can store more energy in the same space. Thus, basically, you have a battery with more energy storage capacity. For my build with the Electra Cruiser, I crammed over 600 lb of batteries into the frame. I used 10 Trojan Group 27 TMH deep-cycle batteries with a peak voltage of 120 V dc. Looking at the 30 percent rule, it is apparent that I went up to about 52 percent battery weight to gross vehicle weight. The Cruiser's battery pack, also counting the auxiliary 12-V battery, brings the pack weight up to a whopping 600 lb! To accommodate the extra weight, I had to make changes in the design. Such changes were in the load capacity of the tires, frame strength, and suspension loading. Part of this is covered in Chapter 5, and more will be covered in Chapter 13 when we get to the actual build.

Streamline Your EV

Inherently, motorcycles are not very aerodynamic, especially if you look at nature's finest and most common example of aerodynamic perfection, the falling raindrop—rounded and bulbous in front and tapering to a point at the rear—the optimal aerodynamic shape. In fact, the newer bicycle-racing helmets adhere perfectly to this principle. One of the areas an EV designer needs to examine is the aerodynamic drag of his or her machine. For a motorcycle, the coefficient of drag is high, only to be superseded by a truck and a tractor trailer (maybe a flat piece of wood is at the top of the drag list). A motorcycle has a drag coefficient of 0.50, which is the lower limit, least drag; the coefficient is 0.90 for medium drag and moves up to 1.0, the highest coefficient of drag. Because of wind resistance and wind drag, your vehicle will consume more energy.

I have noticed myself and also have been told that once you start traveling over 40 mph, you actually can see the energy usage start to climb. This is viewed easily with your amp meter if you install one. An amp meter is like a fuel flow meter for an EV. It is the first sign of energy usage.

All is not lost, though. There are some things you can do to reduce wind drag on a motorcycle. First and most important is the addition of fairings. These will help to streamline your vehicle a little bit. The other big factor is the rider. Yes, human beings not very aerodynamic; we are much like a big flat piece of wood sitting on your motorcycle sucking the range out of it. If you are building just a regular cruiser or touring bike, there is not too much you can do about it. Clothing that is not loose or that does not catch the wind like a sail helps. However, if you are building more of a sport bike, where the rider is crunched forward, you can pick up a lot of aerodynamic savings. In this section we will look at aerodynamic drag and learn about the factors that come into play and how they affect your vehicle.

Aerodynamic Drag Force Defined

As stated earlier, most of your drag force will not be realized until you start to reach 40 mph. You also should take head winds into consideration. Head winds are prevailing winds that occur naturally. If you are cruising down the road at 40 mph and you are heading into the wind on a windy day and the head wind is 30 mph, you are actually battling wind speeds of 70 mph. In essence, therefore, you are using energy as if you were traveling at 70 mph. Thus, when a manufacturer says that its machine has a 60-mile range at 60 mph, that is under perfect, ideal conditions. In the real world, you would be lucky to get that range. This is one of the major things people forget about real-world mileage calculations.

A perfect example occurred during filming of the *Coolfuel Roadtrip* in Florida. The Electra Cruiser under ideal conditions was achieving a 60-mile range per charge at highway speeds, which was a good number for the Cruiser. During heavy-wind conditions on a straight, flat highway during the filming, head winds were zapping the energy and range right out of the Cruiser. We were lucky during the heavy winds to squeeze even a 35-mile range out of the bike. Here again, these are all some of the things you need to consider during your planning and build.

The aerodynamic drag force can be expressed as

$$F_d = (C_d A V^2)/391$$

where F_d is the aerodynamic drag force in pounds, C_d is the coefficient of drag of your vehicle, A is its frontal area in square feet, and V is the vehicle speed in mph. To minimize drag for any given speed, you must minimize C_d, the coefficient of drag, and A, the bike's frontal area.

Choose the Lowest Coefficient of Drag

The coefficient of drag C_d has to do with streamlining and air-turbulence flows around your vehicle. The characteristics that are inherent in the shape and design of your motorcycle cannot be changed much. You are stuck with drag coefficients in the range of 0.50–1.00. A drag coefficient of 0.50 is the lowest for a streamlined sport bike, an average or medium drag coefficient would be 0.90, and the highest would be 1.00, which would apply to a large sport bike with all the dressings and maybe a not-so-aerodynamic rider or riding position (see Figure 6-4). For either high-speed or long-range performance goals, it's important that you keep this critical factor foremost in mind when you make your design calculations for your vehicle.

Unfortunately, little data are available concerning drag coefficients on motorcycles, but the figure gives you the basics. Below are the typical coefficients

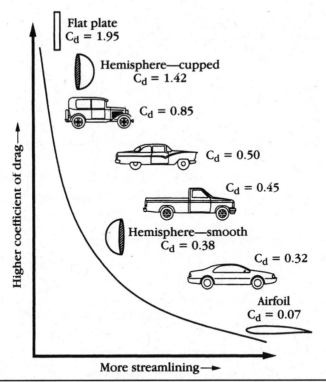

FIGURE 6-4 Common values for the coefficient of drag for different shapes and types of vehicles. From *Build Your Own Electric Vehicle*, Figure 5-4, p. 105.

of drag. Table 6-3 lists the contribution of each component on a car to total coefficient of drag using as an example a vintage 1970s car.

Coefficient of Drag

- Cars: 0.30–0.35
- Motorcycles: 0.50–1.00

TABLE 6-3 Coefficient of Drag Summary for Different Components on a Vehicle Added to the Overall C_d

Car Area	C_d Value	Percentage of total
Body–Rear	0.14	33.3
Wheel wells	0.09	21.4
Body–Under	0.06	14.3
Body–Front	0.05	11.9
Projections and indentations	0.03	7.1
Engine compartment	0.025	6.0
Body–Skin friction	0.025	6.0
Total	0.42	100.0

From *Build Your Own Electric Vehicle*, Table 5-4, p. 106.

- Pickup trucks: 0.42–1.00
- Tractor trailers: 0.60–1.20

Frontal Area

The frontal area A of typical late-model cars, trucks, and vans is in the 18- to 24-ft^2 range. A 4- by 8-ft sheet of plywood held up vertically in front of your vehicle would have a frontal area of 32 ft^2. Aerodynamics has to do with the effective area your vehicle presents to the onrushing airstream. The frontal area on your motorcycle will not change much, but apply the same calculations to that frontal area. Also remember to include you, the rider, in the equation because you may constitute almost half the drag force of the vehicle.

Relative Wind Contributes to Aerodynamic Drag

Drag force is measured nominally at 60°F and a barometric pressure of 30 Hg in still air. Normally, these are adequate assumptions for most calculations. Very few locations, however, have still air, so an additional drag component owing to relative wind velocity has to be added to your aerodynamic drag force calculation. This is the additional wind drag pushing against the vehicle from the random local winds. The equation defining the relative wind factor C_w is

$$C_w = [0.98(w/V)^2 + 0.63(w/V)]C_{rw} - 0.40(w/V)$$

where w is the average wind speed of the area in mph, V is the vehicle speed, and C_{rw} is a relative wind coefficient that is approximately 1.4 for typical sedan shapes, 1.2 for more streamlined vehicles, and 1.6 for vehicles displaying more turbulence or sedans driven with their windows open. For your calculations, I would use a drag force of 1.6 pertaining to a motorcycle.

Table 6-4 shows C_w calculated for seven different vehicle speeds, assuming the U.S. average value of 7.5 mph for wind speed, for the three different C_{rw} values.

TABLE 6-4   Relative Wind Factor C_w at Different Vehicle Speeds for Three C_{rw} Values

C_{rw} at average	C_w factor	C_w factor	C_w factor	C_w factor	C_w factor	C_w factor	C_w factor
wind= 7.5 mph	at V= 5 mph	at V= 10 mph	at V= 20 mph	at V= 30 mph	at V= 45 mph	at V= 60 mph	at V= 75 mph
1.2	3.180	0.929	0.299	0.163	0.159	0.063	0.047
1.4 avg sedan	3.810	1.133	0.374	0.206	0.185	0.082	0.062
1.6	4.440	1.338	0.449	0.250	0.212	0.101	0.076

From *Build Your Own Electric Vehicle*, Table 5-5, p. 107.

Aerodynamic Drag Force Data You Can Use

Table 6-4 puts the C_d and A values for actual vehicles together and calculates their drag force for seven different vehicle speeds. Notice that drag force is lowest on a small car and greatest on a small pickup. From these numbers, I would tend to use the higher numbers for a motorcycle, staying in line with the wind resistance of a truck.

To calculate the aerodynamic drag force of your EV, pick out your vehicle type in Table 6-5, and then multiply its drag force number by the relative wind factor at the identical vehicle speed using the appropriate C_d row for your vehicle type. For example, the 1,100-lb Electra Cruiser has a drag force of 24.86 lb at 30 mph using Table 6-5. Multiplying this by the relative wind factor of 0.250 from the bottom row ($C_{rw} = 1.6$) of Table 6-4 gives you 6.22 lb. Your total aerodynamic drag forced then is $24.86 + 6.22 = 31.08$ lb.

TABLE 6-5   Aerodynamic Drag Force F_d at Different Vehicle Speeds for Typical Vehicle C_d and A Values

Vehicle	C_d	A	V=\n5 mph	V=\n10 mph	V=\n20 mph	V=\n30 mph	V=\n45 mph	V=\n60 mph	V=\n75 mph
Small car	0.3	18	0.35	1.38	5.52	12.43	27.97	49.72	77.69
Larger car	0.32	22	0.45	1.80	7.20	16.20	36.46	64.82	101.28
Van	0.34	26	0.57	2.26	9.04	20.35	45.78	81.39	127.17
Small pickup	0.45	24	0.69	2.76	11.05	24.86	55.93	99.44	155.37
Roadster	0.6	18	0.69	2.76	11.05	24.86	55.93	99.44	155.37

From *Build Your Own Electric Vehicle*, Table 5-6, p. 107.

Wheel Well and Underbody Airflow

Next, pay some attention to the wheels and wheel-well area. Table 6-3 indicates that the tire and wheel-well area by itself contributes approximately 21 percent of the C_d, so small streamlining changes here can have some benefits. Using smooth wheel covers, thinner tires, anything can help. Keep in mind any large intrusions in the airflow around your vehicle. Every little bit helps, so anything you can do to reduce drag will add up.

Roll with the Road

As they said in the movie *Days of Thunder*, "Tires is what wins the race." Today, tires are fat, have wide tread, and are without low-rolling-resistance characteristics; they've been optimized for good adhesion instead. As an electric vehicle owner, you need to go against the grain of current thinking on tires and learn to roll with the road to win the performance race. Figure 6-5 shows Shaun and Sparky rolling through the Midwest.

Figure 6-5   Shaun, Sparky, and the Electra Cruiser rolling through the Midwest. (Courtesy of Shaun Murphy and Gus Roxburgh, Balance Vector Productions, www.balancevector. com.)

In this section we will look at rolling resistance and learn how to maximize efficiency from those four (or three or two) tire-road contact patches that are no bigger than your hand. In this area, there is not too much you can do to improve rolling resistance except maybe to pay attention to tire inflation and using properly rated tires. At best, you can use the data you have to further calculate any losses in the full equation of your conversion.

Rolling Resistance Defined

The rolling resistance force is defined as

$$F_r = CW \cos \Phi$$

where C_r is the rolling-resistance factor, W is the vehicle weight in pounds, and Φ is the angle of incline, as shown in Figure 6-2. Notice that cos Φ varies from 1 degree at no incline (maximum effect) to 0–90 degrees (no effect). Again, vehicle weight is a factor, this time modulated by the vehicle's tire friction. The rolling-resistance factor C_r might at its most elementary level be estimated as a constant. For a typical EV under 1,500-lb., it is approximately

- 0.006–0.01 on a hard surface (concrete)
- 0.02 on a medium-hard surface
- 0.30 on a soft surface (sand)

If your calculations require more accuracy, C_r varies linearly at lower speeds and can be represented by

$$C_r = 0.012(1 + V/100)$$

where V is vehicle speed in mph.

Pay Attention to Your Tires

Tires are important to an EV owner. They support the vehicle and battery weight while cushioning against shocks and develop front-to-rear forces for acceleration and braking. Tires are almost universally of radial-ply construction today. Typically, one or more steel-belted plies run around the circumference of a tire (hence *radial*). These deliver vastly superior performance to the bias-ply types (several plies woven crosswise around the tire carcass, hence *bias* or "on an angle") of earlier years that were replaced by radials as the standard in the 1960s. A tire is characterized by its rim width, the size of the wheel rim it fits on, section width (maximum width across the bulge of the tire), section height (distance from the bead to the outer edge of the tread), aspect ratio (ratio of height to width), overall diameter and load, and maximum tire pressure. In addition, the Tire and Rim Association defines the standard tire-naming conventions. For example, for a tire labeled "130/90H × 16," a typical Harley-style bias tire, *130* denotes the section width in inches ($= 5.4$ in), *16* denotes the rim diameter in inches, and H denotes the load range of the tire, meaning the rated load carrying ability in pounds or kg. Look up the manufacturers' ratings for your specific tire, as these ratings are subject to change.

Table 6-6 provides a comparison of the published motorcycle tire sizes. There are many more than this. You will need to look up the specific tire and rating for your vehicle.

For some of your calculations, you will need revolutions per mile, which is a nominal value calculated directly from the overall diameter rather than using actual measured data. The calculated value is slightly lower than the measured value when tires are new, and as tread wears down, you are looking at a difference of 0.4–0.8 in less in the tire's diameter, which translates into even more revolutions per mile. The difference might be 30 revolutions out of 900—a difference of 3 percent—but if this figure is important to your calculations, measure the actual tire circumference with a tape measure. If the vehicle is still rolling, place some weight on it and yourself. Next mark the road or your driveway and move the bike so the tire rotates one full revolution, noting the distance it traveled. When using the tape measure, you cannot take into account the compression of the tire, which changes the rolling distance.

From engineering studies on the rolling loss characteristics of solid rubber tires, we get the following equation:

$$F_t = C_t(W/d)(t_h/t_w)^{1/2}$$

where F_t is the rolling-resistance force, C_t is a constant reflecting the tire material's elastic and loss characteristics, W is the weight on the tire, d is the outside diameter of the tire, and t_h and t_w are the tire section height and width, respectively. This is the last you will see or hear of this equation in this book, but the point is that the rolling-resistance force is affected by the material (harder is better for EV owners), the loading (less weight is better), the size (bigger is better), and the aspect ratio (a lower t_h:t_w ratio is better). The variables in more conventional tire rolling-resistance equations are usually tire inflation pressure (resistance decreases with increasing inflation pressure—harder is better), vehicle speed (increases with increasing speed), tire warm-up (warmer is better), and load (less weight is better).

TABLE 6-6   Standard Tire Size for Motorcycles

Size	Rim	Overall Width	Overall Diameter
120/80V16	2.75	4.7	23.8
130/90H16	3	5	25.4
130/90V16	3	5.2	25
500S16	3	5.2	26.4
MT90H16	3	5.3	25.3
130/90H16	3	5.4	25.6
140/90H16	3.5	5.8	25.6
140/80VB16	3.5	5.9	24.8
140/90H16	3.5	6	25.8
150/80V16	3.5	6.2	25.4
160/80H16	4	6.4	26.1
160/80H16	4	6.8	26.1
200/60VB16	5.5	7.9	25.9
120/80V18	2.75	4.8	25.9
120/90V18	2.75	4.8	26.4
120/90H16	2.75	4.9	26.3
130/80V18	3	5.2	26.3
130/70VB18	3.5	5.4	25.4
150/70VB18	4	5.9	26.2
140/70V18	4	6.1	25.7
170/60VB18	4.5	6.9	26
180/55VB18	5.5	7	26.3
230/50 X 15	7.00 to 8.00	9.5	25.3

Use Radial Tires

Radial tires are nearly universal today, so tire construction is no longer a factor. However, some tire manufacturers still offer bias-ply tires, so check to be sure because bias-ply or bias-belted tires deliver far inferior performance to radials in terms of rolling resistance versus speed, warm-up, and inflation. You will find that many different tire variations are available for your motorcycle.

Use High Tire Inflation Pressures

While you don't want to overinflate and balloon out your tires so that they pop off their rims, there is no reason not to inflate your EV's tires to their limit to suit your purpose. The upper limit is established by your discomfort level from the road vibration transmitted to your body. Rock-hard tires are fine; the only real caveat is not to overload your tires. For motorcycle handling, safety, and performance, the tire pressure may need to be adjusted to your needs.

Brake Drag and Rolling Resistance

In addition to tires, rolling resistance comes from brake drag. Brake drag usually goes away as the vehicle is broken in. Be aware of your brakes, and make adjustments as needed to reduce any drag.

Rolling-Resistance Force Data You Can Use

For most purposes, the nominal C_r of 0.010 (for concrete) with the nominal brake drag of 0.001 added to it (= 0.011) is all you need. This generates 18.0 lb of rolling-resistance force for a 1,000-lb. vehicle. The 1,100-lb Electra Cruiser would have a rolling resistance of 12.1 lb (1,100 lb of bike weight $\times$ 0.011, or 1.1×11 lb). At 30 mph, the aerodynamic drag force on the Cruiser is 31.08 lb—more than double the contribution of its 12.41 lb of rolling-resistance drag.

Figure 6-6 shows the aerodynamic example of drag force and rolling-resistance force for several vehicle speeds. These two forces, along with acceleration and hill-climbing forces, constitute the *propulsion* or *road load*. Notice that the 12.1 lb of rolling-resistance force is the main component of drag until the aerodynamic drag force takes over above 45 mph. Adding the force required to accelerate at a 1 mph/s rate, nominally equivalent to that required to climb a 4.5 percent incline, merely shifts the combined aerodynamic-drag–rolling-resistance-force curve upward by 60.17 lb (1.1×54.7 lb) for the Cruiser. We'll look at these forces once again further in this chapter.

Less Is More with Drivetrains

In this section we will look at the drivetrain for the motorcycle adopted for your EV conversion. The drivetrain in any vehicle consists of the components that transfer its motive power to the wheels and tires. The problem is that two separate

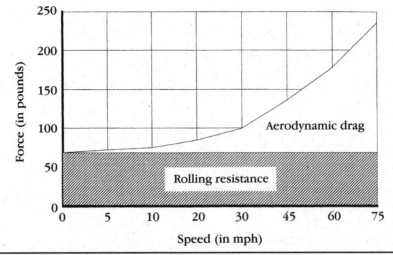

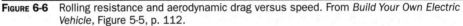

FIGURE 6-6   Rolling resistance and aerodynamic drag versus speed. From *Build Your Own Electric Vehicle*, Figure 5-5, p. 112.

vocabularies are used when talking about drivetrains for electric motors as opposed to those for internal combustion engines. This section will discuss the basic components, cover differences in motor versus engine performance specifications, discuss transmission selection, and look at the tradeoffs of manual transmission versus belt or chain drive. In addition, we will look at the influence of fluids on drivetrain efficiencies.

Drivetrains

Let's start with what the drivetrain in a conventional internal combustion engine vehicle must accomplish. In practical terms, the power available from the engine must be equal to the job of overcoming the tractive resistances discussed earlier for any given speed.

The obvious mission of the drivetrain is to apply the engine's power to driving the wheel and tire with the least loss (highest efficiency). Overall, though, the drivetrain must perform a number of tasks:

- Convert torque and speed of the engine to vehicle motion/traction
- Change directions, enabling forward and backward vehicle motion
- Overcome hills and grades
- Maximize fuel economy

The drivetrain layout shown in simplified form in Figure 6-7 is the one used most widely to accomplish these objectives today. You have a few choices in this area, one of which is the choice between using a transmission, a chain or belt drive, or maybe a shaft drive unit. The function of each component of the drivetrain is as follows:

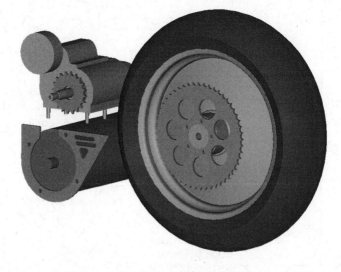

FIGURE 6-7   Simplified EV motorcycle drivetrain layout from the Electra Cruiser.

- *Engine (or electric motor)*—provides the raw power to propel the vehicle.
- *Clutch* (optional)—separates or interrupts the power flow from the engine so that transmission gears can be shifted and, once engaged, the vehicle can be driven from standstill to top speed.
- *Manual transmission*—provides a number of alternative gear ratios to the engine to meet vehicle needs—maximum torque for hill climbing or minimum speed to economical cruising at maximum speed.
- *Chain or belt drive*—connects the motor to the drive wheel.
- *Shaft drive*—geared or connected directly to the drive wheel at 90 degrees in rear wheel to provide a speed reduction with a corresponding increase in torque.

Difference in Motor versus Engine Specifications

Comparing electric motors and internal combustion engines is not an "apples to apples" comparison. If someone offers you either an electric motor or an internal combustion engine with the same rated horsepower, take the electric motor—it's far more powerful. Also, a series-wound electric motor delivers peak torque on startup (0 rpm), whereas an internal combustion engine delivers nothing until you wind up its revolutions per minute (rpm).

An electric motor is so different from an internal combustion engine that a brief discussion of terms is necessary before going further. There is a substantial difference in the ways electric motors and internal combustion engines are rated in horsepower. Figure 6-8 shows at a glance that an electric motor is more powerful than an internal combustion engine of the same rated horsepower. All internal combustion engines

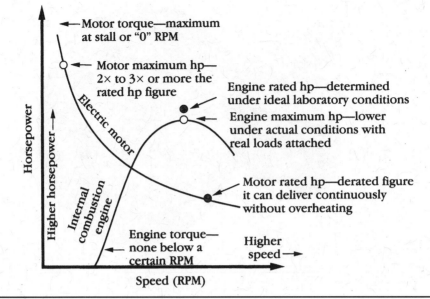

FIGURE·6-8 Comparison of electric motor versus internal combustion engine characteristics. From *Build Your Own Electric Vehicle*, Figure 5-7, p. 115.

are rated at specific rpm levels for maximum torque and maximum horsepower. Internal combustion engine maximum horsepower ratings typically are derived under idealized laboratory conditions (for the bare engine without accessories attached), which is why the rated horsepower point appears above the maximum peak of the internal combustion engine horsepower curve in Figure 6-8. Electric motors, on the other hand, typically are rated at the continuous output level that the motor can maintain without overheating.

As you can see from the figure, the rated horsepower point for an electric motor is far down from its short-term output, which is typically two to three times higher than its continuous output. There is another substantial difference. While an electric motor can produce a high torque at zero speed, an internal combustion engine produces negative torque until some speed is reached. An electric motor therefore can be attached directly to the drive wheels and accelerate the vehicle from a standstill without the need for the clutch, transmission, or torque converter, all of which are required by an internal combustion engine.

Everything can be accomplished by controlling the drive current to the electric motor. While an internal combustion engine can deliver peak torque only in a relatively narrow speed range and requires a transmission and different gear ratios to deliver its power over a wide vehicle speed range, electric motors can be designed to deliver their power over a broad speed range with no need for a transmission at all.

All these factors mean that current EV conversions put a lighter load on vehicle drivetrains, and future EV conversions will eliminate the need for several drivetrain components altogether.

Let's briefly summarize:

- *Clutch*—Although basically unused, the clutch is handy to have in an EV for shifting when needed. For most motorcycle conversions, you may only need to use a straight belt or chain drive. In the future, when widespread the use of alternating-current (ac) motors and controllers may eliminate the need for a complicated mechanical transmission, the electric motor can be coupled directly to the drive wheel or used with a two-gear ratio transmission, eliminating any other components.
- *Transmission*—This is a handy item depending on your performance needs. The transmission's gears not only match the vehicle you are converting to a variety of off-the-shelf electric motors, but in the future, when widespread adoption of ac motors and controllers provides directional control and eliminates the need for a large number of mechanical gears, you will still get the torques and speeds you need.

Going through the Gears

The transmission gear ratios adapt the internal combustion engine's power and torque characteristics to maximum torque needs for hill climbing or maximum economy needs for cruising. Figure 6-9 shows these at a glance for a typical internal combustion engine with four manual gears—horsepower/torque characteristics versus vehicle speed appear above the line and rpm versus vehicle speed appear below. The constant-engine-power line is simply Equation 5, namely, hp = $FV/375$ (V in mph), less any drivetrain losses. The tractive-force line for each gear is simply the characteristic internal combustion engine torque curve (similar to the one shown in Figure 6-8) multiplied by the ratios for that gear. The superimposed incline-force lines are the typical propulsion or road-load-force components added by acceleration or hill-climbing forces (recall the shape of this curve in Figure 6-6). The intersection of the incline or road-load curves and the tractive-force curves is the maximum speed that can be sustained in that gear.

The upper half of Figure 6-9 illustrates how low first gearing for startup and high fourth gearing for high-speed driving apply to engine torque capabilities. The lower part of the figure shows road speed versus engine speed—for each gear. The point of this drawing is to illustrate how gear selection applies to engine speed capabilities. Normally, the overall gear ratios are selected to fall in a geometric progression: first/second = second/third, etc. Then individual gears are optimized for starting (first), passing (second or third), and fuel economy (fourth or fifth). Table 6-7 shows how these ratios turn out in the Electra Cruiser. The table also calculates the actual motor to transmission to drive wheel and overall gear ratios from start to finish.

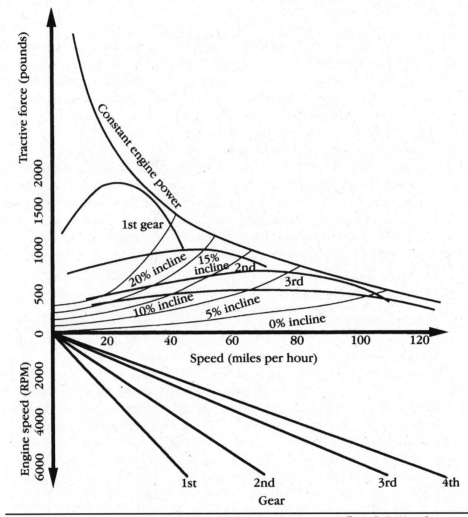

FIGURE 6-9   Transmission gear ratio versus speed and power summary. From *Build Your Own Electric Vehicle*, Figure 5-8, p. 117.

Manual Transmission versus Chain or Shaft Drive

This part of the conversion will depend on a lot of things, mostly what kind of bike you are building or converting. This decision will weigh heavily on your personal preference, the size of the bike, and what you expect to gain performance-wise. There are a lot of factors to consider. The simplest solution is just to use a belt or chain drive directly to the wheel. For a larger, heavier bike, I would choose a chain drive, or if you want to spend a little more money, you can go with a synchronous belt, also referred to as a *timing belt*. This is the same style belt Harley-Davidson

TABLE 6-7 Transmission Gear Ratios for the Electra Cruiser with 1948 Four-Speed Harley Transmission

Motor Rpm	Motor Torque (Ft/Lb)	Motor Amps (Max)	Primary Gear Ratio	Secondary Gear Ratio	Gear Ratio 1st	Gear Ratio 2nd	Gear Ratio 3rd	Gear Ratio 4th	Tire Dia Inches	Tire Rpm 1st Gear	Tire Rpm 2nd Gear	Tire Rpm 3rd Gear	Tire Rpm 4th Gear	Mph 1st Gear	Mph 2nd Gear	Mph 3rd Gear	Mph 4th Gear
			1.68	2.55	3.00	1.82	1.23	1.00	26								
					Combined Ratio	Combined Ratio	Combined Ratio	Combined Ratio									
					12.85	7.80	5.27	4.28									
500	550	750								38.90	64.13	94.89	116.71	3.01	4.96	7.34	9.03
1000	406	750								77.81	128.26	189.78	233.43	6.02	9.92	14.68	18.06
1500	275	750								116.71	192.38	284.67	350.14	9.03	14.88	22.02	27.09
2000	205	750								155.62	256.51	379.56	466.85	12.04	19.84	29.36	36.12
2500	163	750								194.52	320.64	474.44	583.57	15.05	24.80	36.70	45.14
3000	121	675								233.43	384.77	569.33	700.28	18.06	29.77	44.04	54.17
3500	72	460								272.33	448.90	664.22	816.99	21.07	34.73	51.38	63.20
4000	47	330								311.24	513.03	759.11	933.71	24.08	39.69	58.72	72.23
4500	35	260								350.14	577.15	854.00	1050.42	27.09	44.65	66.07	81.26
5000	28	220								389.04	641.28	948.89	1167.13	30.10	49.61	73.41	90.29
5500	23	180								427.95	705.41	1043.78	1283.85	33.11	54.57	80.75	99.32
6000	18	165								466.85	769.54	1138.67	1400.56	36.12	59.53	88.09	108.35
6500	16	150								505.76	833.67	1233.56	1517.27	39.13	64.49	95.43	117.38
7000	13	130								544.66	897.80	1328.44	1633.99	42.13	69.45	102.77	126.40
7500	10	110								583.57	961.92	1423.33	1750.70	45.14	74.41	110.11	135.43
8000										622.47	1026.05	1518.22	1867.41	48.15	79.38	117.45	144.46

motorcycles use for the secondary drive (drive belt for the wheel). For a smaller, light weight bike, you could use a smaller belt.

I liked using a transmission for my motorcycle, but it was a lot more work and meant a significant increase in cost. Just the transmission alone in the Electra Cruiser cost over $3,000 dollars. Then add to that the cost of the clutch, clutch basket, and hydraulic clutch assembly, and now you have a transmission costing over $4,500 dollars. With the Cruiser, it was essential to have the different gear ratios because of the weight of the bike (approaching 1,100 lb). I also wanted the best of both worlds, acceleration and speed. The bike is a beast, with a low-gear ratio of 12:1 and the power to snap 1.5-in-wide Kevlar timing belts. If we look at the torque from the motor at 200 ft · lb, and we take the gear ratio of 12:1 (i.e., 200 × 12 = 2,400 ft · lb), that adds up to 2,400 ft · lb of torque to the rear wheel—that's a lot of power! Depending again on the bike you chose, another solution would be to use a shaft drive and connect the motor directly to it or maybe insert a slight gear reduction. As I said, you have a lot of choices.

Drivetrains and Fluids

Depending on whether you use a transmission or not, your drivetrain will eat up a small amount of power by going through gears, chains, and belts. One of the ways to increase some of your efficiencies is to use a lighter synthetic oil that is more durable in reducing friction. I asked long-time friend of mine Bill Phelan, who also is an AMSOIL distributor, questions about alternate transmission oils I could use to reduce friction. He actually recommended a few products that were synthetic and lighter in viscosity that would do the job. After I added them to the Cruiser's transmission, it did become quieter and shifted smoother. How much added range I achieved I am not sure, but every little bit helps.

Design Your EV

This is step two. Look at your "big picture" first. Before you buy, build, or convert, decide what the main mission of your EV will be: a high-speed dragster to quietly blow away unsuspecting opponents at a stoplight, a long-range cruiser to be a winning candidate at Electric Auto Association meetings, or a utility commuter vehicle to take you to work or grocery shopping with capabilities midway between the other two. Your EV's weight is of primary importance to any design, but high acceleration off the line will dictate one type of design approach and gear ratios, whereas a long-range design will push you in a different direction. If it's a commuter EV you seek, then you'll want to preserve a little of both while optimizing your design flexibility toward either highway commuting or neighborhood traveling needs.

In this section you'll learn how to match your motor-drivetrain combination to the performance level and style you seek by going through the following steps:

- Learn when to use horsepower, torque, or current units and why.
- Look at a calculation overview.
- Determine the required torque needs of your selected vehicle's frame.
- Determine the available capabilities of your selected electric motor and drivetrain.

The design process described herein can be adapted infinitely to any EV you want to buy, build, or convert.

Horsepower, Torque, and Current

Let's start with some basic formulas. Earlier in this chapter, Equation 2 casually introduced you to the fact that

$$1 \text{ hp} = 550 \text{ (ft} \cdot \text{lb)}/\text{s}$$

This was then conveniently bundled into Equation 5:

$$1 \text{ hp} = FV/375$$

where V is speed expressed in mph and F is force in pounds. Horsepower is a rate of doing work. It takes 1 hp to raise 550 lb 1 foot in 1 second. But the second equation, which relates force and speed, brings horsepower to you in more familiar terms. It takes 1 hp to move 37.5 lb at 10 mph. Great, but you also can move 50 lb at 7.5 mph with 1 hp. The first instance might describe the force required to push a vehicle forward on a level slope; the second describes the force required to push the same vehicle up an incline.

Horsepower is equal to force times speed, but you need to specify the force and speed you are talking about. For example, since we already know that 146.19 lb is the total drag force on the 1,100-pound Electra Cruiser at 50 mph, and Equation 5 relates the actual power required at a vehicle's wheels as a function of its speed and the required tractive force, then

$$\text{hp} = (146.19 \times 50)/375 = 19.49 \quad \text{(or approximately 20 hp)}$$

This means that only about 20 hp is necessary—at the wheels—to propel this motorcycle along at 50 mph on a level road without wind. In fact, a rated 20-hp electric motor will easily propel a 4,000-lb vehicle at 50 mph—a fact that might amaze those who think in terms of the typically rated 90- or 120-hp internal combustion engine replaced with an electric motor. The point here is to condition yourself to think in terms of force values, which are relatively easy to determine, rather than in terms of a horsepower figure that is arrived at differently for engines versus electric motors and that means little until tied to specific force and speed values anyway.

Another point (covered in more detail in the discussion of electric motors in Chapter 8 and the discussion of the electrical system in Chapter 12) is to think in terms of current when working with electric motors. The current is directly related to motor torque. Through the torque-current relationship, you can link the mechanical and electrical worlds directly. (*Note:* The controller gives current multiplication. In other words, if the motor voltage is one-third the battery voltage, then the motor current is slightly less than three times the battery current. The motor and battery current would be the same only if you used a very inefficient resistive controller.)

Calculation Overview

Notice that the starting point in the calculations was the ending point of the force value required. Once you know the forces acting on your vehicle chassis at a given speed, the rest is easy. For your calculation approach, first determine these values, and then plug in your motor and drivetrain values for its design center operating point, be it a 100-mph speedster, a 20-mph economy cruiser, or a 50-mph touring bike. A speed of 50 mph will be the design center for our vehicle example.

In short, you need to select a speed, select an electric motor for that speed, choose the rpm value at which the motor delivers that horsepower, choose the target gear ratio based on that rpm value, and see if the motor provides the torque over the range of level and hill-climbing conditions you need. Once you go through the equations, worksheets, and graphed results covered in this section—and repeat them with your own values—you'll find the process quite simple.

The entire process is designed to give you graphic results that you can quickly use to see how the torque available from your selected motor and drivetrain meets your vehicle's torque requirements at different vehicle speeds. If you have a computer with a spreadsheet program, you can set it up once, and afterwards, you can graph the results of any changed input parameter in seconds. In equation form, what I am saying is this:

$$\text{Available engine power} = \text{tractive resistance demand}$$

$$\text{Power} = (\text{acceleration} + \text{climbing} + \text{rolling} + \text{drag} + \text{wind}) \text{ resistance}$$

Plugging this into the force equations gives you

$$\text{Force} = F_a + F_h + F_r + F_d + F_w$$

$$\text{Force} = C_i Wa + W \sin \Phi + C_r W \cos \Phi + C_d A V^2 + C_w F_d$$

You've determined every one of these earlier in the chapter. Under steady-speed conditions, acceleration is zero, so there is no acceleration force. If you are on a level surface, $\sin \Phi = 0$, $\cos \Phi = 1$, and the force equation can be rewritten as

$$\text{Force} = C_r W \cos f + C_d A V^2 + C_w F_d$$

This is the propulsion or road-load force you met at the end of the rolling-resistance section and graphed in Figure 6-6. You need to determine this force for your vehicle at several candidate vehicle speeds and add back in the acceleration and hill-climbing forces. This is easy if you recall that the acceleration force equals the hill-climbing force over the range from 1–6 mph/s. You now can calculate your electric motor's required horsepower for your EV's performance requirements:

$$\text{Horsepower (hp)} = (\text{torque} \times \text{rpm})/5{,}252 = 2\pi/60 \times FV/550$$

$$\text{Wheel rpm} = (\text{mph} \times \text{rev/mi})/60$$

The preceding equation can be substituted to give

$$\text{hp}_{\text{wheel}} = (\text{torque}_{\text{wheel}} \times \text{mph} \times \text{rev/mi})/(5{,}252 \times 60)$$

$$\text{hp}_{\text{motor}} = \text{hp}_{\text{wheel}}/n_o$$

where n_o is the overall drivetrain efficiency. Substituting the preceding equation into this one gives

$$\text{hp}_{\text{motor}} = (\text{torque}_{\text{wheel}} \times \text{mph} \times \text{rev/mi})/(315{,}120 \times n_o)$$

Plugging the values for torque, speed, and revolutions per mile (based on your vehicle's tire diameter) into the equation will give you the required horsepower for your electric motor.

After you have chosen your candidate electric motor, the manufacturer usually will provide you with a graph or table showing its torque and current versus speed performance based on a constant voltage applied to the motor terminals. From these figures or curves, you can derive the rpm value at which your electric motor delivers closest to its rated horsepower. Using this motor rpm figure and the wheel rpm figure from your target speed and rpm, you can determine your best gear or gear ratio from

$$\text{Overall gear ratio} = \text{rpm}_{\text{motor}}/\text{rpm}_{\text{wheel}}$$

This—or the one closest to it—is the best gear for the transmission in your selected vehicle to use; if you were setting up a one-gear-only EV, you would pick this ratio.

With all the other motor torque and rpm values, you then can calculate wheel torque and vehicle speed using the following equations for the different overall gear ratios in your drivetrain:

$$\text{Torque}_{\text{wheel}} = \text{torque}_{\text{motor}}/(\text{overall gear ratio} \times n_o)$$

$$\text{Speed}_{\text{vehicle}} \text{ (in mph)} = (\text{rpm}_{\text{motor}} \times 60)/(\text{overall gear ratio} \times \text{rev/mi})$$

You now have the family of torque-available curves versus vehicle speed for the different gear ratios in your drivetrain. All that remains is to graph the torque-required data and the torque-available data on the same grid. A quick look at the graph tells you whether you have what you need or need to go back to the drawing board.

Torque-Required Worksheet

Tables 6-8 and 6-9 compute the torque-required data for the Electra Cruiser, the vehicle I created using this book. You've met all the values going into the level drag force before, but not in one worksheet. Now they are converted to torque values using Equation 11, and new values of force and torque are calculated for incline values from 2–15 percent. Conveniently, these correspond rather closely to the acceleration values for 1–5 mph/s, respectively, and the two can be used interchangeably. The vehicle assumptions all appear in Table 6-8. If you were preparing a computer spreadsheet, all this type of information would be grouped in one section so that you could see the effects of changing chassis weight, C_dA, C_r, and other parameters. You also might want to graph speed values at 5-mph intervals to present a more accurate picture.

Torque-Available Worksheet

There are a few preliminaries to go through before you can prepare the torque-available worksheet. First, you have to determine the horsepower of an electric motor using the following equation:

$$hp_{motor} = (torque_{wheel} \times mph \times rev/mi)/(315,120 \times n_o)$$

You do this using the numbers from the Advanced DC Motors Model FB1-4001, rated at 22 hp. From the manufacturer's torque versus speed curves for this motor driven at a constant 120 V and using this equation, we get

$$hp = (torque \times rpm)/5,252 = (25 \times 4,600)/5,252 = 21.89$$

This motor produces approximately 22 hp at 4,600 rpm at 25 ft · lb of torque and 170 A.

Next, calculate the wheel rpm using the following equation:

$$rpm_{wheel} = (mph \times rev/mi)/60 = (50 \times 808)/60 = 673.33$$

You then can calculate the best gear using

$$Overall\ gear\ ratio = rpm_{motor}/rpm_{wheel} = 4,600/673.33 = 6.83$$

From Table 6-7, you can use this as an example to create your own spreadsheet. Depending on whether you want a transmission or not, you want to gather all the data you can. If you only use a belt or straight chain drive system, place all the belt or chain ratios in the spreadsheet, and try to balance out the rpm value of the motor with the speed of the vehicle. Optimize your numbers to work with in the most efficient rpm of your electric motor. From these spreadsheets, you can create graphs that give you a full picture of where your numbers need to be. Pay particular attention to the number of amps the electric motor will consume at varying speeds or gear ratios and under inclines or at high speeds. If you can acquire any data from the electric motor manufacturer for torque and rpm, place those data in your

TABLE 6-8 Torque-Required Worksheet for Electra Cruiser at Different Speeds and 2 Percent Incline

Coefficient of Drag Cd	Frontal Area in Sq Ft	Speed in Mph	Tire Dia in In	Speed in Ft/Sec	Rolling Resistance Factor	Relative Wind Factor	Wind Factor Crw (1)	Vehicle Weight in Pounds	Angle of Incline in Degrees	Wheel Rpm	Aerodynamic Drag Force in (Lbs)	Aerodynamic Drag Force w/Wind Factor (Lbs)	Angle of Incline Force in Lbs	Rolling Resistance Force (Lbs)	Hp Required No Acceleration	Required Torque at Rear Wheel
0.6	6	0.1	26.00	0.15	0.01	#####	1.6	1200	2	1.29	0.00	0.82	41.88	12.00	0.01	59.25
0.6	6	2	26.00	2.93	0.01	24.330	1.6	1200	2	25.86	0.04	0.93	41.88	12.00	0.29	59.38
0.6	6	4	26.00	5.87	0.01	6.653	1.6	1200	2	51.72	0.15	1.13	41.88	12.00	0.59	59.59
0.6	6	6	26.00	8.80	0.01	3.210	1.6	1200	2	77.59	0.33	1.40	41.88	12.00	0.89	59.88
0.6	6	8	26.00	11.74	0.01	1.948	1.6	1200	2	103.45	0.59	1.74	41.88	12.00	1.20	60.25
0.6	6	10	26.00	14.67	0.01	1.338	1.6	1200	2	129.31	0.92	2.15	41.88	12.00	1.52	60.70
0.6	6	12	26.00	17.60	0.01	0.993	1.6	1200	2	155.17	1.33	2.64	41.88	12.00	1.85	61.23
0.6	6	14	26.00	20.54	0.01	0.776	1.6	1200	2	181.04	1.80	3.20	41.88	12.00	2.20	61.84
0.6	6	16	26.00	23.47	0.01	0.630	1.6	1200	2	206.90	2.36	3.84	41.88	12.00	2.56	62.53
0.6	6	18	26.00	26.41	0.01	0.526	1.6	1200	2	232.76	2.98	4.55	41.88	12.00	2.95	63.30
0.6	6	20	26.00	29.34	0.01	0.449	1.6	1200	2	258.62	3.68	5.33	41.88	12.00	3.35	64.15
0.6	6	22	26.00	32.27	0.01	0.390	1.6	1200	2	284.49	4.46	6.19	41.88	12.00	3.79	65.08
0.6	6	24	26.00	35.21	0.01	0.343	1.6	1200	2	310.35	5.30	7.12	41.88	12.00	4.24	66.09
0.6	6	26	26.00	38.14	0.01	0.306	1.6	1200	2	336.21	6.22	8.13	41.88	12.00	4.73	67.17
0.6	6	28	26.00	41.08	0.01	0.275	1.6	1200	2	362.07	7.22	9.21	41.88	12.00	5.25	68.34
0.6	6	30	26.00	44.01	0.01	0.250	1.6	1200	2	387.94	8.29	10.36	41.88	12.00	5.80	69.59
0.6	6	32	26.00	46.94	0.01	0.229	1.6	1200	2	413.80	9.43	11.58	41.88	12.00	6.39	70.92
0.6	6	34	26.00	49.88	0.01	0.210	1.6	1200	2	439.66	10.64	12.88	41.88	12.00	7.02	72.33
0.6	6	36	26.00	52.81	0.01	0.195	1.6	1200	2	465.52	11.93	14.26	41.88	12.00	7.69	73.81
0.6	6	38	26.00	55.75	0.01	0.181	1.6	1200	2	491.39	13.30	15.70	41.88	12.00	8.40	75.38
0.6	6	40	26.00	58.68	0.01	0.169	1.6	1200	2	517.25	14.73	17.22	41.88	12.00	9.16	77.03
0.6	6	42	26.00	61.61	0.01	0.159	1.6	1200	2	543.11	16.24	18.82	41.88	12.00	9.96	78.75
0.6	6	44	26.00	64.55	0.01	0.149	1.6	1200	2	568.97	17.83	20.48	41.88	12.00	10.82	80.56
0.6	6	46	26.00	67.48	0.01	0.141	1.6	1200	2	594.84	19.48	22.23	41.88	12.00	11.73	82.45
0.6	6	48	26.00	70.42	0.01	0.133	1.6	1200	2	620.70	21.21	24.04	41.88	12.00	12.69	84.41

continued on next page

TABLE 6-8 Torque-Required Worksheet for Electra Cruiser at Different Speeds and 2 Percent Incline (continued)

Coefficient of Drag Cd	Frontal Area in Sq Ft	Speed in Mph	Tire Dia in In	Speed in Ft/Sec	Rolling Resistance Factor	Relative Wind Factor	Wind Factor Crw (1)	Vehicle Weight in Pounds	Angle of Incline in Degrees	Wheel Rpm	Aerodynamic Drag Force in (Lbs)	Aerodynamic Drag Force w/Wind Factor (Lbs)	Angle of Incline Force in Lbs	Rolling Resistance Force (Lbs)	Hp Required No Acceleration	Required Torque at Rear Wheel
0.6	6	50	26.00	73.35	0.01	0.126	1.6	1200	2	646.56	23.02	25.93	41.88	12.00	13.71	86.46
0.6	6	52	26.00	76.28	0.01	0.120	1.6	1200	2	672.42	24.90	27.89	41.88	12.00	14.79	88.59
0.6	6	54	26.00	79.22	0.01	0.115	1.6	1200	2	698.29	26.85	29.93	41.88	12.00	15.93	90.79
0.6	6	56	26.00	82.15	0.01	0.110	1.6	1200	2	724.15	28.87	32.04	41.88	12.00	17.14	93.08
0.6	6	58	26.00	85.09	0.01	0.105	1.6	1200	2	750.01	30.97	34.22	41.88	12.00	18.42	95.44
0.6	6	60	26.00	88.02	0.01	0.101	1.6	1200	2	775.87	33.15	36.48	41.88	12.00	19.76	97.89
0.6	6	62	26.00	90.95	0.01	0.096	1.6	1200	2	801.74	35.39	38.81	41.88	12.00	21.18	100.41
0.6	6	64	26.00	93.89	0.01	0.093	1.6	1200	2	827.60	37.71	41.21	41.88	12.00	22.67	103.02
0.6	6	66	26.00	96.82	0.01	0.089	1.6	1200	2	853.46	40.11	43.69	41.88	12.00	24.23	105.70
0.6	6	68	26.00	99.76	0.01	0.086	1.6	1200	2	879.32	42.57	46.24	41.88	12.00	25.88	108.46
0.6	6	70	26.00	102.69	0.01	0.083	1.6	1200	2	905.19	45.12	48.87	41.88	12.00	27.60	111.31
0.6	6	72	26.00	105.62	0.01	0.080	1.6	1200	2	931.05	47.73	51.56	41.88	12.00	29.41	114.23

TABLE 6-9 Torque-Required Worksheet for Electra Cruiser at Different Speeds and 15 Percent Incline

Coefficient of Drag Cd	Frontal Area in Sq Ft	Speed in Mph	Tire Dia in Inches	Speed In Ft/Sec	Rolling Resistance Factor	Relative Wind Factor	Wind Factor Crw (1)	Vehicle Weight in Pounds	Angle of Incline in Degrees	Wheel Rpm	Aerodynamic Drag Force in Lbs	Aerodynamic Drag Force w/Wind Factor (Lbs)	Angle of Incline Force in Lbs	Rolling Resistance Force (Lbs)	Hp Required No Acceleration	Required Torque at Rear Wheel
0.6	6	0.1	26.00	0.15	0.01	#####	1.6	1200	15	1.29	0.00	0.82	310.58	12.00	0.09	350.35
0.6	6	2	26.00	2.93	0.01	24.330	1.6	1200	15	25.86	0.04	0.93	310.58	12.00	1.73	350.48
0.6	6	4	26.00	5.87	0.01	6.653	1.6	1200	15	51.72	0.15	1.13	310.58	12.00	3.45	350.69
0.6	6	6	26.00	8.80	0.01	3.210	1.6	1200	15	77.59	0.33	1.40	310.58	12.00	5.19	350.98
0.6	6	8	26.00	11.74	0.01	1.948	1.6	1200	15	103.45	0.59	1.74	310.58	12.00	6.93	351.35
0.6	6	10	26.00	14.67	0.01	1.338	1.6	1200	15	129.31	0.92	2.15	310.58	12.00	8.68	351.80
0.6	6	12	26.00	17.60	0.01	0.993	1.6	1200	15	155.17	1.33	2.64	310.58	12.00	10.45	352.33
0.6	6	14	26.00	20.54	0.01	0.776	1.6	1200	15	181.04	1.80	3.20	310.58	12.00	12.23	352.94
0.6	6	16	26.00	23.47	0.01	0.630	1.6	1200	15	206.90	2.36	3.84	310.58	12.00	14.03	353.63
0.6	6	18	26.00	26.41	0.01	0.526	1.6	1200	15	232.76	2.98	4.55	310.58	12.00	15.85	354.39
0.6	6	20	26.00	29.34	0.01	0.449	1.6	1200	15	258.62	3.68	5.33	310.58	12.00	17.69	355.24
0.6	6	22	26.00	32.27	0.01	0.390	1.6	1200	15	284.49	4.46	6.19	310.58	12.00	19.55	356.17
0.6	6	24	26.00	35.21	0.01	0.343	1.6	1200	15	310.35	5.30	7.12	310.58	12.00	21.44	357.18
0.6	6	26	26.00	38.14	0.01	0.306	1.6	1200	15	336.21	6.22	8.13	310.58	12.00	23.36	358.27
0.6	6	28	26.00	41.08	0.01	0.275	1.6	1200	15	362.07	7.22	9.21	310.58	12.00	25.31	359.44
0.6	6	30	26.00	44.01	0.01	0.250	1.6	1200	15	387.94	8.29	10.36	310.58	12.00	27.30	360.69
0.6	6	32	26.00	46.94	0.01	0.229	1.6	1200	15	413.80	9.43	11.58	310.58	12.00	29.32	362.01
0.6	6	34	26.00	49.88	0.01	0.210	1.6	1200	15	439.66	10.64	12.88	310.58	12.00	31.38	363.42
0.6	6	36	26.00	52.81	0.01	0.195	1.6	1200	15	465.52	11.93	14.26	310.58	12.00	33.48	364.91
0.6	6	38	26.00	55.75	0.01	0.181	1.6	1200	15	491.39	13.30	15.70	310.58	12.00	35.63	366.48
0.6	6	40	26.00	58.68	0.01	0.169	1.6	1200	15	517.25	14.73	17.22	310.58	12.00	37.82	368.12
0.6	6	42	26.00	61.61	0.01	0.159	1.6	1200	15	543.11	16.24	18.82	310.58	12.00	40.06	369.85
0.6	6	44	26.00	64.55	0.01	0.149	1.6	1200	15	568.97	17.83	20.48	310.58	12.00	42.34	371.66
0.6	6	46	26.00	67.48	0.01	0.141	1.6	1200	15	594.84	19.48	22.23	310.58	12.00	44.69	373.54
0.6	6	48	26.00	70.42	0.01	0.133	1.6	1200	15	620.70	21.21	24.04	310.58	12.00	47.08	375.51

continued on next page

111

TABLE 6-9 Torque-Required Worksheet for Electra Cruiser at Different Speeds and 15 Percent Incline (continued)

Coefficient of Drag Cd	Frontal Area in Sq Ft	Speed in Mph	Tire Dia in Inches	Speed In Ft/Sec	Rolling Resistance Factor	Relative Wind Factor	Wind Factor Crw (1)	Vehicle Weight in Pounds	Angle of Incline in Degrees	Wheel Rpm	Aerodynamic Drag Force in Lbs	Aerodynamic Drag Force w/Wind Factor (Lbs)	Angle of Incline Force in Lbs	Rolling Resistance Force (Lbs)	Hp Required No Acceleration	Required Torque at Rear Wheel
0.6	6	50	26.00	73.35	0.01	0.126	1.6	1200	15	646.56	23.02	25.93	310.58	12.00	49.54	377.55
0.6	6	52	26.00	76.28	0.01	0.120	1.6	1200	15	672.42	24.90	27.89	310.58	12.00	52.05	379.68
0.6	6	54	26.00	79.22	0.01	0.115	1.6	1200.	15	698.29	26.85	29.93	310.58	12.00	54.63	381.89
0.6	6	56	26.00	82.15	0.01	0.110	1.6	1200	15	724.15	28.87	32.04	310.58	12.00	57.27	384.17
0.6	6	58	26.00	85.09	0.01	0.105	1.6	1200	15	750.01	30.97	34.22	310.58	12.00	59.98	386.54
0.6	6	60	26.00	88.02	0.01	0.101	1.6	1200	15	775.87	33.15	36.48	310.58	12.00	62.75	388.98
0.6	6	62	26.00	90.95	0.01	0.096	1.6	1200	15	801.74	35.39	38.81	310.58	12.00	65.60	391.51
0.6	6	64	26.00	93.89	0.01	0.093	1.6	1200	15	827.60	37.71	41.21	310.58	12.00	68.52	394.11
0.6	6	66	26.00	96.82	0.01	0.089	1.6	1200	15	853.46	40.11	43.69	310.58	12.00	71.52	396.79
0.6	6	68	26.00	99.76	0.01	0.086	1.6	1200	15	879.32	42.57	46.24	310.58	12.00	74.60	399.56
0.6	6	70	26.00	102.69	0.01	0.083	1.6	1200	15	905.19	45.12	48.87	310.58	12.00	77.76	402.40
0.6	6	72	26.00	105.62	0.01	0.080	1.6	1200	15	931.05	47.73	51.56	310.58	12.00	81.00	405.33

spreadsheet, and try to match everything up. It is not as hard as it sounds, but it does take a little time on your part to set up all the parameters. Once you have the spreadsheets worked out, your job now is a snap—just drop numbers in, and the whole picture will unfold right before your eyes. Figures 6-10 to 6-14 are samples of spreadsheets I created that you can use as samples.

As you look at the motor and drivetrain combination for your vehicle, you can make changes along the way and tweak things. If you want to make minor

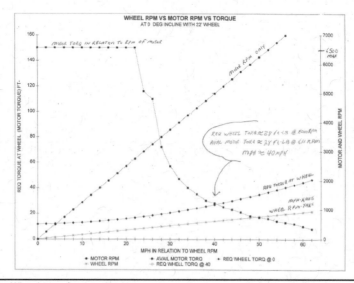

FIGURE 6-10   Wheel rpm versus motor rpm versus torque on a 0-degree incline.

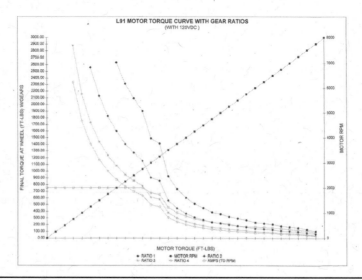

FIGURE 6-11   Advanced DC Motors curves with gear ratios.

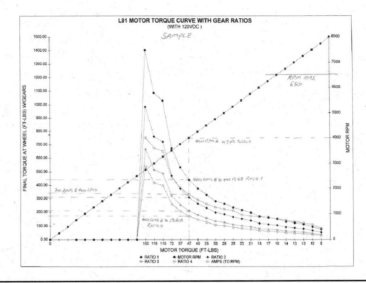

FIGURE 6-12 Advanced DC Motors curves for four-speed transmission with gear ratios.

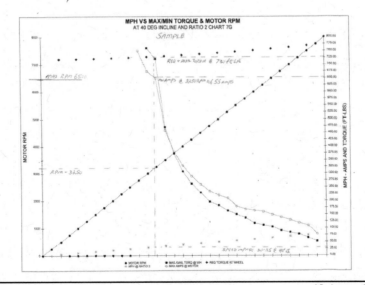

FIGURE 6-13 Wheel rpm value versus max/min torque and motor rpm on a 40-degree incline.

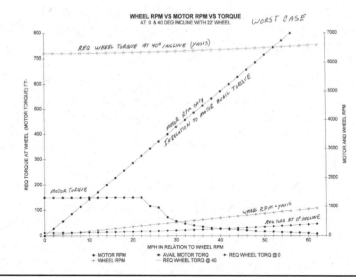

FIGURE 6-14   Wheel rpm versus motor rpm versus torque on 0- and 40-degree inclines.

adjustments, just raise or lower the battery voltage. This will shift the torque-available curve for each gear. A larger motor in your particular vehicle may give you better acceleration and top-end speed and performance. The torque-available curves for each gear would be shifted higher. However, the penalty might be higher weight and increased current draw with shorter range. A smaller motor would shift the torque-available curves lower while returning a small weight and current draw advantage. Beware of underpowering your vehicle, though. A motor that is not sized properly may overheat and have a shorter life. If given the choice, always go for a slightly larger motor rather than slightly less horsepower than you need. The result almost always will be higher satisfaction with your finished EV conversion.

Why Conversion Is Best

In the real world, where time is money, converting an existing internal combustion engine vehicle saves money in terms of large capital investment and a large amount of labor. By starting with an existing late-model vehicle, the EV converter's bonus is a structure that comes complete with body, frame, suspension, and braking systems—all designed, developed, tested, and safety-proven to work together. Provided that the converted electric vehicle does not greatly exceed the original vehicle's Gross Vehicle Weight Rating (GVWR) overall weight or Gross Axle Weight Rating (GAWR) weight per axle specifications, all systems will continue to deliver their previous performance, stability, and handling characteristics. And the EV converter inherits another body bonus—its lights, brakes, and other equipment are already pre-approved and tested to meet all safety requirements and DOT standards.

There's still another benefit—you save more money selling off its pieces for more than you paid for the bike. When you build (rather than convert) an EV, you are on the other side of the fence. Unless you bought a complete kit, building from scratch means buying chassis tubing, angle braces, and sheet stock plus axles/suspension, brakes, bearings/wheels/tires, trim/paint, lights/electrical, gauges, instruments, etc.—parts that are bound to cost you more à la carte than buying them already manufactured and installed on the vehicle.

Sell Your Unused Engine Parts

Somebody somewhere wants that engine you just removed for the EV that you just built for their own bike. This is a great way to recoup some money on your investment. If the parts are no good, in the worst case, you could sell them for scrap and still do your part by recycling.

Equipment Required for Motorcycles (Including Limited-Use Motorcycles)

Equipment must be of a type approved by the commissioner of motor vehicles. Department of transportation (DOT) designation or proof on parts and equipment may be mandatory. If you are building a homemade or custom vehicle, please contact your DMV technical services unit for more information.

Brakes

Brakes must be adequate to control the motorcycle at all times and must be in good working order. All 1971 and newer motorcycles must be equipped with brakes acting on the front and rear wheels to stop the motorcycle within 25 ft from 20 mph on a hard, dry surface.

Horn

The sound produced must be loud enough to serve as a warning but not unnecessarily loud or harsh.

Muffler

Since you are building an EV, this will not apply. If, by chance, you built a hybrid version, these requirements might apply. No person shall operate on any highway a motorcycle which is

- Not equipped with a muffler to prevent excessive or unusual noise
- Equipped with a muffler from which the baffle plates, screens, or other original internal parts have been removed or altered

- Equipped with an exhaust device without internal baffles, known as "straight pipes"
- Equipped with a modified exhaust system that amplifies or increases the exhaust noise so it is louder than the noise made by the original exhaust system

Mirror

A motorcycle must have an adjustable rear-view mirror to give the operator a clear view of the road and traffic conditions behind the motorcycle.

Windscreen

If the motorcycle is equipped with a windscreen, the windscreen and its brackets must be permanently labeled by the manufacturer to ensure that they are approved for highway use (DOT).

Handlebars or Grips

The handlebars or grips must not be higher than the operator's shoulders. Handlebars should be no more than 15 in higher than the seat. This means no "ape hanger" handlebars. Such handlebars are primarily for show and actually adversely affect handling and control of the vehicle.

Seat Height

Measure from the ground to the top of the operator's seat. If the seat is adjustable, the seat must be at its lowest position. Seat height must be at least 25 in from the ground on a two-wheeled motorcycle and 20 in on a three-wheeled motorcycle.

Tires

Tires must be DOT approved with a DOT number. A tire may not be used if there is

- A visible break, that is, a cut, in excess of 1 in that is deep enough to reach body cords
- Any bump, bulge, ply, or cord exposure
- Any portion of tread design that is completely worn and which is of sufficient size to affect the traction or stopping ability of the tire
- Tread depth (when measured with a tire gauge) of less than 2/32 in
- Labeling such as "Not for highway use," "For racing purposes only," or words of similar intent
- A weight rating not sufficient for the vehicle, rider, and equipment combined

Lighting Devices and Reflectors

Headlamps

One unit may be used to accomplish two or more lighting purposes. The motorcycle must display at least one headlamp at the front of the vehicle. When operated with a sidecar attached, it must have at least two headlamps displayed at the front. The headlamp(s) must be capable of projecting a dual beam (high/low). The headlamp(s) must be on whenever the motorcycle is operated on public highways. Lights should be mounted at a height of not more than 54 in or less than 24 in from the ground, measured from the center of the lamp to the level ground on which the motorcycle stands without a load

Stop Lamp

One red stop lamp must be displayed to the rear. Some older motorcycles were equipped with a red-amber stop light. These lights are approved only for use on the original vehicle. The light should be visible from at least 300 ft to the rear in normal sunlight.

Tail Lamp

One red tail lamp must be displayed to the rear. This lamp must be visible from 300 ft, and some states say up to 500 ft. The tail lamp must be on whenever the motorcycle is operated on public highways.

Turn Signal Lamps

Any 1985 or newer motorcycle must be equipped with directional or turn signals. Any motorcycle that was originally equipped with such signals or to which such signals have been added must have them inspected. Turn signals must show amber to the front and red or amber to the rear. Front signals must be mounted at the same level and as widely spaced laterally as practicable and must emit white or amber light. Rear signals must be mounted at the same level and as widely spaced laterally as practicable and must emit red or amber light. Both front and rear lights must be visible from a distance of at least 500 ft.

License Plate Lamp

The plate must be lit with a white light bright enough to make the plate visible from 50 ft.

Reflector

One red reflector must be displayed to the rear of the vehicle (may be a part of the tail lamp).

Speedometer

All 1980 and newer motorcycles must be capable of measuring the motorcycle's speed and of displaying the speed in miles per hour.

Fenders

Wheels must be protected by fenders to prevent the throwing of rocks, dirt, water, or other substances to the rear.

All these requirements are for your safety and that of others. Remember, you want your vehicle to be as visible as possible. What is the old saying among bikers? "Loud pipes save lives?" Well, now we have no pipes and have created a very silent vehicle. It is really cool to cruise with just the wind and little sound—something words just cannot explain; you have to experience it for yourself. In the same respect, it is important to make sure that your vehicle is highly visible and safe to operate.

Since you have an EV, I would plan to keep a few additional safety items on board. This is a subject few people talk about, and I feel that is very important to consider, if not just for the EV motorcycle but for all electric vehicles. Motorcycles are dangerous. We all know this. The problem is not the motorcycle rider, but the other people on the road. Things happen, and you need to be prepared for the worst. I will assume that most of the motorcycle conversions to electric will use some form of lead-acid batteries. It just makes sense; they are cheap, work well, and are easy to get. Well, in a worst-case scenario, you get in an accident. Some jerk hits you, your bike is busted up, and your batteries leak, burst, or explode. What do you do? Now you have acid on you, in your eyes or, worse, in your wounds. My advice is to know your battery chemistry. Know what harm those chemicals can have, and prepare for it. In the case of lead-acid batteries, I would keep a small kit on board with eyewash and baking soda or another substance to neutralize the acid. A few little precautions now could go a long way in the future and may be the deciding factor in preventing a serious injury.

CHAPTER 7

Batteries

From its early beginnings, battery technology is ever evolving. Looking back to the first battery, invented in 1800 by Alessandro Volta, technology has advanced greatly (Figures 7-1 and 7-2). The three major and most important components your electric vehicle (EV) depends on are the batteries, the electric motor, and the controller. In my opinion, the batteries are the most important; they are the key and limiting factor in any EV.

Batteries power our daily lives, and the multibillion-dollar industry fuels the worldwide economy. Without batteries, our cars would not start, and we would have no backup power in buildings, no emergency lighting, no security systems, no telecommunications, and no EVs.

If you look at all of society's technological advancements from electronics to materials and so much more, you would think that since 1800, over 200 years later, batteries would be so much more advanced. Yes, battery technology has gained many leaps and bounds, but where are these batteries? Why have the masses, you and I, been unable to purchase this advanced technology? Why is it so expensive? Is there a conspiracy? Why did Texaco/Chevron ("big oil") buy the controlling interests in the General Motors' Ovonic high-efficiency, nickel–metal hydride (NiMH) battery technology? Why have the patents on NiMH batteries, previously owned by GM Ovonic Battery Company (during the EV1 battery era) and later sold to Texaco/Chevron, been used to prevent anyone from making large NiMH batteries suitable for use in EVs? All NiMH battery production (such as the common AA rechargeables) must be licensed from Chevron, and its licensing terms forbid batteries from being made above a certain specified size.

Since January 2000, GM has been gradually taking steps to eliminate its EV program, going as far as taking EV1s and Chevy S10 trucks out of service (see Figure 7-3), with plans to send them to the crusher. Is it coincidence that in the same year of 2000 Texaco/Chevron bought GM's 60 percent share of an existing joint

FIGURE 7-1   Early 6-V battery by Exide. (www.powerstream.com/1922/battery_1922_WITTE/batteryfiles/fig.001.jpg.)

FIGURE 7-2   Early 6-V lead acid battery. (www.powerstream.com/1922/battery_1922_WITTE/batteryfiles/fig.171.jpg; www.powerstream.com/1922/battery_1922_WITTE/batteryfiles/chapter11.htm.)

venture with Energy Conversion Devices (ECD) (maker of the Ovonic battery)? ECD is a firm in which Texaco already holds a 20 percent interest. These stories and many others make you think, "Maybe there is more behind our lack of battery technology advancements?" Or is there no conspiracy? Was it that the government only granted GM a special 36-month permission allowing it to give the prototype EV to the public with the stipulation that it had to be removed from the roads? I will leave you to your own conclusions. David Findley researched this topic and found even more information and came to a number of different conclusions. His special article can be found at www.exploresynergy.org.

In this chapter you will learn about different battery technologies and their advantages and disadvantages. I will discuss the many batteries available on the market today and future batteries to come. I will touch on some of the basic chemistry and makeup of batteries for your basic knowledge. Then we will look at the basic calculations, capacity, and rating of batteries.

Battery Overview

Your EV's construction up to now involved many mechanical aspects involving transmissions, gear ratios, geometry, and other design considerations. Here, we

FIGURE 7.3 .Ovonic EV1 battery in an S-10 pickup. (Courtesy of Mike Anzalone of Long Island Electric Auto Association [LIEAA].)

will review the electrochemical actions that turn chemical energy into electrical energy. In essence, your batteries are your fuel tank. The goal of your fuel tank (batteries) is to achieve the greatest storage possible in a limited space, giving your EV as much range as possible.

While battery development and advancements are an ongoing process, the objective here is to give you some basic background and knowledge. For your EV conversion, I will assume that lead-acid batteries will be the battery of choice. Considering your conversion and the limited space available, you may opt for advanced battery technology to cram more power in a smaller space. The batteries may represent the largest replacement-cost item and possibly your largest initial-expense item depending on the number and type of battery you use. The cost of batteries for your EV should be half to one-quarter what a normal EV conversion might cost depending on the size of your conversion. Considering this cost savings, you might be able to spend a little more money on advanced batteries. Remember, the batteries are the heart of your EV, one of three very important areas that are crucial in your EV build.

You probably can find many good-quality books about batteries and a few good Web sites with excellent data. Curtis Instruments has a great Web site link just dedicated to batteries. While the information was written in 1980 as a book, it is still as valid today as it was then. Curtis now has made this information available to everyone by publishing its works on the Web at evbatterymonitoring.com.

As you read this chapter, I will help you to become familiar with a few basic areas:

- What goes on inside a battery and the chemical reactions taking place
- A battery's external characteristics, mounting, and connections
- Calculations and formulas to understand battery rating and to evaluate range and performance

Knowledge in these areas gives you a strong background and understanding of your choices and your batteries.

Battery History

The battery is one of the most important inventions in the history of humankind. The invention is now taken for granted but was not always so commonplace. You couldn't just walk into a store and buy a battery off a shelf as we do now. Volta's pile was at first a technical curiosity, but this new electrochemical phenomenon very quickly opened a myriad of discoveries, inventions, and applications. The electronics, computer, and communications industries; power engineering; and much of the chemical industry of today were founded on discoveries made possible by the battery. Below is a brief history and timeline of just some of the pioneers of the past. There are many more to be added to the list that literally will fill four or five more pages.[1]

Early Pioneers in Battery Technology

- 1748: Benjamin Franklin first coined the term *battery* to describe an array of charged glass plates.
- 1780–1786: Luigi Galvani demonstrated what we now understand to be the electrical basis of nerve impulses. This was accomplished by placing a voltage across a frog's leg and making it twitch. This provided the cornerstone of research for later inventors such as Volta.
- 1800: Alessandro Volta invented the voltaic pile and discovered the first practical method of generating electricity. Alessandro Volta's voltaic pile was the first "wet-cell battery" that produced a reliable, steady current of electricity.
- 1836: Englishman John F. Daniel invented the Daniel cell that used two electrolytes, copper sulfate and zinc sulfate. The Daniel cell was somewhat safer and less corrosive then the Volta cell.
- 1839: William Robert Grove developed the first fuel cell, which produced electricity by combining hydrogen and oxygen.
- 1859: Gaston Planté, a French physicist, invented the lead-acid battery The lead-acid battery eventually became the first rechargeable electric battery marketed for commercial use.

- 1881: Carl Gassner invented the first commercially successful dry-cell battery (zinc-carbon cell).
- 1899: Waldmar Jungner invented the first nickel-cadmium rechargeable battery.

And this list goes on and on.

For our initial discussions, I will review lead-acid batteries because they are the most popular battery for EVs. The basics of battery operation hold true for other types of batteries, most using an anode and cathode that I will explain in more detail below.

Battery Types

The basic batteries this book will explain are *secondary batteries*. These are the most popular of all batteries. Secondary batteries are rechargeable batteries, the battery of choice used most in EVs. They have the advantage of being more cost-efficient over the long term. Secondary batteries are the best solution for high-drain applications. If you look at primary batteries, you see that they do not fit the requirements of an EV. First off, primary batteries are not rechargeable; once you use them, they are discarded. They do have higher energy density and voltage because no design compromises were necessary to accommodate recharging. Primary batteries are not suitable for high-drain applications owing to their short lifetime.

Most of this chapter will focus on lead-acid batteries because they are most popular and most likely the battery of choice. I will explain various advanced battery technologies currently available and new technologies for the future. Even though the focus may lean toward lead acid, that does not rule out other batteries and battery technologies for EVs. A major design consideration is power-to-weight ratio because your EV must carry the batteries, and any weight you can save means more range for the EV. In the next few paragraphs I will briefly explain additional battery types and chemistry starting from the bottom up. I will not be able to cover all battery types, only the ones that apply to EVs.

Starting Batteries

The starting battery is designed to deliver quick bursts of energy, and generally such batteries are used for starting engines with a short burst of power. Typically this battery sees only a 2 percent discharge under normal conditions. This type of battery has a greater plate count internally, and the plates are usually thinner and somewhat different in material composition. The thin plates allow for more plates in the battery, increasing the surface area. The plates generally are around 0.04 in. thick.[2] With more surface area, the battery is able to provide greater bursts of current.

The starting battery cannot withstand more than a few deep discharges before failure. Generally, a starting battery should not be discharged more than 20 percent of its total charge. A starting battery, if deeply discharged, may last only 30–150 deep cycles until failure. Normally, the battery will see only 2–5 percent discharge, allowing it to last thousands of cycles. This is why it is unable to start your car if you accidentally leave the lights on and fully discharged it more than a couple of times. Discharges of more than 50 percent over time will degrade the battery and damage it. Since the plates are thin, they are only lightly loaded with active material. A starting battery is not suitable nor designed for an EV. For the conventional 12-V system on your vehicle, a starting battery (Figure 7-4) can be used or replaced with a direct current (dc)-to-dc converter. More will be explained in Chap. 11 on dc-to-dc converters.

Deep-Cycle Batteries

A deep-cycle battery is designed to provide a steady amount of current over a long period of time (Figure 7-5). A deep-cycle battery can provide a surge when needed, but nothing like the surge a car battery can. A deep-cycle battery is also designed to be deeply discharged over and over again (something that would ruin a car battery very quickly). To accomplish this, a deep-cycle battery uses thicker plates. Plates normally are anywhere from two or three times thicker than in starting batteries at around 0.7–0.11 in. thick. A deep-cycle battery is designed to discharge to 80 percent depth of discharge (DOD). Typical discharge-cycle life is 400–1,000 cycles depending on the care taken of the batteries. Any depth of charge lower than 80 percent will shorten the life of the battery and the number of cycles.

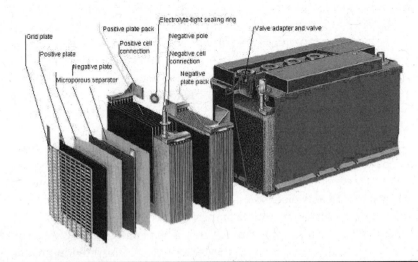

FIGURE 7-4 Typical starting battery. Notice the thin plates. (www.offroaders.com/tech/images/lead-acid_battery.jpg.)

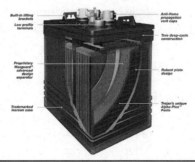

Figure 7-5   Typical Trojan 6-V Deep-Cycle Battery T105-T145. (www.trojan-battery.com.)

Industrial Batteries

These are deep-cycle batteries designed more for stationary applications or where weight is needed. Typical uses are battery backups for home or power storage, such as wind and solar generation applications. Other uses are for forklifts or other motive machinery that benefits from the extra weight as a counterbalance. Industrial batteries have a great depth of discharge and a cycle life of more than 1,000 cycles. What makes these batteries such workhorses is the size of the internal plates. As you may recall, the plates of a starting battery are about 0.04 in. thick. Well, the plates in an industrial battery measure 0.25 in. thick. Plate thickness and the heavy-duty construction of the battery casing make this battery very heavy. This is not the kind of battery you want for your EV. They are great for what they were designed for, but they're just too heavy for an EV. Figure 7-6 shows a cutaway of a Deka industrial battery.

Sealed Batteries

Sealed batteries are made with vents that (usually) cannot be removed. The so-called maintenance-free batteries are also sealed, but they are not usually leakproof. Sealed batteries are not totally sealed because they must allow gas to vent during charging. If they are overcharged too many times, some of these batteries can lose

Figure 7-6   Cutaway of one cell on a Deka industrial battery. (www.eastpenncanada.com/images/industrial_cutaway.jpg.)

enough water that they will die before their time. Most smaller deep-cycle batteries (including AGM batteries) use lead-calcium plates for increased life, whereas most industrial and forklift batteries use lead-antimony for greater plate strength to withstand shock and vibration.

Absorbed Glass Mat (AGM) Batteries

A newer type of sealed battery uses absorbed glass mats between the plates. The mat consists of a very fine fiber boron-silicate glass. These type of batteries have all the advantages of gelled batteries but can take much more abuse. AGM batteries are also called *starved-electrolyte batteries* because the mat is about 95 percent saturated rather than fully soaked. This also means that they will not leak acid, even if broken (Figure 7-7).

Since all the electrolyte (acid) is contained in the glass mats, these batteries cannot spill, even if broken. This also means that since they are nonhazardous, the shipping costs are lower. In addition, since there is no liquid to freeze and expand, they are practically immune from freezing damage.

The charging voltages are the same as for any standard battery; no need for any special adjustments or problems with incompatible chargers or charge controls. And since the internal resistance is extremely low, there is almost no heating of the battery even under heavy charge and discharge currents.

AGM batteries do not have any liquid to spill, and even under severe overcharge conditions, hydrogen emission is far below the 4 percent maximum specified for aircraft and enclosed spaces. The plates in AGM batteries are tightly packed and rigidly mounted and will withstand shock and vibration better than any standard battery.

Even with all the advantages just listed, there is still a place for the standard flooded deep-cycle battery. AGM batteries cost two to three times more than flooded batteries of the same capacity. In many installations where the batteries are set in an area where you don't have to worry about fumes or leakage, a standard or industrial deep-cycle is

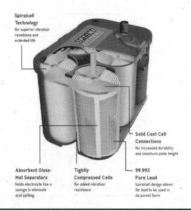

FIGURE 7-7   Optima deep-cycle red-top AGM battery. (www.optimabatteries.com/_media/images/optima_edge/diagram_large.jpg.)

Batteries   129

a better economic choice. The main advantages of AGM batteries are the lack of maintenance; the complete seal against fumes, hydrogen, or leakage; the fact that they are nonspilling even if they are broken; and that they can survive most freezes.

Charging Lead-Acid Batteries

Charging for most lead-acid batteries varies little, but always check with the manufacturer for proper charging methods and rates. Four methods exist to control the dc current and voltage supplied to a battery in the charging process: two rate, voltage detect and time, taper, and pulsed. Some chargers, such as the Zivan and Brusa chargers, are programmable to match the battery's charging specifications and curves. I will go into more detail on the various chargers in Chapter 10.

For most lead-acid batteries, charging at 15.5 V will give you a 100 percent charge. Once the charging voltage reaches 2.583 V per cell, charging should stop or be reduced to a trickle charge. Note that flooded batteries must bubble (gas) somewhat to ensure a full charge and to mix the electrolyte. Float voltage for lead-acid batteries should be about 2.15–2.23 V per cell, or about 12.9–13.4 V for a 12-V battery. At higher temperatures (>85°F), this should be reduced to about 2.10 V per cell.

Nickel-Cadmium Batteries

NiCad batteries are another secondary battery that might be viable for EVs (Figure 7-8). They far outperform lead-acid batteries, providing twice as much energy storage. The NiCad battery has an incredible cycle life that is four to seven times that of lead-acid batteries, achieving 2,500–3,500 lifetime cycles. Energy output in cold temperatures diminishes very little. The upfront cost of NiCad batteries is not cheap; they are expensive. If you take the cost and apply it to the lifetime of the battery and the number of cycles, they come out almost the same as a standard deep-cycle battery. You would need to replace your lead-acid battery pack seven to eight times before you had to replace one NiCad battery pack. One drawback besides price is the environmental concern expressed about the dangers of cadmium as a heavy metal, and much has been made of the disposal problem associated with NiCad batteries. This could be a significant issue for the millions of small flashlight cells used in rechargeable drills, vacuum cleaners, electric razors, and thousands of

FIGURE 7-8   SAFT NiCad battery. (www.saftbatteries.com/images/Produits/Photos/uptimax.jpg.)

other appliances. However, if these batteries are handled and disposed of/recycled properly, this problem can be avoided.

Charging Nickel-Cadmium Batteries

NiCad batteries require a somewhat different charging regimen than lead-acid batteries. In the first charging phase, they are charged at constant current until a temperature-compensated voltage threshold is reached or until all the ampere-hours consumed in driving have been replaced, whichever comes first. The charger notes how many ampere-hours are added in this phase. Then, in the second phase, a lower constant-current finish charge is applied until a percentage of the ampere-hours in phase one has been added. Obviously, a programmable smart charger is required for NiCad batteries. Brusa manufactures a number of chargers that meet these requirements.

Lithium Batteries

Lithium batteries over recent years have received a considerable amount of attention and media coverage. Many of the car and motorcycle manufacturers are increasingly using lithium battery technology. Lithium may be the battery of today and for future EVs. Lithium batteries, when cared for properly, perform exceptionally well. When seeking lithium batteries for an EV, be sure to check the manufacturer and the history and track record of each company thoroughly for quality. Many new battery companies are entering the market, several from Asia. Lithium batteries tend to be costly, but you get what you pay for. An inexpensive battery from a foreign county may save you money today, but in the end may cost you. In the simple case, you may have poor battery performance and life. In the worst case, you may have a catastrophic thermal runaway causing fire, vehicle damage, or worse, personal injury. Know your batteries and your manufacturer (Figure 7-9).

Figure 7-9   Thunder Sky lithium battery.

In a typical lithium cell, the anode, or negative electrode, is based on carbon, and the cathode, or positive electrode, is made from lithium-cobalt-dioxide or lithium-manganese-dioxide (other chemistries are also possible). Since lithium reacts violently with water, the electrolyte is composed of nonaqueous organic lithium salts and acts purely as a conducting medium, not taking part in the chemical action. Since no water is involved in the chemical action, the evolution of hydrogen and oxygen gases, as in many other batteries, is also eliminated (Figure 7-10). As noted earlier, lithium reacts intensely with water, forming lithium hydroxide and highly flammable hydrogen gas. When these two elements converge, a violent reaction occurs, creating heat and flammable gases that will ignite. A simple Internet search will uncover videos of such reactions and tests for your own eyes. Short-circuiting a lithium battery can cause it to ignite or explode, and as such, any attempt to open or modify a lithium-ion battery's casing or circuitry is dangerous.

Types of Lithium Chemicals Used
- LCPositive pole of lithium-cobalt-oxide ($LiFCoO_2$)
- LFPositive pole of lithium-iron-phosphate ($LiFePO_4$)
- LMPositive pole of lithium-manganese-oxide ($LiFNiMnO_2$)

Charging Lithium Batteries
Most lithium batteries are supplied with some type of battery management system (BMS). This is a system that manages charging and balance of the battery voltage. I will go into more detail below. All lithium batteries require some type of BMS system. What happens if a battery is inadvertently overcharged? The lithium battery is designed to operate safely within normal operating voltage, but it

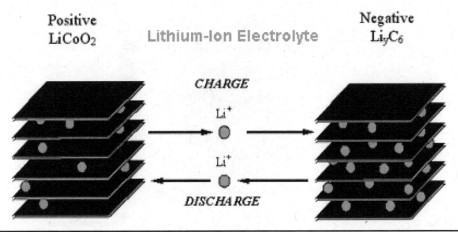

FIGURE 7-10 Lithium-ion electrolytes. (Courtesy of Electropaedia, www.mpoweruk.com/images/swingcell.gif.)

becomes unstable if it is charged to higher voltages above designed thresholds. When charging above 4.30 V, the cell causes plating of metallic lithium on the anode; the cathode material becomes an oxidizing agent, loses its stability, and releases oxygen. Overcharging causes the cell to heat up. If left unattended, the cell could vent with flammable gases, catch fire, and set off adjacent batteries, causing a chain reaction. Lithium batteries may explode if overheated or if charged to an excessively high voltage.[3]

Battery Construction

This section will provide you with an overview of the basics of lead-acid battery construction (Figure 7-11). For our purpose of keeping things simple, we will look at the construction of standard lead-acid batteries. The lead-acid battery is still the most popular battery. Global lead-acid battery production is estimated to be worth more than $17.45 billion per year and is growing steadily.[4] In the United States, over 88 percent of all lead production goes into batteries.[5]

Earlier in this chapter I touched on plate thickness in batteries and how it affects the performance of a lead-acid battery. Now I will review just a few of the basics that make up the standard lead-acid battery. Since many battery types exist, my focus for now is on lead-acid batteries.

Battery Case

Most heavy-duty lead-acid battery casings are manufactured from polypropylene copolymers—essentially durable plastic that resists the corrosive effects of battery

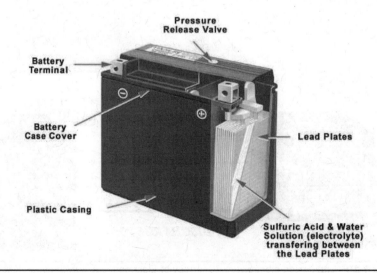

FIGURE 7-11   Basic lead-acid battery construction. (www.infinitecables.com/images/battery-cutaway.jpg.)

acid. Some applications use a hard-rubber rectangular container. Most casings have three, four, or six cells molded into them.

Each cell has molded-in ribs running across the width of its bottom or down the long dimension of the battery. The plates are mounted at right angles to the ribs, whose purpose is to stiffen the case, support the plates in a non–electrically conductive manner, and act as collection channels for the active material shed from the plates. A battery is usable until the active material it sheds makes a pile that eventually reaches the plates and shorts them out. Using a deeper case will allow more material to accumulate before reaching the plates. Large industrial batteries can be rebuilt by opening them, dumping the used active material, cleaning out any cell residue, and replacing the plates, separators, and electrolyte as needed.

Plates

The lead-acid battery is made up of plates, lead, and lead oxide (various other elements are used to change density, hardness, porosity, etc.). Flat-plate cells typically used in lead-acid batteries have over a hundred years of history and development. The plates are manufactured in varying sizes and thicknesses according to the type of battery. As described earlier, batteries with thinner plates usually contain multiple plates, creating more surface area and higher current (amperes). The tradeoff with thin plates limits the depth of discharge of the battery. If we look at a battery with thick plates, the output current is not as much as a thin-plate battery, but the ability of the battery to store more energy and to discharge to a greater depth of discharge is increased significantly. The easiest way to tell if a battery has thick or thin plates is by its weight. An overly heavy battery will contain more lead and thus have thicker plates (Figures 7-12 and 7-13).

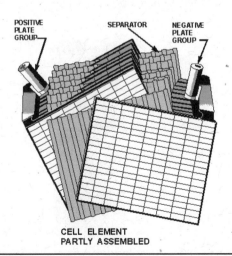

FIGURE 7-12   Illustration of battery plates with separators. (www.tpub.com/neets/book1/chapter2/2-10.gif.)

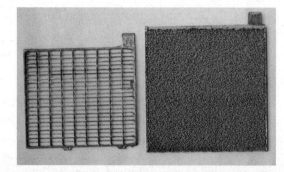

FIGURE 7-13   Photograph of both negative and positive battery plates. (http://thefraserdomain. typepad.com/photos/uncategorized/power_currentcollectorcomparison.jpg.)

Separators are used between the positive and negative plates of a lead acid battery to prevent short-circuit through physical contact, mostly through dendrites (a crystal that develops with a typical multibranching treelike form, much like a snowflake) but also through shedding of the active material.

Sulfation

Sulfation is the result of grain-size growth of lead sulfate that has been deposited on battery plates during discharge (Figure 7-14). Normally, the lead sulfate deposit is so fine grained that during recharge it easily reverts back to sulfuric acid, lead, and lead dioxide—the components of a lead-acid battery that produce electricity. When sulfation occurs, the grains of lead sulfate, or "hard sulfate," as it is commonly called, are too large to react effectively during recharge. The finite life of the battery is caused by the fact that all the sulfate (SO_4) radicals cannot be removed from the plates on recharge. The longer the sulfate radicals stay bonded to the plates, the harder it is to dislodge them. To postpone the inevitable as long as possible, the

FIGURE 7-14   Sulfation of battery plates. (www.surfacematics.com/Cell_sediment.jpg.)

battery should be kept in a charged state, and equalizing charging should be done regularly. In Chapter 10, I provide greater detail about chargers, equalizing, and ways to safely charge and extend the life of your battery.

Terminal Posts

Batteries are supplied in a few different arrangements of terminal posts; some even have dual connection capabilities. Under high-power conditions, a heavy-duty post is desirable for use with a bolt and a washer. In certain cases, high-current draw at the connection of a standard tapered post can soften the lead, thus loosening the connection. A loose connection can cause increased heat, arcing, and resistance. Following is some relevant terminal post terminology:

- *Automotive*—the round post familiar on starting batteries in gasoline-powered cars. The cable lug fits around the terminal (Figure 7-15).
- *Universal*—like an automotive post but with an extra stud in the center of the post. The cable lug fits over the stud, and a nut holds them together (Figure 7-16).
- *L*—a flat tang with a hole through it. A bolt through the hole connects the terminal to the cable lug (Figure 7-17).

Figure 7-15   An automotive terminal.

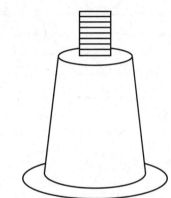

Figure 7-16   A universal terminal.

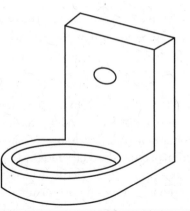

FIGURE 7-17   An L-type terminal.

Battery Group Size

Every battery manufacturer conforms to a standardized designated battery group size number in accordance with the Battery Council International (BCI). This number is part of a standardized system that allows you to look at any battery chart or designation number and determine the size and voltage for that particular battery group by the battery group number. This only applies to the size; you will need to look up the manufacturer's rating and capacity for its particular brand. Table 7-1 provides a short list of common group numbers.

TABLE 7-1   Typical Battery Dimensions

	Battery Group								Units
	21	24	27	31	T105	T125	T145	6-V Gel	
Voltage	12	12	12	12	6	6	6	6	Volts
Length	8.19	10.25	12.06	13	10.38	10.38	10.35	10.25	Inches
Width	6.81	6.81	6.81	6.72	7.13	7.13	7.13	7.13	Inches
Height	8.75	8.87	8.75	9.44	10.68	10.87	11.5	10.87	Inches

Note: Dimensions are approximate and vary by manufacturer. Consult manufacturer data sheets for exact dimensions of container, location, and types of terminals.

Inside Your Battery

Battery improvements have occurred steadily, but the basic principles have remained unchanged. Battery action takes place in the cell, the basic battery building block that transforms chemical energy into electrical energy. A cell contains the two active materials, or electrodes, and the solution, or electrolyte, that provide the conductive environment between them. An electrolyte is any substance containing free ions that behaves as an electrical conductor. An ion is an atom or molecule that has lost or gained one or more electrons, giving it a positive or negative electrical charge.

As stated earlier, there are two kinds of batteries. In a *primary* battery, the chemical action eats away one of the electrodes (usually the negative), and the cell must be discarded or the electrode replaced; in a *secondary* battery, the chemical process is reversible, and the active materials can be restored to their original condition by recharging the cell. A battery can consist of only one cell, such as the primary battery that powers your flashlight, or several cells in a common encasement, such as the secondary battery that powers your automobile starter.

Active Materials

Active materials are defined as electrochemical couples. This means that one of the active materials, the positive pole, or anode, is electron-deficient; the other active material, the negative pole, or cathode, is electron-rich. The active materials usually are solid (lead-acid) but can be liquid (sodium-sulfur) or gaseous (zinc-air, aluminum-air). Table 7-2 lists comparisons of a few of these elements.

TABLE 7-2   Electrodes: Common Chemicals

Anode Materials (Negative Terminals) Best + Most Positive	Cathode Materials (Positive Terminals) Best − Most Negative
Lithium	Ferrate
Magnesium	Iron Oxide
Aluminum	Cuprous Oxide
Zinc	Iodate
Chromium	Cupric Oxide
Iron	Mercuric Oxide
Nickel	Cobaltic Oxide
Tin	Manganese Dioxide
Lead	Lead Dioxide
Hydrogen	Silver Oxide
Copper	Oxygen
Silver	Nickel Oxyhydroxide
Palladium	Nickel Dioxide
Mercury	Silver Peroxide
Platinum	Permanganate
Gold	Bromate
Worst Least Negative	*Worst* Least Positive

In simple terms, batteries can be considered to be electron pumps. The internal chemical reaction within the battery between the electrolyte and the negative metal electrode produces a buildup of free electrons, each with a negative charge, at the battery's negative (–) terminal, the anode. The chemical reaction between the electrolyte and the positive (+) electrode inside the battery produces an excess of positive ions (atoms that are missing electrons, thus with a net positive charge) at the positive terminal, the cathode. The electrical (pump) pressure or potential difference between the positive and negative terminals is called *voltage*.

Different metals have different affinities for electrons. When two dissimilar metals (or metal compounds) are put in contact or connected through a conducting medium, there is a tendency for electrons to pass from the metal with the smaller affinity for electrons, which becomes positively charged, to the metal with the greater affinity, which becomes negatively charged. A potential difference between the metals therefore will build up until it just balances the tendency of the electron transfer between the metals. At this point, the *equilibrium potential* is that which balances the difference between the tendency of the two metals to gain or lose electrons.

When a load is connected across the battery, the surplus electrons flow in the external circuit from the negatively charged anode, which loses all its charge, to the positively charged cathode, which accepts it, neutralizing its positive charge. This action reduces the potential difference across the cell to zero.

To make an ideal battery, you'd choose the active material that gives the greatest oxidation potential at the anode coupled with the material that gives the greatest reduction potential at the cathode that are both supportable by a suitable electrolyte material. This means pairing the best reducing material—lithium (+3.045 V with respect to hydrogen as the reference electrode)—with something that just can't wait to receive its electrons, or the best oxidizing material—fluorine (–2.87 V with respect to hydrogen)—with something that just can't wait to give electrons to it (Table 7-3). In practice, many other factors enter the picture, such as availability of material, ease in making them work together, ability to manufacture the final product in volume, and cost. As a result of the tradeoffs, only a few electrochemical couple possibilities make it into the realm of commercially produced batteries that you will meet later in this chapter.

Electrolytes

The electrolyte in a lead-acid battery is a mixture of sulfuric acid and water. Sulfuric acid is a very active compound of hydrogen, sulfur, and oxygen. The chemical formula of sulfuric acid is H_2SO_4. In water, the sulfuric acid molecules separate into two ions, hydrogen and sulfate. Sulfate is made up of sulfur and oxygen atoms. Each sulfate ion contains two "excess" electrons, and each therefore carries two negative electrical charges. Each hydrogen ion, having been stripped of one electron, carries one positive electrical charge.

Table 7-3 Common Chemicals for Electrodes

Percentage Charge	Specific Gravity	Open Circuit Voltage		
		Cell	6 Volt	12 Volt
100	1.277	2.122	6.37	12.73
90	1.258	2.103	6.31	12.62
80	1.238	2.083	6.25	12.50
70	1.217	2.062	6.19	12.37
60	1.195	2.04	6.12	12.24
50	1.172	2.017	6.05	12.10
40	1.148	1.993	5.98	11.96
30	1.124	1.969	5.91	11.81
20	1.098	1.943	5.83	11.66
10	1.073	1.918	5.75	11.51

Because sulfuric acid is highly reactive, it ionizes almost completely, so there are very few fully assembled molecules of sulfuric acid in the electrolyte at any instant. Furthermore, the ions are in constant motion, attracted and repelled by one another, by the water, and by any impurities in the mixture. This constant random motion eventually causes the ions to diffuse evenly throughout the electrolyte. If any force disturbs this even distribution, the random motion eventually restores it. However, since the electrolyte is contained in a complex structure of cells, redistribution takes a relatively long time. This fact turns out to play a key role in your ability to measure the exact state of charge of a battery at any instant.

The electrolyte within the battery provides a path for electron migration between the electrodes. The electrolyte is usually in the form of a liquid (an acid, salt, or alkali added to water) but can be in jelly or paste form. For simpler terms, a battery consists of an electrode and an electrolyte operating in a cell or container in accordance with certain chemical reactions (see Table 7-3).

Figure 7.18 shows the inside battery reaction, which consists of an electrode made of sponge lead (Pb), another electrode made of lead peroxide (PbO_2), and an electrolyte made of a mixture of sulfuric acid (H_2SO_4) diluted with water (H_2O).

Overall Chemical Reaction

Combining active-material elements into compounds that further combine with the action of the electrolyte significantly alters their native properties. The true operation of any battery is best described by the chemical equation that defines its operation. In the case of the lead-acid battery, this equation is given as

$$Pb + PbO_2 + 2H_2SO_4 = 2PbSO_4 + 2H_2O$$

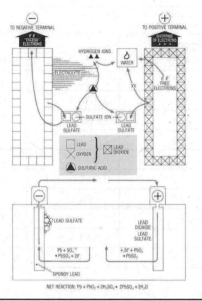

FIGURE 7.18   Chemical reaction inside a lead-acid battery under charging conditions. (Courtesy of Curtis Instruments, www.curtisinst.com.)

The equation in Figure 7-19 represents the cell in the charged condition. In a charged lead-acid battery, the positive anode plate is nearly all lead peroxide (PbO_2), the negative cathode plate is nearly all sponge lead (Pb), and the electrolyte is mostly sulfuric acid (H_2SO_4). In a discharged condition, both plates are mostly lead sulfate ($PbSO_4$), and the acid electrolyte solution used in forming the lead sulfate becomes mostly water (H_2O).

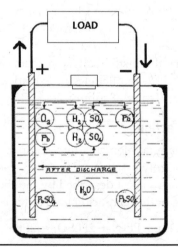

FIGURE 7-19   Discharging reaction. (www.powerstream.com/1922/battery_1922_WITTE/batteryfiles/chapter11.htm.)

Discharging Chemical Reaction

The general equation gives a more accurate view when separately analyzed at each electrode. The discharging process is described at the anode[6] as

$$PbO_2 + 4H^- + SO_4^{2-} = 2e^- + PbSO_4 + 2H_2O$$

The discharging process is described at the cathode as

$$Pb + SO_4 - 2e^- \rightarrow 4PbSO_4$$

When discharging, the cathode acquires the sulfate (SO_4) radical from the electrolyte solution and releases two electrons in the process. These electrons are acquired by the electron-deficient anode. The electron flow from negative cathode to positive anode inside the battery is the source of the battery's power and external current flow from positive anode to negative cathode through the load. In the process of discharging, both electrodes become coated with lead sulfate ($PbSO_4$)—a good insulator that does not conduct current—and the sulfate (SO_4) radicals are consumed from the electrolyte. At the same time, the physical area of the spongelike plates available for further reaction decreases as it becomes coated with lead sulfate; this increases the internal resistance of the cell and results in a decrease of its output voltage.

At some point before all the sulfate (SO_4) radicals are consumed from the electrolyte, there is no more area available for chemical reaction, and the battery is said to be fully discharged.

Charging Chemical Reaction

The charging process is described at the anode as

$$PbSO_4 + 2H_2O - 2e^- \rightarrow PbO_2 + 4H^- + SO_4$$

The charging process is described at the cathode as

$$PbSO_4 + 2e^- \rightarrow Pb + SO_4$$

The charging process (Figure 7-20) reverses the electronic flow through the battery and causes the chemical bond between the lead (Pb) and the sulfate (SO_4) radicals to be broken, releasing the sulfate radicals back into solution. When all the sulfate radicals are again in solution with the electrolyte, the battery is said to be fully charged.

Electrolyte Specific Gravity

The *specific gravity* of any liquid is the ratio of the weight of a certain volume of that liquid divided by the weight of an equal volume of water. Alternatively, the specific gravity of a material can be expressed as its density divided by the density of water because the density of any material is its mass-to-volume ratio. Water has a specific gravity of 1.000.

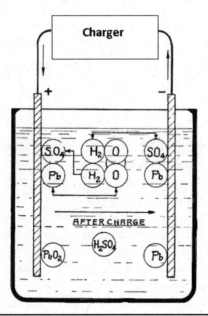

FIGURE 7-20   Charging reaction. (www.powerstream.com/1922/battery_1922_WITTE/
batteryfiles/chapter11.htm.)

Concentrated sulfuric acid has a specific gravity of 1.830—1.83 times as dense as water. In a fully charged battery at 80°F, water and sulfuric acid mix in roughly a 4:1 volume ratio (25 percent sulfuric acid) to produce a 1.275 specific gravity, and the sulfuric acid represents about 36 percent of the electrolyte by weight.

While specific gravity is not significant in other battery types, it is important in lead-acid batteries because the amount of sulfuric acid combining with the plates at any one time is directly proportional to the discharge rate (current × time, usually measured in ampere-hours) and therefore is a direct indicator of the state of charge.

State of Charge

State of charge (SOC) is the amount of energy left in a battery compared with the energy it had when it was fully charged. This gives the user an indication of how much longer a battery will continue to perform before it needs recharging.

Battery voltage, internal resistance, and amount of sulfuric acid combined with the plates at any one time are all indicators of how much energy is in a battery at any given time. Frequently, this is given as a percentage of its fully charged value; for example, "75 percent" means that 75 percent of the battery's energy is still available and 25 percent has been used.

Traditionally, the specific gravity of the electrolyte was measured using a hydrometer, the device used to measure specific gravity. As the battery discharges, its active electrolyte, sulfuric acid, is consumed, and the concentration of the sulfuric acid in water is reduced. With reduction of the sulfuric acid, the specific gravity becomes less. It was common practice with flooded lead-acid batteries to use a hydrometer (Figures 7-21 and 7-22). The hydrometer worked fairly well, but with some inaccuracy and ability to contaminate battery cells. With the latest sealed batteries and new battery chemistry, measurements are no longer done this way.

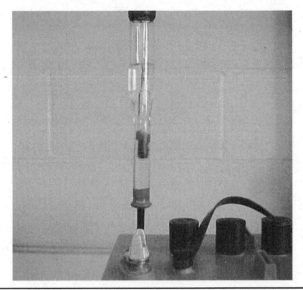

FIGURE 7-21   Glass tube hydrometer measuring specific gravity in a battery cell. (www2.tech. purdue.edu/at/courses/aeml/airframeimages/hydrometerinbatt.jpg.)

FIGURE 7-22   Inexpensive plastic hydrometer for measuring specific gravity.

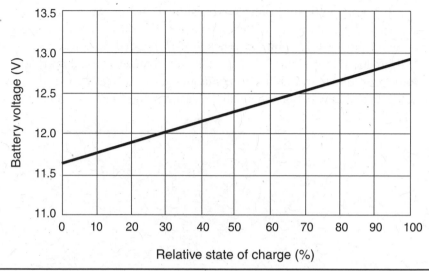

FIGURE 7-23   Graph of voltage versus capacity.

Today, a battery's voltage is used to determine the state of charge electronically. Voltage of the battery cell is used as the basis for calculating SOC or the remaining capacity. Results can vary widely depending on actual voltage level, temperature, discharge rate, and age of the cell. Note that the cell voltage will diminish in direct proportion to the remaining capacity of the battery (Figure 7-23).

Gassing

As charging nears completion, another phenomenon takes place: Hydrogen gas (H_2) is given off at the negative cathode plate, and oxygen gas (O_2) is given off at the positive anode plate. This occurs because any charging current beyond that required to liberate the small amount of sulfate radicals from the plates ionizes the water in the electrolyte and begins the process of electrolysis (separating the water into hydrogen and oxygen gas).

While most of the hydrogen and oxygen gas recombines to form water vapor, some of the hydrogen and oxygen will escape from the battery[7] (the main reason why periodic replenishing of the water is needed in this type of battery).

Additionally, batteries will start to gas when you attempt to charge them faster than they can absorb energy or when you overcharge them. Hydrogen bubbles are produced at the negative plates and oxygen bubbles at the positive plates during charging. After the battery reaches full charge, almost all added energy goes into this gassing. The gassing process begins in the range of 2.30–2.38 V/cell depending on cell chemistry and construction. After full charge, gassing releases about 1 ft³ of hydrogen per cell for each 63 A · h supplied. About 4 percent concentration of hydrogen in air is extremely explosive, so excessive charging can lead to an explosion. An exploding battery is like a bomb (hydrogen bomb) that sprays chunks

Figure 7-24   Battery explosion resulting from gassing.

of metal, plastic casing, and sulfuric acid toward anyone or anything nearby. The most vulnerable part of your body in such accidents is your eyes, which can sustain lacerations and acid burns resulting in loss of eyesight (Figure 7-24).

Equalizing

Equalization is very important and must be performed correctly, but only as required. *Equalizing* is an overcharge performed on flooded lead-acid batteries after they have been fully charged. It reverses the buildup of negative chemical effects such as stratification, a condition in which acid concentration is greater at the bottom of the battery than at the top. Equalizing also helps to remove sulfate crystals that may have built up on the plates. If left unchecked, this condition, called *sulfation*, will reduce the overall capacity of the battery. Equalization should be performed only when required or once every 6 months.

In any cyclic application, a series of batteries always will need to be equalized from time to time to ensure that the battery cells remain at the same voltage throughout the pack. Over time, cells of a lead-acid battery begin to show differences in their state of charge. No two battery cells or batteries are created equal. During both charge and discharge, each and every cell/battery will react in a minutely different way from its neighbor. This could mean that each battery may be holding a different quantity of charge. In order to get the most out of the total battery pack, it is necessary to make sure, as far as possible, that each and every battery is holding a similar amount of charge.

During the charge cycle, the voltages of the different batteries will vary. To bring them all to the same level, it is necessary to give some a slight overcharge to bring the other up to full charge.

Equalization is done by allowing the voltage to rise while allowing a small constant current to enter the batteries. The voltage is allowed to rise above the normal finish voltage to allow the weaker batteries/cells to draw more current. The stronger batteries will not be adversely affected, provided that the current is added gently and the period and frequency of overcharging are not too high. The stronger batteries will absorb the overcharge by gently boiling and giving off heat and gassing more heavily. Once the weaker batteries have absorbed the required current, the equalization charge can be halted. The equalization time should be long enough to bring all the batteries up to a full state of charge. Since the time factor will vary, the most reliable way to check the charge state is with a voltmeter on each cell or individual battery.

Over time, the differences can be caused by temperature, materials, construction, electrolyte, and even electrolyte stratification (the tendency of the heavier sulfuric acid to sink to the lower part of the cell), causing premature aging of the plates in that part. The only cure for these differences is to use a controlled overcharge, equalizing the characteristics of the cells by raising the charging voltage even higher after the battery is fully charged and maintaining it at this level for several hours until the different cells again test identical. Obviously, this produces substantial gassing, so the precautions of a well-ventilated area and no smoking definitely apply.

Cell Balancing

Cell balancing is defined as the application of differential currents to individual cells (or combinations of cells) in a series string. Normally, of course, cells in a series string receive identical currents. A battery pack in some cases requires additional components and circuitry to achieve cell balancing. In the simplest form, an equalizing charge is performed to balance cells or strings of batteries in a pack. If this does not work sufficiently, other components are added to the battery pack, such as a BMS, to balance the string of batteries. I will cover more on battery balancing and battery management systems in Chapter 10.

Battery-pack cells are balanced when all the cells in the battery pack meet two conditions:

- If all cells have the same capacity, then they are balanced when they have the same SOC. In this case, the open-circuit voltage (OCV) is a good measure of the SOC. If, in an out-of-balance pack, all cells can be differentially charged to full capacity (balanced), then they will subsequently cycle normally without any additional adjustments. This is mostly a one-shot fix.
- If the cells have different capacities, they are also considered balanced when the SOC is the same. But since SOC is a relative measure, the absolute amount of capacity for each cell is different. To keep the cells with different capacities at the same SOC, cell balancing must provide differential amounts of current to cells in the series string during both charge and discharge on every cycle.

Battery Explosions

After talking about gassing and equalization, I need to emphasize the dangers of mishandling and battery abuse. Your battery can burst and, even worse, explode if

FIGURE 7-25   Exploded battery. (www.rayvaughan.com/images/battery/MVC-172F.jpg.)

not treated property. Always make sure while charging or using a battery under any heavy load that the area is well ventilated. Always keep all sparks, flames, or anything else that can ignite gases away from a battery.

As you discovered in the sections about gassing and equalizing, excessive charging of a lead-acid battery will cause the release of hydrogen and oxygen from each cell. Wet cells have open vents to release any gas produced, and valve-regulated lead-acid (VRLA) batteries rely on valves fitted to each cell. Wet cells may be equipped with catalytic caps to recombine any emitted hydrogen. A VRLA cell normally will recombine any hydrogen and oxygen produced into water inside the cell, but malfunction or overheating may cause gas to build up. If this happens (e.g., by excessively overcharging the cell), the valve is designed to vent the gas and thereby normalize the pressure, resulting in a characteristic acid smell around the battery. Valves can fail if dirt and debris accumulate in the device, and pressure can build up inside the affected cell, creating the potential for an explosion.

If the accumulated hydrogen and oxygen within either a VRLA or wet cell is ignited, an explosion results. The force is sufficient to burst the plastic casing or blow the top off the battery, can injure anyone in the vicinity, and can spray acid and casing shrapnel throughout the immediate environment (Figure 7-25). An explosion in one cell also may set off the combustible gas mixture in remaining cells of the battery or, even worse, set off an explosion in other batteries in the pack.

As we examine other batteries, this danger increases as the stored energy in "exotic chemistry" batteries increases. Lithium-ion batteries, for example, store more energy than conventional batteries—as much as six times that of lead-acid batteries and two to three times as much as nickel-metal-hydride batteries. These batteries, if abused, can have unfortunate and explosive side effects.

Battery Calculations and Capacity

This is a very important subject and one that I once was confused about. So now that we have all this great knowledge about batteries, gassing, and how not to blow ourselves up, how do we begin to select and decide on the battery we need? I will give you the information and tools to help you make the best choice. The biggest task in choosing a battery is balancing all the information and placing it into some form to compare it for each battery.

Your considerations involve cost, stored energy, weight, size, cycle life, power output, and depth of discharge. Remember, not all batteries are the same. Many of your steps may depend on other components, such as the motor, motor controller, and operating voltage of your EV. You may need to change or tweak things as you plan. Gather all the information you can about each particular battery you are considering for use in your vehicle. See Table 7-4 for an example of a battery comparison spreadsheet I created during my build.

Some things to consider initially:

- What voltage do you want to use?
- What amount of current do you plan to draw from the pack?
- Do you want continuous power rating of the battery?
- Do you want intermittent power rating of the battery with a time limit?
- Do you want very short burst rating for heavy accelerating?

Current and Amperes

Current flow is the means by which a battery releases its energy in electrical form. *Current* is the flow of electric charge from the positive terminal of the battery through the *load* (controllers and motor) of your vehicle and back to the negative terminal of the battery. The flow of current from the battery depletes the battery's stored charge. The rate of that depletion or current drain is measured in *amperes*.

The Volt

The *volt* is the unit of electrical potential, or pressure, that "forces" the current from the battery through the motor and back to the battery. Since batteries are made up of many cells connected in series, the total voltage of a battery, naturally, is the sum of the voltages of all its cells. A typical lead-acid battery pack used in a vehicle may contain four 12-V batteries. If the batteries are connected in series, the nominal battery voltage is therefore 48 V.

Power or Watts

The *watt* is a unit of electricity measuring the rate at which work is done. The equation is watts = volts × amperes. One watt is equivalent to about 0.00134 hp. If we look at an example, for instance, a battery or, let us say, a battery pack has a particular draw of 50 A at 48 V.

Our equation would be as follows:

$$48 \text{ V} \times 50 \text{ A} = 2{,}400 \text{ W, or } 2.4 \text{ kW}$$

If we equate that to horsepower, we get

$$2,400 \text{ W} = 3.22 \text{ hp}$$

Battery Storage Capacity

The *ampere-hour* (A · h) capacity of a battery is the total amount of electric charge transferred when a current of 1 A flows for 1 hour. Therefore, the total usable charge stored in a battery can be stated in terms of ampere-hours, that is, how long a current of a particular amperage can be drawn from the battery.

The ampere-hour rating accurately predicts the battery's capacity at a specified load current; batteries therefore are rated in ampere-hours at specified currents. A battery that can be discharged at 125 A for 6 hours before reaching its end-point voltage is rated at 125 A × 6 h = 750 A · h. Its *capacity* therefore is stated as "750 ampere-hours at the 6-hour discharge rate (at +25°C)." All things equal, the greater the physical volume of a battery, the larger is its total storage capacity. Storage capacity is additive when batteries are wired in parallel but not if they are wired in series.

Battery Configurations: Series and Parallel

In the battery pack in your vehicle, you most likely will connect your batteries in a series configuration to increase the voltage. This is very much like a flashlight with two or more batteries, where we place the batteries back to back, adding the voltage up. In your design and conversion, it is best to keep the voltage as high as possible for the total pack voltage. The higher the voltage, the more efficient your vehicle will become. It will not be a lot, but every little bit helps. With an increase in voltage, your current requirement will decrease for the controller and the motor. As another added benefit, you can reduce the wire gauge size, thus reducing weight and cost.

Series Battery Configuration

When two 6-V, 50-A · h batteries are wired in series, the voltage is doubled, but the ampere-hour capacity remains 50 A · h (total power = 600 Wh) (Figure 7-26). You may decide to wire batteries in series to increase your voltage. Installing larger batteries may not fit well in a small space or may be awkward to fit into place. Batteries consisting of fewer cells (and hence lower voltage) in series can provide the same storage capacity yet be more flexible.

If we use another example of four 12-V, 50-A · h batteries connected in series, we would get

$$12 \text{ V} \times 4 = 48 \text{ V}$$

$$(50 \text{ A} \cdot \text{h} \times 12 \text{ V}) \times 4 = 2,400 \text{ Wh, or } 2.4 \text{ kWh}$$

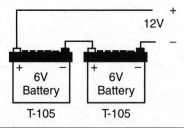

FIGURE 7-26   Series battery connection.

Parallel Battery Configuration

If you were to wire two 6-V, 50-A · h batteries in parallel, you would yield a total storage capacity of 100 A · h at 6 V (or 600 Wh) (Figure 7-27). Battery banks wired in parallel are not common on EVs, where the goal most often is to go as high as possible with the voltage. If such a configuration is used, make sure that your wire meets the required minimum size for cabling. However, the wiring must have the capacity to deal with a full battery bank. You should fuse each battery individually in such a bank to ensure that a battery gone bad will not affect the rest of the bank.

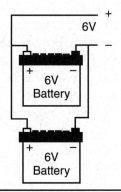

FIGURE 7-27   Parallel battery connection.

Battery C Rating: C/20, C/3, C/1, etc.

The C rating of a battery is an expression describing rate of discharge. The number indicates the number of hours to completely discharge the battery at a constant current. Thus C/20 is the current draw at which the battery will last for 20 hours; C/1 is the current at which the battery will last 1 hour. The useful capacity of a battery changes depending on the discharge rate, so battery capacities are stated with respect to a particular rate. For instance, a particular model battery is rated at 42 A · h at the C/10 rate of 4.2 A but only 30 A · h at the C/1 rate of 30 A. These are also written as the 20-hour rate, 1-hour rate, etc.

Available Capacity versus Total Capacity

Since batteries depend on a chemical reaction to produce electricity, their *available capacity* depends in part on how quickly you attempt to charge or discharge them relative to their total capacity. The *total capacity* is frequently abbreviated to C and is a measure of how much energy the battery can store. Available capacity is always less than total capacity.

Typically, the ampere-hour capacity of a battery is measured at a rate of discharge that will leave it empty in 20 hours (aka the C/20 rate). If you attempt to discharge a battery faster than the C/20 rate, you will have less available capacity, and vice versa. The more extreme the deviation from the C/20 rate, the greater is the available (as opposed to total) capacity difference.

However, as you will discover, this effect is nonlinear. The available capacity at the C/100 rate (i.e., 100 hours to discharge) is typically only 10 percent more than at the C/20 rate. Conversely, a 10 percent reduction in available capacity is achieved just by going to a C/8 rate (on average). Thus you are most likely to notice this effect with engine starts and other high-current applications such as inverters, windlasses, desalination, or air-conditioning systems.

For example, the starter in an engine typically will quickly outstrip the capacity of the battery to keep cranking it for any length of time—hence the tip from mechanics to wait some time between engine start attempts. Not only does it allow the engine starter to cool down, but it also allows the chemistry in the battery to "catch up." As the battery comes to a new equilibrium, its available capacity increases. An equation developed in 1897 by a scientist named Peukert describes the charging and discharging behavior with a value that indicates how well a lead-acid battery performs under heavy currents.[8] This formula will generate a more accurate real-life ampere-hour rating.

Peukert Equation

$$C = I^n T$$

where C = theoretical capacity of the battery
I = current
T = time
n = the Peukert number

To help you even further if you need to calculate and learn more about the Peuket number and equation, you can visit www.smartgauge.co.uk/peukert.html. In addition to explaining the calculations in more detail, the site has a page that does all the work for you. Just plug in the numbers, and it calculates the real ampere-hour capacity and generates a graph.

Energy Density

Energy density is the amount of energy contained in an exact quantity of the fuel source, typically stated in watthours per pound (Wh/lb) or watthours per kilogram (Wh/kg). For example, flooded lead-acid batteries generally contain about 25 Wh/kg, the latest advanced lead-acid designs claim about 50 Wh/kg, and newer advanced battery technologies such as NiMH and LiON are in the 80–135 Wh/kg range.

Cold-Cranking Amperes

This rating is not normally used for calculations for an EV, but more as a performance rating for automobile starting batteries. It might appear handy if you want to calculate a 30-second all-out acceleration. It is defined as the current that the battery can deliver for 30 seconds and maintain a terminal voltage greater than or equal to 1.20 V per cell at 0°F (–18°C) when the battery is new and fully charged. Starting batteries also may be rated for cranking amperes, which is the same thing but rated at a temperature of 32°F (0°C).

Depth of Discharge (DOD)

The *depth of discharge* is the amount of energy removed from a battery or the total battery pack (see Table 7-4). DOD is usually expressed as a percentage of the total capacity of the battery. For example, 50 percent DOD means that half the energy in the battery has been used; 80 percent DOD means that 80 percent of the energy has been discharged. Check with the battery manufacturer for detailed specifications. The general rule for deep-cycle batteries is never to go past 80 percent DOD. Any discharge below 80 percent will degrade the life of the battery and lessen the cycle life.

Basic Battery Spreadsheet

Table 7-4 is a basic spreadsheet I used for my own calculations when I was building the first Electra Cruiser. With this spreadsheet, I was able to take all the batteries I had considered with all the numbers and weigh out my options. I had many objectives—voltage, weight, size, cycle life, cost, energy density, pack ampere-hours, and total pack energy. By creating the spreadsheet, I could see every option, play around with the numbers, and tweak it as I needed. This just made the planning so much easier.

The table is just a sample of one page. I actually put together six or seven pages of batteries that made the list. At the end of the day, I chose a standard deep-cycle lead-acid battery by Trojan Batteries, a Group 27 TMH 12-V battery. It is not that I did not consider other batteries; I actually bought 100 lithium batteries for the new bike. These batteries were 200 lb lighter, had twice the energy storage, and used less space. Sounds like a home run, right? It was, except that I did not do my homework on a key ingredient, the BMS. At the time, there was no BMS to handle 100 batteries; it was still in development. The closest system I found had a price tag of $30,000. It goes without saying that this was not an option. Moral of the story: Make sure you plan ahead; the

TABLE 7-4 Battery Comparison Spreadsheet

BATTERY TYPE: TROJAN 27TMH

BATTERY WEIGHT EACH	56	TOTAL # OF BATTERIES	10
BATTERY PRICE EACH	$75.00	BATTERY 20 HR CAP	115.00
BATTERY VOLTAGE EACH	12	TOTAL VOLTAGE	120.00
BATTERY DIMENTIONS L,W,H	12 · 6.563 · 9.75	BATTERY TOTAL CUBIC FT	4.44
TOTAL BATTERY WEIGHT	560	TOTAL BATTERY Watt-Hrs	13800.00
ENERGY DENSITY WATT-HRS/LB	24.64		
BATTERY CAPACITY C/3		TOTAL BATTERY Watt-Hrs @ 74%	10212.00
TOTAL COST OF BATTERIES	$750.00	BATTERY CYCLE LIFE 80% DOD	350.00

BATTERY TYPE: OVONIC 12-HEV-60

BATTERY WEIGHT EACH	24.3	TOTAL # OF BATTERIES	23
BATTERY PRICE EACH	$0.00	BATTERY 20 HR CAP	60.00
BATTERY VOLTAGE EACH	12	TOTAL VOLTAGE	276.00
BATTERY DIMENTIONS L,W,H	15.27 · 4.02 · 4.9	BATTERY TOTAL CUBIC FT	4.00
TOTAL BATTERY WEIGHT	558.9	TOTAL BATTERY Watt-Hrs	16560.00
ENERGY DENSITY WATT-HRS/LB	29.63		
BATTERY CAPACITY C/3		TOTAL BATTERY Watt-Hrs @ 74%	12254.40
TOTAL COST OF BATTERIES	$0.00	BATTERY CYCLE LIFE 80% DOD	800.00

BATTERY TYPE: Thunder Sky TS-8581A

BATTERY WEIGHT EACH	6.12	TOTAL # OF BATTERIES	55
BATTERY PRICE EACH	$150.00	BATTERY 20 HR CAP	100.00
BATTERY VOLTAGE EACH	3.4	TOTAL VOLTAGE	187.00
BATTERY DIMENTIONS L,W,H	5.17 · 2.48 · 9.06	BATTERY TOTAL CUBIC FT	3.70
TOTAL BATTERY WEIGHT	336.6	TOTAL BATTERY Watt-Hrs	18700.00
ENERGY DENSITY WATT-HRS/LB	55.56		
BATTERY CAPACITY C/3		TOTAL BATTERY Watt-Hrs @ 74%	13838.00
TOTAL COST OF BATTERIES	$8,250.00	BATTERY CYCLE LIFE 80% DOD	800.00

BATTERY TYPE: OPTIMA

BATTERY WEIGHT EACH	45	TOTAL # OF BATTERIES	14
BATTERY PRICE EACH	$120.00	BATTERY 20 HR CAP	60.00
BATTERY VOLTAGE EACH	12	TOTAL VOLTAGE	168.00
BATTERY DIMENTIONS L,W,H	10 · 6.875 · 7.8125	BATTERY TOTAL CUBIC FT	4.35
TOTAL BATTERY WEIGHT	630	TOTAL BATTERY Watt-Hrs	10080.00
ENERGY DENSITY WATT-HRS/LB	16.00		
BATTERY CAPACITY C/3		TOTAL BATTERY Watt-Hrs @ 74%	7459.20
TOTAL COST OF BATTERIES	$1,680.00	BATTERY CYCLE LIFE 80% DOD	700-900

(continued on next page)

TABLE 7-4 Battery Comparison Spreadsheet (continued)

BATTERY TYPE: YARDNEY YS300 SILVER-CADMIUM

BATTERY WEIGHT EACH	11		
BATTERY PRICE EACH			
BATTERY VOLTAGE EACH	1.02		
BATTERY DIMENTIONS L,W,H	17.5	4.19	1.78
TOTAL BATTERY WEIGHT	660		
ENERGY DENSITY		WATT-HRS/LB	38.95
BATTERY CAPACITY C/3			
TOTAL COST OF BATTERIES	$0.00		
TOTAL # OF BATTERIES	60		
BATTERY 20 HR CAP	420.00		
TOTAL VOLTAGE	61.20		
BATTERY TOTAL CUBIC FT	4.53		
TOTAL BATTERY Watt-Hrs	25704.00		
TOTAL BATTERY Watt-Hrs @ 74%	19020.96		
BATTERY CYCLE LIFE 80% DOD	500-1000		

simplest oversight could be a big problem later. For me, I was left sitting on $5,000 in batteries, a $10,000 Siemens 100-hp ac drive system, and a $3,000 Brusa charger. It was a great system setup, but without the batteries, I couldn't use it.

Battery Disposal

Lead-acid batteries have the highest recycling rate of any product sold in the United States (Figure 7-28). This is so because of the ease of returning a used battery when purchasing a new battery and the value of the lead and plastic components of the used battery.

Environmental Benefits

Many states require a core charge of up to $5 when purchasing a new battery. Imported lead-acid batteries have entered the United States in new cars, which account for almost half of all new battery sales, but even more are imported for the replacement market.[9] Imports of lead-acid batteries to the United States are rising rapidly as production shifts to developing countries with fewer environmental regulations and less enforcement capacity. Data from the U.S. International Trade Commission indicate that imports rose more than 282 percent from 1989 to 2007. The United States has taken steps to protect the environment and recycle, but unfortunately, developing third-world countries have not taken the same care for the environment or their workers.

Lead-acid batteries are the environmental success story of our time. More than 97 percent of all battery lead is recycled. Compared with 55 percent of aluminum soft drink and beer cans, 45 percent of newspapers, 26 percent of glass bottles, and 26 percent of tires, lead-acid batteries top the list of the most highly recycled consumer product.

Figure 7-28   Consumer batteries for recycling. (From Marty Jerome, "Firefly Gives New Life to Lead Acid Batteries," *BusinessWeek*, July 23, 2007, http://blog.wired.com/./ photos/uncategorized/2007/07/21/lead_acid_batteries.jpg.)

The lead-acid battery is part of a closed-loop life cycle that's good for the environment. Typical new lead-acid batteries contain 60–80 percent recycled lead and plastic. When a spent battery is collected, it is sent to a qualified recycler, where, under strict environmental regulations, the lead and plastic are reclaimed and sent to a new battery manufacturer. The recycling cycle continues indefinitely. This means that the lead and plastic in the lead-acid battery in your car, truck, boat, or motorcycle have been and will continue to be recycled many times. This makes lead-acid battery disposal extremely successful from both environmental and cost perspectives.

During the first part of the process, the battery is broken apart in a hammer mill (a machine that hammers the battery into pieces). Sometimes a battery saw is also used (Figure 7-29). The broken battery pieces go into a vat, where the lead and heavy materials fall to the bottom and the plastic rises to the top. At this point, the polypropylene pieces are scooped away, and the liquids are drawn off, leaving the lead and heavy metals. Each of the materials goes into a different "stream." We'll begin with the plastic, or polypropylene.

Plastic

The polypropylene pieces are washed, blown dry, and sent to a plastic recycler, where the pieces are melted together into an almost-liquid state. The molten plastic is put through an extruder that produces small plastic pellets of uniform size. Those pellets are sold to the manufacturer of battery cases, and the process begins all over again.

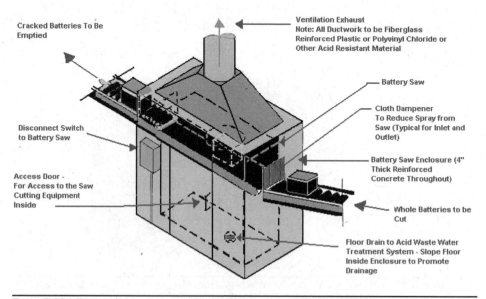

FIGURE 7-29   Battery saw used in recycling batteries. (www.osha.gov/SLTC/etools/leadsmelter/ popups/batterysaw_popup.html.)

Lead

The lead grids, lead oxide, and other lead parts are cleaned and then melted together in smelting furnaces. The molten lead is poured into ingot molds. Large ingots, weighing about 2,000 lb, are called hogs. Smaller ingots, weighing 65 lb, are called pigs. After a few minutes, the impurities, otherwise known as dross, float to the top of the still-molten lead in the ingot molds. The dross is scraped away, and the ingots are left to cool. When the ingots are cool, they are removed from the molds and sent to battery manufacturers, where they are remelted and used in the production of new lead plates and other parts for new batteries (Figures 7-30 and 7-31).

FIGURE 7-30 Cycle life of a lead-acid battery. (Courtesy of the Battery Council International, www. batterycouncil.org/portals/0/images/RecycleChart.gif.)

FIGURE 7-31 Tesla electric car battery pack being recycled and reclaimed. (www.treehugger.com/ tesla-battery-recycled-002.jpg.)

Sulfuric Acid

Old battery acid can be handled in four ways:

- It can be neutralized with an industrial compound similar to household baking soda. The resulting effluent is treated to meet clean water standards and then released into the public sewer system.
- It can be reclaimed and, after topping up with concentrated acid, used as the electrolyte in new batteries.
- It can be chemically treated and converted to either agricultural fertilizer using ammonia or powdered sodium sulfate, an odorless white powder that is used as a filler or stabilizer in laundry detergent, or for use in glass and textile manufacturing.
- It can be converted to gypsum for use in the production of cement or by the construction industry in the manufacture of fiberboard.

General Battery Requirements

It goes without saying that low cost, long life (>1,000 cycles), low self-discharge rates (<5 percent per month), and low maintenance are basic requirements for all battery applications. Traction batteries generally operate in very harsh operating environments and must withstand wide temperature ranges (–30 to +65°C) as well as shock, vibration, and abuse. Low weight, however, is not always a priority because heavy weight provides stability for materials handling equipment such as forklift trucks and the grip needed by aircraft tugs for pulling heavy loads. Low weight, however, is essential for high-capacity automotive EV and Hybrid Electric Vehicle (HEV) batteries used in passenger vehicles.

Purchasing Specifications

Traction batteries are very expensive, and like all batteries, they deteriorate during their lifetime. Consumers expect a minimum level of performance even at the end of the battery's life, so the buyer is likely to specify the expected performance at the end of life (EOL) rather than the beginning of life (BOL). Under normal circumstances for EV applications, the EOL capacity is specified as not less than 80 percent of BOL capacity. For HEV applications, a change in internal impedance is often used as an indicator of lifetime. In this case, the EOL internal impedance may be specified as not more than 200 percent of BOL internal impedance.

EV Battery Operating Requirements

Large-capacity batteries are required to achieve reasonable range. A typical electric car uses around 150–250 Wh/mi depending on the terrain and the driving style. A smaller vehicle such as a motorcycle may only require 100–150 Wh/mi.

- The battery must be capable of regular deep discharge to 80 percent DOD.
- The battery is designed to maximize energy content and deliver full power even with deep discharge to ensure long range.
- A range of capacities will be required to satisfy the needs of different sized vehicles and different usage patterns.
- The battery must accept very high repetitive pulsed charging currents (>5/C) if regenerative braking is required.
- Without regenerative braking, controlled charging conditions and lower charging rates are possible (at least 2/C is desirable).
- The battery must routinely receive a full charge.
- The battery often must reach nearly full discharge.
- Fuel-gauging is critical near the "empty" point.
- The battery needs an integrated BMS.
- The battery needs thermal management for severe hot or cold conditions.
- Typical voltage should surpass 300 V.
- Typical capacity should be greater than 20–60 kWh for passenger vehicles and 10–30 kWh for motorcycles.
- The battery must have a typical discharge current up to a specified C rate continuous and 3/C peak for short durations.

Because these batteries are physically very large and heavy, they need custom packaging to fit into the available space in the intended vehicle. Likewise, the design layout and weight distribution of the pack must be integrated with the chassis design so as not to upset vehicle dynamics. These mechanical requirements are particularly important for passenger cars.

Safety

The safety issues of battery EVs are largely dealt with by the international standard ISO 6469.[10] This document is divided in three parts dealing with specific issues:

- On-board electrical energy storage, that is, the battery
- Functional safety means and protection against failure
- Protection of persons against electrical hazards

With the emergence of more EVs in the future, firefighters and rescue personnel now receive special training in dealing with the higher voltages and chemicals encountered in EV and hybrid EV accidents. While Battery Electric Vehicle (BEV) accidents may present unusual problems, such as fires and fumes resulting from rapid battery discharge, there is apparently no available information regarding whether they are inherently more or less dangerous than gasoline or diesel internal combustion vehicles that carry flammable fuels.

Electric Shock

One of the topics that I feel is very important is that of electric shock. Since we are talking about batteries, I mean their potential and the amount of energy they contain and can release in an instant. If I told you to hold a wire with 120-V dc connection and the potential of 2000 A, would you touch it? This is no joke. Your EV could kill you in a second after all the time you put into it and not even care.

You can view your body as containing an electrical network, passing tiny nerve signals around and enabling you to do all those essential things you like to do so much, such as breathing, thinking, and moving. Your body's function can be severely disrupted by the presence of an extraneous current. Your body also contains a network of canals transporting oxygen to the muscles and the brain in a salty solvent called *blood*, which, incidentally, is a good conducting medium for electricity. To the battery, however, the body is a poorly insulated vessel containing electrolyte.

Voltage is not a reliable indicator of the severity of an electric shock. The most important indicators are the actual current that flows through the body and its duration. Current passing through the heart or the brain is infinitely more damaging than current passing across a finger or the palm of the hand caught between the terminals of a battery. A sustained current also will do more damage than a short current pulse. Table 7-5 lists electric shock hazards.

Additional Effects and Results of Electric Shock (Courtesy of Electropaedia)

- Low voltages do not mean low hazard.
- Other things being equal, the degree of injury is proportional to the length of time the body is in the circuit.
- It is extremely important to free a shock victim from contact with the current as quickly as possible. The difference of a few seconds in starting artificial respiration may spell the difference between life or death for the victim. Don't give up unless the victim has been pronounced dead by a doctor.
- Women tend to be more susceptible to electric currents than men.
- Lower body weight increases the susceptibility to electric currents.
- A shock from dc is more likely to freeze or stop the victim's heart.
- The current range 100–200 mA is particularly dangerous because it is almost certain to result in lethal ventricular fibrillation, the shocking of the heart into a useless flutter rather than a regular beat.
- The fibrillation threshold is a function of current over time. For example, fibrillation will occur with 500 mA over 0.2 second or 75 mA over 0.5 second.
- Alternating current (ac) is more dangerous than dc, causing more severe muscular contractions. Ac is also more likely to cause a victim's heart to fibrillate, which is a more dangerous condition. Safe working thresholds are consequently much lower for ac voltages.

TABLE 7-5 Electric Shock Hazards

Current (contact 1 second)	Physiological Effect
Less than 1mA	No sensation
1mA	Threshold of feeling. Tingling sensation
5mA	Maximum harmless current
8–15 mA	Mild shock
	Start of muscular contraction
	No loss of muscular control
15–20 mA	Painful shock
	Sustained muscular contraction
	Can't let go of conductor
20–50 mA	Can't breathe. Paralysis of the chest muscles
	Possibly Fatal
50–100 mA	Intense pain
	Impaired breathing
	Ventricular fibrillation
	Possibly fatal—Fatal if continued
100–200 mA	Ventricular fibrillation
	Probably fatal—Fatal if continued
	Respiratory function continues
Over 200 mA	Sustained ventricular contractions followed by normal heart rhythm (defibrillation)
	Chest muscles clamp the heart and stop it for the duration of the shock. This also prevents ventricular fibrillation improving the chances of survival, but other factors come into play.
	Burns
	Temporary respiratory paralysis.
	Possibly fatal—Fatal if continued
Over 1 Amp	Severe burns.
	Internal organs burned
	Death
	Survivable if vital organs not in current path—e.g. across a finger or hand

Table, Carl Vogel; source Electropaedia www.mpoweruk.com

- It is easier to restart a stopped heart once the source of the electric shock has been removed than it is to restore a normal beating rhythm to a fibrillating heart. A heart that is in fibrillation cannot be restored to normal by closed-chest cardiac massage. Defibrillators give the heart a jolt of dc to stop fibrillation to allow the heart to restart with a normal beat.

- Victims of a high voltage shock usually respond better to artificial respiration than do victims of a low voltage shock, probably because the higher voltage and current clamp the heart and hence prevent fibrillation. The chances of survival are good if the victim is given immediate attention.
- Shock victims may suffer heart trouble up to several hours after being shocked. The danger of electric shock does not end after the immediate medical attention.
- Don't expect a circuit breaker or fuse to protect you. They trip at 15 A.

Additional Risks

- There are huge variations in contact resistance of each person's skin.
- Working with minor wounds to the hands seriously increases the risk of shock.
- Once a shock has been initiated, the resulting electrical burn can puncture the skin and increase the shocking current.
- Rings, bracelets, and other jewelry decrease the contact resistance to the body and increase the potential for electric shock.
- Use only one hand (keeping one hand in your pocket) while working on high-voltage circuits to avoid the risk of the body becoming part of the circuit.
- Risks can be minimized by using insulated hand tools (e.g., pliers, screwdrivers, wrench, etc.) and by wearing rubber gloves and shoes.

Battery Solutions Today

The simplest battery solution for today that enables EV enthusiasts to build quickly and get a reliable vehicle on the road is lead-acid batteries. This is not ruling out any other battery chemistry, and I think that even today with the newer battery technology we can start using NiCad or the lithium batteries. You have the advantage and the ability to make use of the new technology because your EV is smaller, uses fewer batteries, and is easily monitorable. Compared with a large electric car, your upfront cost is considerably less for a battery pack, so purchasing that exotic battery may not be out of reach.

CHAPTER 8

Electric Motors

This chapter will guide you through the central part of your electric vehicle (EV), the electric motor. Electric motors come in all types, shapes, and sizes. Unlike the internal combustion engine, they emit zero pollutants. The electric motor has only one moving part and needs very little service, if any. Your electric motor will outlast its internal combustion engine counterpart several times over.

Electric motors are the most efficient mechanical devices known at this time. Between 85 and 90 percent of the energy used by an electric motor is transferred to the wheels of your vehicle, whereas with an internal combustion engine, only 15–20 percent of the energy makes it to the drive wheels. Just think, you are losing 80–85 percent burning fossil fuels and converting their energy to mechanical energy. This is a considerable amount of loss and a waste of energy. Most of the energy is lost as heat and some to friction from all the moving parts in the internal combustion engine and transmission.

Your selection of an electric motor is a very important decision in the design of your EV. Do not be fooled by their size; electric motors are powerful and deliver a force you would not believe! Power from an electric motor is instantaneous, full power being available from the start.

History of Electric Motors

The development of the electric motor belongs to more than one individual. Throughout the early 1800s, you will find a great deal of research and development by many ingenious individuals. The electric motor was developed through a process of research and discovery beginning with Hans Oersted's discovery of electromagnetism in 1820 and involving additional work by William Sturgeon, Joseph Henry, Andre Marie Ampere, Michael Faraday, Thomas Davenport, and a few others.[1] Some of the most documented sources on the electric motor all point to the work of Michael Faraday. In 1821, Faraday demonstrated by a simple device

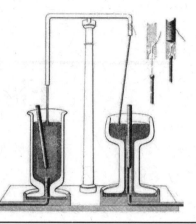

FIGURE 8-1 The first electric motor—Michael Faraday, 1821. (www.sparkmuseum.com/MOTORS. HTM.)

that mechanical energy could be created by electromagnetic means. Faraday's device consisted of a free-hanging wire dipping into a pool of mercury. A permanent magnet was placed in the middle of the pool of mercury. When an electric current passed through the wire, the wire would begin to rotate around the magnet, demonstrating that the current gave rise to a circular magnetic field around the wire[2] (Figure 8-1).

The first real electric motor, using electromagnets for both stationary and rotating parts, was demonstrated by Anyos Jedlik in 1828 in Hungary.[3] He is considered by many to be the unsung father of the electric motor. Jedlik at the time was not the only one creating simple machines; many others experimented with similar devices around the same time.

In 1873, the modern direct-current (dc) motor was invented by accident by Zénobe Gramme during an inventors' fair. During the fair, a careless worker connected the terminals of a Gramme dynamo to another dynamo (a generator that produces direct current) that was producing electricity, and Gramme's dynamo

FIGURE 8-2 Example of an early dc motor. (http://upload.wikimedia.org/wikipedia/en/3/34/ World's_first_electric_motor_Jedlik's_motor_(1828).jpg.)

began to spin on its own. Gramme found that his device would act as an electric motor when a constant voltage was applied. The Gramme machine was the first electric motor that was successful in the industry. His work and the help of a careless worker ushered in the development of large-scale electric motors[4] (Figure 8-2).

Choosing the Right Motor for You

The selection of your electric motor is one of the most important choices you will make. What type of performance do you want? A tire-burning quarter mile all-out race machine? On the other hand, maybe a cruising machine with good power and considerable range? Throughout this section I will help to educate you in the selection of the right motor for your application. You may have to make some compromises and work with what is available, what may fit, or within a certain budget.

This book will explain both dc motors and alternating-current (ac) motors. The motor is one of the three crucial components in your design and build, those components being the batteries, the controller, and the motor. Many decisions need to be made, and planning is the key to the performance of the final vehicle. In your build, every choice and every change you make will have a great effect. Remember, you are working with a much smaller vehicle; space, size, and power all make a big difference. Always keep in mind that one major change could create a domino effect through the whole design. Unlike the conversion of a car to electric, in which you have plenty of room to stash a few more batteries or play with motor size, with your EV, you are limited. Plan carefully, and you will have great results. Believe me, I know this all too well and have made the mistakes to prove it.

Try to lay out the basics of what you want. If you have an idea about what batteries you will use, list their capacity. In Chapter 7, I provided you with all the information to get you started. Battery selection is one of the first few steps before selecting your electric motor. Battery type, amperage, and voltage all will be determining factors in the selection of your motor. Based on your battery selection, you already will know the voltage and maximum amperage draw. If your batteries or your complete battery pack has a nominal voltage of 120 V dc and is limited to 400 A maximum intermediate current draw, then your motor will need to be selected with these parameters in mind. Additionally, keep motor controller selection in mind because that could be your limiting factor (see Chap. 10). You can use the motor controller to limit current to protect your batteries and electric motor. Your motor selection will have limitations around the power supplied by the batteries and by the controller. In contrast, your batteries and/or your controller may supply more power over the rating of your motor. If your battery pack has a limit on amperage output available, you may need to increase the voltage. Later in this chapter I will go into more detail on the formulas and mathematics you might need.

Electric Motor Horsepower

Electric motors are powerhouses, delivering hundreds of horsepower in a fraction of a second. In selecting your electric motor, you need to have an understanding of the rated power set by the engine manufacturer. Electric motors have a continuous rating and an intermittent or 5-minute rating. Electric motors are capable of a power output of two to more than four times their continuous rating, but only for a few minutes. The 5-minute power rating generally is used for acceleration and hill climbing. A large part of this rating is due to heat buildup under heavy load and high-current draw (amperes). Therefore, keeping your motor running cool is very important. The rated power is listed on the motor, or the manufacturer can supply you with the appropriate data and charts. Your vehicle's performance will greatly rely on the rated power of the motor. Table 8-1 provides an example of motor rating.

TABLE 8-1   Sample Series DC Motor Rating

Length	Diameter	Weight	Input Voltage	Efficiency	
14.50"	8.0"	107.0 lbs.	96-120 V	89.00%	
Test Data @ 96 V Input					
Time On	**Volts**	**Amps**	**RPM**	**HP**	**KW**
5 min.	86	322	3600	31.5	23.8
1 hr.	90	190	4800	20.6	15.5
Continuous	91	178	5000	19	14.4
Peak Horsepower				68	
Test Data @ 120 V Input					
Time On	**Volts**	**Amps**	**RPM**	**HP**	**KW**
5 min.	111	300	4650	37	28
1 hr.	114	180	6200	24	18
Continuous	115	165	6500	21.7	16.3
Peak Horsepower				83	
Peak Torque @ 120 V & 500 A				85 ft. lbs.	

Carl Vogel—Advanced DC Motors

Later in this chapter I will provide more details on how each motor works and the advantages and disadvantages of each type. Other books have listed in great detail motor designs and formulas, such as reluctance, magnetic fields, magnetomotive force, flux, and flux density. This sounds like something from *Back to the Future*, very cool but not fully relevant unless you are building an electric motor. I will keep it simple and give you the basics that you need to know on these topics.

Some Simple Points and Notes

Even though electric motors are given a continuous rating, this does not mean that the motor cannot run at less horsepower. If only 5 hp is required to operate your vehicle at a certain speed, your motor can run at a reduced load. Controlling the speed and load is a function of the motor controller (see Chapter 9).

The continuous rating is there for a reason. Operating your motor over this rated horsepower eventually will overheat and damage the motor. A motor rated for 100 A may be able to run at 300 A for a few minutes, but operating the electric motor above the rating for any extended periods of time will easily damage it by overheating the field coils, armature, and brushes, causing permanent damage.

Available horsepower increases with the amount of voltage supplied to the motor. For example, if a motor is rated at 15 hp continuous at 72 V, the same motor also may be rated at 30 hp at 144 V. As voltage is increased, so are the horsepower and revolutions per minute (rpm). Horsepower is a function of torque × rpm. Additionally, if you increase the voltage, the amperage stays the same or less. Remember, increased amperage means an increase in motor temperature.

Select the right-sized motor for your application. An undersized motor will not last long. The increased current over the maximum rating will overheat your motor. High current (amperes) will result in too much heat and damage.

If your motor has a limit, try to select a motor controller that meets the specifications of your electric motor. Some motor controllers are very advanced, allowing the user to program limits and parameters. Some controllers have the ability to measure motor rpm and temperature. When your motor reaches its thermal limit, a controller can cut back power and reduce the risk of damage.

The greater the highway speed required, the more horsepower you will need. The horsepower required at 70 mph can be over four times the power needed to propel your vehicle at 35 mph. Remember, the higher the speed, the less range you will achieve and the more amperes you will consume.

Some Basic Terms to Know

Magnetic flux   This is a measure of the quantity of magnetism, represented by the Greek capital letter Φ (phi), taking into account the strength and the extent of a magnetic field.

Magnetism   This is the means by which materials exert attractive or repulsive forces on other materials. Some well-known materials that exhibit easily detectable magnetic properties (called *magnets*) are nickel, iron, cobalt, and their alloys; however, all materials are influenced to a greater or lesser degree by the presence of a magnetic field.

Magnetic field   This is a vector field that can exert a magnetic force on moving electric charges. Magnetic fields can be created by supplying voltage to a winding of copper wires around a piece of steel. The steel with the windings now creates a magnetic field with both north and south poles.

Permanent magnets   These are objects that stay magnetized and produce their own magnetic fields. All permanent magnets have both a north and a south pole.

Back electromotive force (EMF) An electric motor in addition to supplying mechanical power also can act as a generator. This is true in a sense even when the motor functions as a motor. The EMF a motor generates is referred to as *back EMF*. Back EMF is produced when the armature begins to spin. It will produce a voltage that is of opposite polarity to that of the power supply. The overall effect of this voltage will be subtracted from the supply voltage, so the motor windings will see a smaller voltage potential. The motor acts as a generator at the same time, opposing the current supplied to the motor or holding back the voltage supplied to the motor. As an unloaded dc motor spins, it generates a backward-flowing electromotive force (back EMF) that resists the current being applied to the motor. The current through the motor drops as the rotational speed increases; the free-spinning motor has very little current. It is only when a load is applied to the motor that the rotor slows, thus allowing current draw through the motor to increase. In most cases, if the motor has no load, it turns very quickly and speeds up until the back EMF plus the voltage drop equal the supply voltage. Back EMF acts as a "regulator," limiting the motor's maximum rotational speed.[5] Note that in some types of motors, the back EMF can be reduced, creating a serious condition under no load where the motor can run away and explode. Never apply full power to an electric motor with no load!

DC Motors

The classic dc motor design is a device that converts electrical energy into mechanical energy. This holds true for any electric motor, whether the motor is dc or ac.

A simple dc motor has a coil of wire that can rotate in a magnetic field. The current in the coil of wire is supplied via two brushes that make moving contact with a split ring known as a *commutator*. The coil lies in a steady magnetic field in the simplest form from permanent magnets. In other types of dc motors, such as the series motor, the permanent magnets are replaced with coils of wire producing their own magnetic field when current is applied. The forces exerted on the current-carrying wires generate a magnetic field creating north and south magnetism. This magnetism creates a force on the coil, also known as an *armature*. As current is applied to the armature, an opposite north and south pole is created, causing them to repel or attract one another, creating rotational movement. Figure 8-3 demonstrates how magnetic fields and poles repel and attract one another. Notice how opposite poles attract and like poles repel.

To demonstrate this, you can create a magnetic field simply with a source of electricity, a wire, and a piece of steel. Using a piece of steel, wrap a few turns of insulated copper wire around it, and apply electric current from a battery to it. Now you have just transformed the steel into a bar-style magnet with a north and south pole (Figure 8-4).

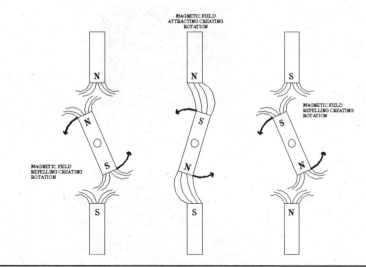

FIGURE 8-3 Simple rotation.

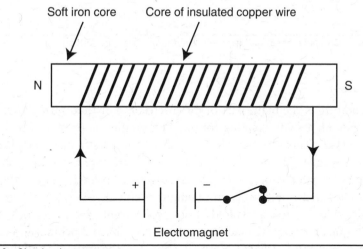

FIGURE 8-4 Simple electromagnet.

DC Motor Basic Construction

In this section I will explain some of the basic parts that make up the typical dc motor. These same parts are similar in a few ac motor designs. Figure 8-5 displays the fundamental parts of a permanent-magnet dc motor in the simplest form (see also Figure 8-6).

FIGURE 8-5   Sample of basic dc motor. (www.physclips.unsw.edu.au/jw/electricmotors.html.)

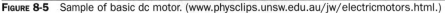

FIGURE 8-6   Three-dimensional (3D) representation of basic motor components.

Armature

The armature is the main part of the electric motor that normally rotates on two bearings with a shaft, creating torque. The rotation is produced by current in the coil windings. The armature usually consists of a shaft surrounded by laminated steel pieces called the *armature core*. The armature core is divided in sections with windings of coated copper wire. When current is applied to one of the windings, it creates a magnetic field, thus producing movement.

The armature's role is twofold: (1) to carry current crossing the field, thus creating shaft torque (in a rotating machine) or force (in a linear machine) and (2) to generate an electromotive force (EMF). Notice in Figure 8-7 the armature and the heavy-gauge copper wires to carry high current and to produce strong magnetic fields.

FIGURE 8-7   Basic dc armature.

Commutator

The commutator normally consists of a set of copper segments fixed around part of the circumference of the armature (Figs. 8-8 and 8-9). Each segment of the commutator is separated from the other. A set of spring-loaded brushes is fixed to the frame of the electric motor. An external source of current is supplied to the brushes. The commutator acts as a switch for each segment of the armature. Current flows through only the winding of the armature with which the brushes are in contact. This flow of current creates an EMF, producing torque and rotating the shaft. As the shaft rotates, the brushes contact the next segment of the commutator, alternating the magnetic poles and continuing the rotation of the armature.

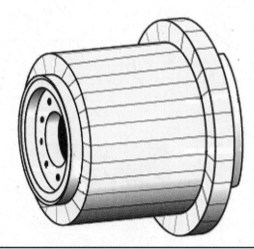

FIGURE 8-8   CAD drawing of a simple commutator.

FIGURE 8-9   Photograph of a simple commutator.

Field Poles

Electromagnets and permanent magnets are referred to as *field poles*. The electromagnet is created by winding turns of wire. The poles are normally curved to match the circumference of the armature. The poles can be composed of either a permanent magnet or an electromagnet. For most of the motors used in EVs, an electromagnet is used; on smaller motors, permanent magnets sometimes are used (Figure 8-10).

The strength of an electromagnet is determined by a number of factors:

- The strength is proportional to the number of turns in the coil.
- The strength is relative to the current flowing in the coil.
- The strength is inversely proportional to the length of the air gap between the poles.

In general, an electromagnet is often considered better than a permanent magnet because it can produce very strong magnetic fields, and its strength can be controlled by varying the number of turns in its coil or by changing the current flowing through the coil (Figure 8-11).

FIGURE 8-10   Field pole in the housing of a series motor.

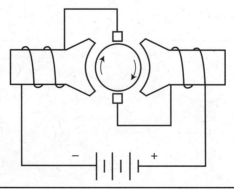

FIGURE 8-11   Drawing of a field coil.

Brushes

The brushes are made of carbon-composite material, usually in a rectangular shape (Figure 8-12). Typically, the brushes have copper added to aid in conduction, and sometimes another material is also added to reduce wear. The brushes are held securely in place by the rigging normally at the tail end of the motor housing. The rigging, while holding the brushes in place, uses a spring to provide the proper amount of tension on the brushes so that they make proper contact with the commutator. Brush tension is important. If the tension is too light, the brushes will bounce and arc, and if the tension is too heavy, the brushes will wear down prematurely. The end of the brush that contacts the commutator is contoured to fit the commutator for better current transfer. In a typical motor, half the brushes will be connected to the positive voltage, and half will be connected to the negative voltage. In most motors, the number of brushes will be equal to the number of field poles. Current is applied through copper wire connected to the brushes. This allows higher current loads and flexibility as the brushes wear. In most applications, a brush set can be replaced through access from the side of the motor housing when replacement is necessary.

Figure 8-12 Brushes.

The classic dc motor exhibits some limitations owing to the need for brushes pressing against the commutator. Friction is one result. At higher speeds, brushes have difficulty maintaining uninterrupted contact with the commutator. At high rotational speeds, brushes may bounce off the irregularities in the commutator surface, creating sparks. Sparks inevitably may be created by the brushes making and breaking contact as the brushes cross the insulating gaps between commutator sections. The making and breaking of electric contact also causes electrical noise, and the sparks additionally cause radiofrequency interference (RFI).

Motor Timing

Just like the timing on an internal combustion engine, you can advance or retard the timing on many electric motors. In the electric motor, the magnetic field is never perfectly uniform. Instead, as the armature spins, it induces field effects that drag and distort the magnetic lines of the outer nonrotating stator.

The faster the armature spins, the greater the degree of magnetic field distortion becomes. Because the electric motor operates most efficiently with the armature field at right angles to the stator field (field poles), it is necessary to either retard or advance the brush position to put the rotor's field into the correct position to be at a right angle to the distorted field, producing the most magnetic force or rotating torque.

As a general rule of thumb, the brushes are neutral when they line up inline with the motor's field coil pole shoe bolts on the motor's sides. To advance the motor's timing, you must move the brushes opposite the motor's rotation by x degrees depending on voltage.

If brush timing seems a bit confusing, it basically refers to the position of the brushes in the motor and the position to which they are set physically during manufacture. The position to which they are normally set by the manufacturer is a "neutral" position. This neutral position allows the motor to operate and perform almost identically in counterclockwise (CCW) and clockwise (CW) rotations at normal voltages. A normal voltage for most series-wound motors in a neutral timed arrangement is generally less than 96 V. Above this range, motors almost always should be advanced in the direction opposite to their normal rotation in order to reduce arcing and provide increased performance at higher voltages. *Caution:* If a motor is advanced and then powered to run in the opposite direction, significant arcing could result! Regenerative braking should not be attempted with motors that have significantly advanced timing. Running an advanced-timing motor in reverse at low speed is okay, but do not operate in reverse at high speeds or for any prolonged period of time. Significant arcing will occur, resulting in damage to the brushes and armature.

DC Motor Types

Now that you have a little background in basic motor operations, I would like to explain the different motor types:

- Series
- Shunt
- Compound
- Permanent magnet
- Brushless
- Universal

Series DC Motor

The series dc motor is a popular motor of choice (Figures 8-13 and 8-14). This type of motor develops a very large amount of turning force, called torque, from a standstill. Because of this characteristic, the series dc motor can be used in many

FIGURE 8-13   Advanced DC BL5-4001 series motor.

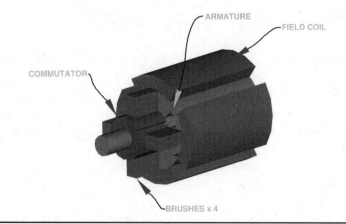

FIGURE 8-14   Series dc motor.

applications. For traction applications, such as powering an EV, this motor works very well. The series motor acquires the name because its field winding is connected in series with the armature. The current must flow through the field windings and the armature itself. As a result, the field current and armature current are equal. Heavy currents flow directly from the supply to the field windings. To carry this huge load, the field windings are very thick and have few turns. Usually, copper bars form the stator windings or very heavy-gauge copper wire with few turns. These thick copper bars or heavy-gauge wire dissipate the heat produced by the heavy flow of current extremely effectively.

Torque

The series motor can develop an enormous amount of torque at startup. The torque varies with the square of the current. If you view the graph in Figure 8-15, you can actually see the torque versus the armature current. At startup of a series motor,

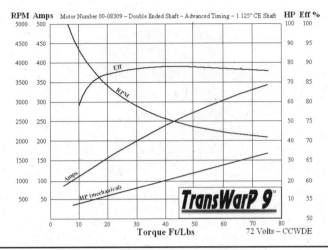

FIGURE 8-15   Nine-inch motor curves. (Courtesy of NetGain Motors, Inc.)

there is no back EMF to limit the flow of current to the armature. The startup torque values can far exceed the stated specifications of the motor. When using a series-wound motor, you might want to take precautions to limit startup current. Because of the high starting torque, the series motor is appealing for use in EV applications. As rpm increase in the series motor, it will reach a point where torque will start to drop dramatically. This point is normally near the high rpm range or limit of the motor. Check your torque curves and specifications for your particular motor.

Speed

A major disadvantage of the series motor is related to speed characteristics. The speed of a series motor with no load connected to it increases to the point where the motor may become damaged, usually by bearing damage or by the windings flying out of the slots in the armature. There is a danger to both equipment and personnel. Think of it as over-revving your internal combustion engine. You would not put the pedal to the floor with no load or the engine in neutral; you would blow your motor. Equally, some form of load always must be connected to a series motor or some way to limit motor speed must be in place before you turn it on. As the series motor accelerates, the armature current decreases, reducing the back EMF to limit the speed. The reduction in field causes the motor to speed up until it self-destructs and flies apart.

The simple way to avoid this is always have a load on the motor. Be actively aware of the speed and load on your motor, just as you would an internal combustion engine. Install a revolution-limiting device. Some motor controllers have the ability to cut power to the motor when limits are reached. There may be units on the market called *rev limiters* that you can install to cut power to the motor. A rev limiter manufactured by K & W Engineering was called the TD-100. This unit was both a rev limiter and a tachometer drive. At this time, the TD-100 is no longer available. From my local Electric Auto Association chapter, a member named Mike Savino from EV-Propulsion is developing a unit to replace the tachometer drive with rev limit capabilities.

Field Weakening

Field weakening is one way to control the series motor speed. If you place a resistor in parallel with the series motor field winding, you divert part of the current through the resistor. If you keep the field current to 50 percent or less of the total current, you can gain up to a 20–25 percent increase in speed at moderate torque. Today, most motor controllers use a variation of field weakening in addition to other capabilities.

Reversing

In the series motor, the same current that flows through the field flows through the armature. By reversing the current polarity, however, you will not reverse the direction of the motor. To reverse the motor, you need to transpose or change the direction of current flow to the field winding with respect to the armature or the armature with respect to the field winding.

Regenerative Braking

All motors exhibit the ability to act as generators, creating a counter EMF. Regenerative braking is a way to use the electric motor to slow down your vehicle without using your brakes. By using your electric motor to slow your vehicle down, you capture energy otherwise wasted as heat in your brakes. It is a way to capture mechanical energy that otherwise would have been lost. This energy is now stored back in your batteries. Imagine all the energy used to power your vehicle up a hill. Now, once you are at the top, a typical vehicle would use its brakes to reduce the speed traveling back down, in addition to maybe downshifting. With regenerative braking, you have the ability to capture and use otherwise wasted potential energy going downhill and place it back in your batteries. What a great way to increase your range and conserve energy!

Series motors in the past exhibited unstable generator properties, leaving them less likely to be used as generators or for regenerative braking. Today, however, with the advancements in motor controllers, using a series motor in regenerative mode is a problem of the past. Now, motor controller technology and programming allow regenerative braking on series motors. I have personally used a series-wound dc motor (Advanced DC L91-4003) on my motorcycle with regenerative braking through a Zapi motor controller for over 5 years without any problems. It provokes a great feeling; you hear a click of a relay and then see 30 A and 140 V dc going back into the batteries. The braking can be controlled either with a brake peddle or with the throttle control.

Shunt DC Motors

The shunt dc motor is similar to the series motor in its basic construction, with the exception of the field windings and the connection to the armature. The shunt motor is connected in parallel with the armature instead of in series. Since the field winding is placed in parallel with the armature, it is called a *shunt winding,* and the motor is called a *shunt motor.* In examining a shunt motor, you will notice that the field terminals are marked "Fl" and "F2," and the armature terminals are marked "Al" and "A2" (Figure 8-16).

The windings in the field coil consist of small-gauge wire with many turns. Since the wire is so small, the coil can have thousands of turns. The small-gauge wire cannot handle as much current as the heavy-gauge wire in the series field, though. Since this field coil consists of more turns of wire, it can still produce an exceptionally strong magnetic field.

The shunt motor has somewhat different operating characteristics than the series motor. Since the shunt field coil is made of fine wire, it cannot handle a large amount of current. This means that the shunt motor develops low starting torque. With a low starting torque, you will need to decrease the shaft load at startup.

The armature for the shunt motor is similar to that of the series motor and will draw current to produce a magnetic field, causing the armature shaft and load to start turning. Because of the high resistance from many windings of wire, the shunt coil keeps the overall current flow low. When the armature begins to turn, it will produce back EMF. The back EMF will decrease the current in the armature as

Figure 8-16 Typical shunt motor. (Courtesy of EVDrives, www.evdrives.com/motor_products. html.)

speed increases to a very small level. The amount of current the armature will draw is directly related to the size of the load when the motor reaches full speed. Since the load is generally small, the armature current will be small. Unlike the series motor, the shunt motor's speed will remain rather constant when the motor reaches full rpm. Also remember that the shunt motor's efficiency will drop off drastically when it is operated below its rated voltage. The motor will tend to overheat when it is operated below full voltage, so motor cooling must be provided.

Torque

The armature's torque increases as the motor gains speed. This is so because the shunt motor's torque is directly proportional to armature current. When the motor is starting and the number of revolutions per minute is very low, the motor has decreased torque. After the motor reaches full rpm, the torque reaches maximum potential. The shunt motor is a good choice for applications where constant speed is required. The speed of the shunt motor stays fairly constant throughout its load range and drops slightly when it is drawing the largest current. For vehicle applications, a lower gear ratio or transmission may be needed to compensate for the low starting torque.

Speed

When the shunt motor reaches full rpm, its speed will remain reasonably constant. The reason the speed remains constant is because of the load characteristics of the armature and shunt coil. The ability of the shunt motor to maintain a set rpm at high speed when the load changes is because of the characteristic of the shunt field and armature. Since the armature begins to produce back EMF as soon as it starts to rotate, it will use the back EMF to maintain its rpm at high speed. If the load increases slightly and causes the armature shaft to slow down, less back EMF will be produced, which will cause more current to flow. The extra current provides the motor with the extra torque required to regain its rpm when this load is increased slightly.

The shunt motor's speed can be varied in two ways: (1) varying the amount of current supplied to the shunt field and (2) controlling the amount of current supplied to the armature. Controlling the current to the shunt field allows the rpm to be changed 10–20 percent when the motor is at full rpm.

The shunt motor's rpm also can be controlled by regulating the voltage that is applied to the armature. This means that if the motor is operated on less voltage, it will run at fewer than full rpm. You also should be aware that the motor's torque is reduced when it is operated below the full voltage level. In addition, lower voltage will increase the heat produced by the motor.

Field Weakening

Field weakening is accomplished by slightly increasing or decreasing the voltage applied to the field. The armature continues to have full voltage applied to it while the current to the shunt field is regulated. When the shunt field's current is decreased, the motor's rpm will increase slightly. When the shunt field's current is reduced, the armature must rotate faster to produce the same amount of back EMF to keep the load turning. If the shunt field current is increased slightly, the armature can rotate at slower rpm and maintain the amount of back EMF to produce the armature current to drive the load.

Reversing

The direction of rotation of a dc shunt motor can be reversed by changing the polarity of either the armature coil or the field coil. In this application, the armature coil is usually changed, as was the case with the series motor.

In most applications, the field leads are connected directly to the power supply, so their polarity is not changed. Since the field's polarity has remained the same, the armature's polarity needs to be reversed. Once the polarity of the armature is switched, the motor will begin to rotate in the reverse direction. The same can be accomplished by switching the polarity of the field leads.

Regenerative Braking

The shunt motor is directly adaptable for use as a generator. In fact, most generators are shunt motors or, should I say, shunt generators. The shunt motor has a high degree of stability when used for regenerative braking. The voltage and power remain linear.

Compound DC Motor

The dc compound motor is a combination of shunt-wound and series-wound types, combining the characteristics of both with a sort of hybrid operating characteristic. It has a series field winding that is connected in series with the armature and a shunt field that is in parallel with the armature. Characteristics may be mixed by varying the combination of the two windings. These motors generally are used where severe starting conditions are needed and constant speed is required at the same time. A compound motor can be safely operated without a load and can have the speed characteristics of a shunt motor and the starting-torque characteristics of a series motor. The compound dc motor combines the properties of both with some slight trade-offs in torque or speed. Look at the manufacturers' specific ratings for exact specifications.

Types of Compound DC Motors

The *cumulative compound motor* is one of the most common dc motors because it provides high starting torque and good speed regulation at high speeds. Since the shunt field is wired with similar polarity in parallel with the magnetic field, aiding the series field and armature field, it is called *cumulative*. When the motor is connected this way, it can start even with a large load and then operate smoothly when the load varies slightly.

Differential compound motors use the same motor and windings as the cumulative compound motor, but they are connected in a slightly different manner to provide slightly different operating speed and torque characteristics. The differential compound motor's characteristics are less like a shunt motor and more like a series motor. This means that the motor will tend to overspeed when the load is reduced, just like a series motor. Its speed also will drop more than that of a cumulative compound motor when the load increases at full rpm. These two characteristics make the differential motor less desirable than the cumulative motor for most applications.

Torque

The dc compound motor has greater torque than a shunt motor owing to the series field. In addition, it has fairly consistent speed owing to the shunt field winding. Depending on whether the motor is connected in the differential or cumulative position, it will yield different torque values (Figure 8-17).

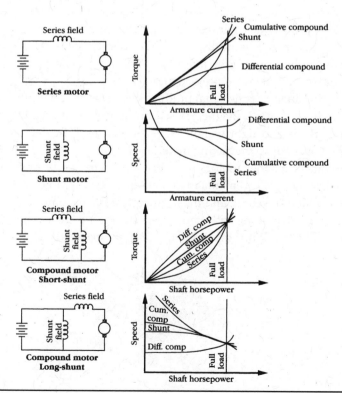

FIGURE 8-17   Curves for series and shunt dc motors. (From *Build Your Own Electric Vehicle*, Figure 6-3, p. 141.)

Speed

The speed of a compound motor can be changed very easily by adjusting the amount of voltage applied to it. Since the advent of solid-state components and microprocessor controls, speed is controlled easily. You can see that the speed of a differential compound motor increases slightly when the motor is drawing the highest current through the armature. The increase in speed occurs because the extra current in the differential winding causes the magnetic field in the motor to weaken slightly.

Reversing

Each type of compound motor can be reversed by changing the polarity of the armature winding. If the motor has interpoles, the polarity of the interpole must be changed when the armature's polarity is changed. Since the interpole is connected in series with the armature, it should be reversed when the armature is reversed. Interpoles help to prevent the armature and brushes from arcing so that the brushes will last longer.

Permanent-Magnet DC Motor

Permanent-magnet dc motors represent the simplicity of dc motor design. The permanent-magnet design is used in countless applications and increasingly today. The alloys from which permanent magnets are made are often very difficult to handle; many are mechanically hard and brittle. They may be cast and then ground into shape or even ground to a powder and formed. The powders are mixed with resin binders and then compressed and heat-treated.

The permanent magnets that produce the largest magnetic flux with the smallest mass are the rare-earth magnets based on samarium and neodymium. Their high magnetic fields and light weight make them useful for demonstrating magnetic levitation over superconducting materials.

Permanent-magnet motors have become increasingly popular owing to new technology and advancements in magnetic materials. Motor designs have become smaller, lighter in weight, and more powerful. Permanent-magnet motors roughly resemble shunt motors with similar speed, torque, reversing, and regenerative braking abilities. With the advancement in materials technology, permanent

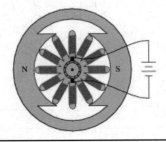

Figure 8-18   Basic dc motor.

magnets have increased dramatically in magnetic force. With these advancements, the permanent-magnet motor has surpassed the typical shunt motor speed and torque curves down to zero. Permanent-magnet motors are now capable of generating several times more starting torque than shunt motors.[6]

One perfect example from the Lynch motor is a unique axial gap permanent-magnet brushed dc motor. The motor was invented by Cedric Lynch (U.S. patent no. 4823039). Its efficiency is around 90 percent, further extending the life of the batteries and improving the range of an EV (Figure 8-19).

LEM-130 Model   LEM-170 Model   LEM - 200 Model

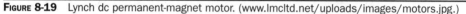

FIGURE 8-19   Lynch dc permanent-magnet motor. (www.lmcltd.net/uploads/images/motors.jpg.)

Universal Motor

The universal dc motor is similar to a regular dc motor but is designed to operate either from dc or from single-phase ac. The stator and rotor windings of the motor are connected in series through the rotor commutator. Therefore, the universal motor is also known as an *ac series motor* or an *ac commutator motor*. The universal motor can be controlled either as a phase-angle drive or as a chopper drive.

In the phase-angle application, the phase-angle control technique is used to adjust the voltage applied to the motor. A phase shift of the gate's pulses allows the effective voltage seen by the motor to be varied. The phase-angle drive requires just a triac, a bidirectional electronic switch which can conduct current in either directions.

In the chopper application, the pulse-width-modulation (PWM) technique is used to adjust the voltage applied to the motor. Modulation of the PWM duty cycle allows the effective voltage seen by the motor to be varied. Compared with a phase-angle drive, a chopper drive requires a more complicated power stage with an input rectifier, a power switch, and a fast power diode. The advantage is higher efficiency, less acoustic noise, and better electromagnetic compatibility EMC behavior.

AC Electric Motors

Now that you have learned a little about dc motors, this section will focus on the basics of ac motors. In the world today, a third of electricity consumption is used for running induction motors driving pumps, fans, compressors, elevators, and machinery of various types. The ac induction motor is a common form of asynchronous motor whose operation depends on three electromagnetic phenomena (Figures 8-20 and 8-21).

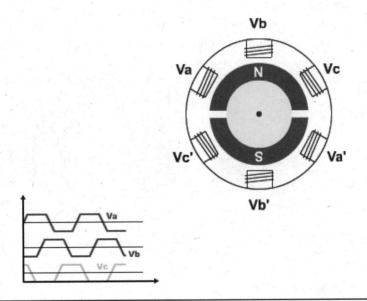

FIGURE 8-20   Ac induction motor with a permanent magnet armature showing phases.

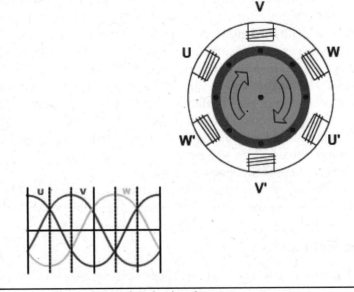

FIGURE 8-21   Ac induction motor rotating showing phases.

While dc motor drive systems were used universally in early EVs, ac drive systems started to emerge because of advances in technology. As the U.S. Department of Energy program for EVs progressed early on, interest in ac drive systems advanced with government funding.[7] The ac motor offers many advantages. First, it requires little or no maintenance because there are no commutators or brushes. Second, ac motors are relatively light and small in size given their voltage power and speed ratings. Third, they are far less expensive, in some cases one-fifth to one-third the expense of a dc motor. Last, the efficiency of the ac motor tends to be a few points higher than that of the dc motor owing to the low copper and iron heat losses (Figures 8-22 and 8-23).

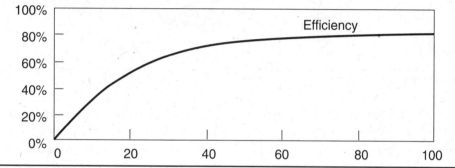

FIGURE 8-22 Typical ac: more efficiency.

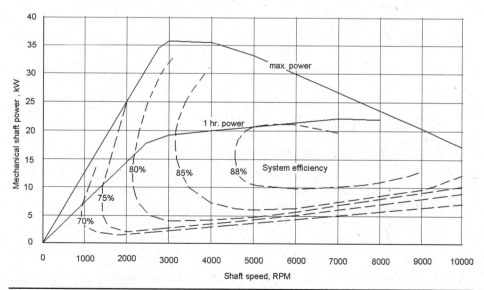

FIGURE 8-23 Combined efficiencies of the Simovert ac inverter at 130 V dc input. (Courtesy Metric Mind Engineering, www.metricmind.com.)

FIGURE 8-24   Siemens ac induction motor (10,000 rpm. 100 hp peak at 400 V).

The ac induction motor is designed to operate from a three-phase source of voltage (Figure 8-24). The stator is a classic three-phase stator with the winding displaced by 120 degrees. The most common type of induction motor has a squirrel-cage rotor in which aluminum conductors or bars are shorted together at both ends of the rotor by cast-aluminum end rings. When three currents flow through the three symmetrically placed windings, a sinusoidally distributed air-gap flux generating the rotor current is produced. The interaction of the sinusoidally distributed air-gap flux and induced rotor currents produces a torque on the rotor. In adjustable-speed applications, ac motors in traction vehicles are powered by inverters. The inverter converts dc power to ac power at the required frequency and amplitude. The output voltage is mostly created by a PWM technique (more about PWM in Chapter 9). The three-phase voltage waves are shifted 120 degrees to each other, and thus a three-phase motor can be supplied. The following sections will explain more about the different types of ac motors.

A Couple of Terms You Should Know

Synchronous speed is the theoretical speed of an ac induction motor at which the motor should spin if the induced magnetic field in the rotor perfectly follows the rotating magnetic field of the stator. Synchronous speed is measured in rotations per minute (rpm) and is given by the following formula:

$$\text{RPM} = 120 \times \text{electric frequency rpm / number of poles}$$

However, to produce torque, an induction motor suffers from slip. *Slip* is the result of the induced field in the rotor windings lagging behind the rotating magnetic field in the stator windings. The energy lost in this discrepancy is what produces the useful work in an induction motor. Slip is expressed as a percentage of synchronous speed and is given by the following formula:

S = [(Synchronous speed – actual speed) / (synchronous speed)] * 100%

Typical slip values at full-load torque range from 1 percent (for large 100-hp motors) to 5 percent (for small ½-hp motors). Slip is not a concern in most applications, unless precise speed control is required. One solution is to use a variable-frequency drive controlled by a feedback encoder to keep the motor at a specific speed.[8]

Single-Phase Induction Motor

The single-phase ac motor is the simplest design. I will just touch base on this ac motor to familiarize you with the various types. This type of ac motor would not be used in traction vehicles. Single-phase induction motors are less efficient than polyphase motors and were developed mainly for domestic use because only single-phase power is available. The single-phase ac motor has no control of speed, and it is designed for one speed only (Figure 8-25).

AC Synchronous Motor

The ac synchronous motor is similar to the induction motor in that it is a polyphase machine in which the stator produces a rotating field. An ac synchronous motor rotates at a fixed speed regardless of any increase or decrease in load. The motor will keep a fixed speed regardless of the torque required until it reaches its stall torque rating. If the load becomes greater than the motor's stall torque, the ac synchronous motor will not slow down until it reaches a point at which it will stall and stop turning. No expensive driver or amplifier is necessary. Most synchronous motors are used where precise timing and constant speed are required. A unique characteristic of the ac synchronous motor is that it is not self-starting. A synchronous motor has no starting torque. It has torque only when it is running at

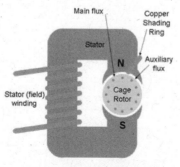

Shaded Pole Induction Motor

Figure 8-25 Basic single-phase ac motor. (www.mpoweruk.com/motorsac.htm.)

synchronous speed. Either a squirrel-cage winding is added to the rotor to cause it to start, or a dc motor is used to bring the rotor to near-synchronous speed, at which time the ac is applied. The synchronous motor is not suited for traction vehicles because of its fixed speed.

Polyphase AC Induction Motor (Three-Phase AC Motor)

The most common type of ac motor is the three-phase induction motor. The term *polyphase* means "more than one phase." The polyphase motor consists of a stator with stator windings and a rotor assembly constructed as a cylindrical frame of metal bars arranged in a squirrel-cage type of configuration (Figure 8-26). Compared with a dc motor armature, there is no commutator. This eliminates the brushes, arcing, sparking, graphite dust, brush adjustment and replacement, and remachining of the commutator.

Synchronous Speed

The synchronous speed of an ac induction motor is the theoretical speed at which the motor should spin if it the induced magnetic field in the rotor perfectly followed the rotating magnetic field of the stator. Synchronous speed is measured in rotations per minute (rpm).

Regenerative Braking

If the motor is fed by a variable-frequency inverter, then regenerative braking is possible. Ac motors can be microprocessor-controlled to a fine degree and can regenerate current down to almost a stop, whereas dc regeneration fades quickly at low speeds.

The induction motor may function as an alternator if it is driven by a torque at greater than 100 percent of the synchronous speed. This corresponds to a few percent of negative slip, say, 1 percent. This means that as we are rotating the motor faster than the synchronous speed, the rotor is advancing 1 percent faster than the stator rotating magnetic field. It normally lags by 1 percent in a motor. Since the rotor is cutting the stator magnetic field in the opposite direction (leading), the

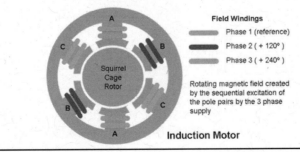

FIGURE 8-26   Three-phase ac motor.

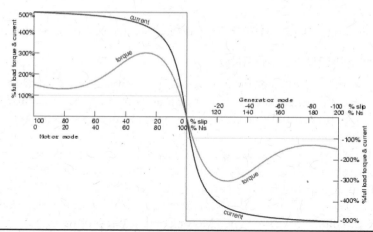

FIGURE 8-27   Basic ac induction motor and regenerative motor curve. (http://electojects.com/ motors/tesla-induction-motors-4.htm.)

rotor induces a voltage into the stator, feeding electrical energy back into the motor controller and thus the batteries (Figure 8-27). The induction ac motor must be excited by a power source to create regenerative braking. No power can be generated in the event of a controller or battery failure.

EV Motor Selection

As you have seen, motors come in numerous variations and types, giving you a large selection of solutions for your EV. Your task is to decide which one to use given the tools and knowledge you have obtained from this book and your vehicle requirements. Remember, many motors are available, and one motor or configuration is not the only solution. Weigh your options, and look at all the available motors on the market. You will find an enormous amount of resources in Chapter 14. Additionally, I have set up an online resource site with more updates to help you as new technology and products become available. From these resources, you can find many companies and distributors of electric motors. In the following sections I will explain a few motor options. I do not advocate any particular motor over any other. So which one is right for you?

Basic Considerations

- Cost
- Power and torque
- Amperes
- Voltage
- Size
- Efficiency

- Shaft size
- Controllers available that work with your motor

Permanent-Magnet DC Motor

The permanent-magnet dc motor is a good choice for a small to midsized EV. Permanent magnets have advanced a long way; the magnets of today are smaller and more powerful. What this means to you is more power and efficiency packed into one motor.

Briggs & Stratton in around 2003 started manufacturing a permanent-magnet motor called the Etek electric motor. This motor is compact with a lot of power in relation to the size. Unfortunately, Briggs & Stratton stopped manufacturing this motor. The good news is that you can purchase this same motor from the original motor manufacturer, the Lynch Motor Company. It produces a few models that will fit many applications.

The Lynch LEM-200-D135 double-magnet motor is extremely efficient: 12–84 V dc (96 V dc), 8-in-diameter single shaft, 200+ A continuous/250+ A intermittent, and reversible. It is a good choice for EVs weighing 400–1200 lb. This motor weighs approximately 25 lb (11 kg) (Figure 8-28; see also Table 8-2).

Series-Wound Motor Examples

The series dc motor is adaptable to many vehicles and available in many sizes and configurations. These motors work well and have stood the test of time, providing great power and reliability. Many motor controllers are readily available in all different sizes and power ratings that work great with the series motor. With recent advances in controller technology, more options are achievable, such as regenerative braking yielding greater programming ability. Pricing of these motors also makes them attractive for EVs. Figures 8-29 and 8-30 provide a couple of examples of the series motors. Note these are only a few of the motors on the market today. For a greater listing, see Chapter 14.

Figure 8-28   Lynch permanent-magnet motor. (www.lmcltd.net.)

TABLE 8-2 Lynch Motor Series 200 Specifications

Motor	No Load Current A	Speed Constant RPM/V	Peak Power kw/HP	Peak Efficiency %	Peak Current	Rated Power kW/ HP	Rated Speed RPM	Rated Voltage	Rated Current A	Rated Torque Nm/ftlb
126	10	105	7.6/10.2	83	400	5.1/6.8	2520	24	270	19.2/14
127	5	54	16.1/21.6	88	400	8.6/11.5	2592	48	215	31.5/23.2
D126	5	100	11.1/14.9	81	400	6.9/9.3	6300	36	250	18.3/13.5
D127	4	50	25.4/34	90	400	12.6/17	6300	72	200	33.3/24.6
D135	3.5	45	29/39	90	400	14.4/19.3	3780	84	200	36.4/27.0
D135RAG	7.4	42	34.3/46	91	400	16.8/22.6	4032	96	200	39.9/29.4

FIGURE 8-29   Warp 8-in series motor. (Courtesy of NetGain Motors www.go-ev.com.)

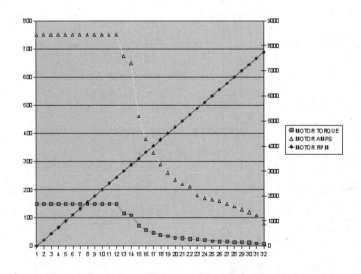

FIGURE 8-30   Advanced DC series motor curves for the L91-4003 at 120 V dc, max. 750 A.

Calculations and Formulas

$$1 \text{ hp} = 746 \text{ W (at 100 percent efficiency)}$$

$$1 \text{ W} = 1/746 \text{ of 1 hp}$$

$$W = V \times A$$

$$W/V = A$$

$$W/A = V$$

$$1{,}000 \text{ W} = 1 \text{ kW}$$

Calculating Horsepower

Electrical power is rated in horsepower or watts. A horsepower is a unit of power equal to 746 W or 33,000 lb · ft/min (550 lb · ft/s). A watt is a unit of measure equal to the power produced by a current of 1 A across the potential difference of 1 V. It is 1/746 of 1 hp. The watt is the base unit of electrical power. Motor power is rated in horsepower and watts. Horsepower is used to measure the energy produced by an electric motor while doing work.[9]

To calculate the horsepower of a motor when current, efficiency, and voltage are known, apply this formula:

$$\text{hp} = (V \times I \times \text{efficiency})/746$$

where hp = horsepower
     V = voltage
     I = current (A)

Example: What is the horsepower of a 230-V motor pulling 4 A and having 82 percent efficiency?

$$\text{hp} = (V \times I \times \text{efficiency})/746$$

$$= (230 \times 4 \times 0.82)/746$$

$$= 754.4/746$$

$$= 1 \text{ hp}$$

Calculating Full-Load Torque

Full-load torque is the torque required to produce the rated power at full speed of the motor. The amount of torque a motor produces at rated power and full speed can be found by using a horsepower-to-torque conversion chart. When using the conversion chart, place a straightedge along the two known quantities, and read the unknown quantity on the third line.

To calculate motor full-load torque, apply this formula:

$$T = (hp \times 5{,}252)/rpm$$

where T   = torque (in lb · ft)
    hp   = horsepower
    5,252 = constant

Example: What is the full-load torque of a 30-hp motor operating at 1,725 rpm?

$$T = (hp \times 5{,}252)/rpm$$

$$= (30 \times 5{,}252)/1{,}725$$

$$= 157{,}560/1{,}725$$

$$= 91.34 \text{ lb} \cdot \text{ft}$$

Conclusion

New technology and an array of motor choices are to your advantage for your EV build. Today, commutated dc motors and series-wound motors are the most common, have worked well for numerous years, and are very economical. Presently, ac induction motors and permanent-magnet brushed and brushless dc motors are the best technologies. The newer motor and controller technologies offer efficiency increases of up to 98 percent, improved reliability, and quiet and dependable operation. Weigh out your options, and go over all the specifications. List the pros and cons. To this day, the simplest and most cost-effective motor of choice is still the dc permanent-magnet motor for smaller applications and the series-wound motor. Both motors provide plenty of power, are plentiful, and most of all, are affordable.

CHAPTER 9

The Motor Controller

The controller by far is one of the most important components of every electric vehicle (EV). The technology and advancements in electronics today make the controller a simpler solution for the EV enthusiasts. Past EV pioneers could only dream of the great advancements of today. Future advancements in technology will yield greater efficiency, more control features, and reductions in size and weight.

Your controller choice is an important decision and needs to be thought out. Just like the process of selecting your electric motor or other components, you need to weigh all your options. Your choice of controller is narrower and depends on your motor selection, but nonetheless, it is very crucial. Your motor, batteries, pack voltage, and available current play a very important roll in controller choice. All these factors must be balanced properly to achieve significant performance and efficiency whether your vehicle is an all-out tire-burning quarter-mile machine or an energy sipper with efficiency and excellent range.

This chapter will introduce you to many different controllers, explaining them in a simple manner. You are not going to build a controller, but it would be nice to have a basic understating of how they work. I will explain the advantages and disadvantages of different controllers, options, technology, and much more. In addition, I will provide a brief explanation of the wiring and accessories that go with the controller.

Controller Overview

In this chapter I will provide a brief background on motor controllers and offer simple solutions to get you up and running in no time at all. EV enthusiasts have more choices today with the advancements that have occurred in electronics and declining costs.

Today, power is not the only thing people are demanding. New features such as programmability, integrated inputs/outputs, tachometer drives, and many safety items are becoming essential. The big feature people are starting to demand is regenerative braking, which is still missing from many controllers. In the face of this demand, manufacturers are adding more features.

Remember, the controller is the brain or computer of your vehicle. The controller "controls," or governs, the performance of the electric motor. The controller integrates motor speed, battery voltage, and system current, yielding power and range. The controller is the key to a vehicle with a long range or an all-out drag bike such as the KillaCycle doing 0–60 mph in 0.97 s (yes, you read that correctly, 0.97 s!) or a quarter mile in 7.890 s at 174 mph (as of October 2008)[1] (Figure 9-1).

The controller on an EV is the device or method by which the speed and power output of the drive motor are controlled, much in the way the throttle of a carburetor controls the power output of a gas-powered engine. The controller is usually interfaced with the accelerator. The controller provides many other features, such as safety interlocks and protection for your electric motor.

Basic Controller Explanation

Controller functions and controlling the speed and power of an electric motor have evolved over the past 100 years. Early control was achieved by multiswitching devices that stepped the voltage up or down. All electric motors on startup require some current limitation. On startup, the electric motor can draw an enormous amount of amperage, as much as your batteries or power source will supply. Amperage draw could be as high as 2,000 A on some vehicles if they are connected directly to the power source. If we applied a 120-V dc pack voltage at 1,000 A, we would yield 120 kW of power (160 hp), if your motor could handle it. However, applying this much power directly to your motor will blow it out. Not good! Once rotation of the motor starts, current can be

Figure 9-1   Bill Dube's KillaCycle burnout! (www.killacycle.com.)

increased. You may remember from Chapter 8 the current-limiting phenomenon called *back EMF* that limits or balances voltage and current as the motor spins. Today, advancements make controlling the speed of your EV much simpler.

Multiswitching Control

Multiswitching dates from the late 1890s. This type of control is the simplest and most basic form of speed control. Multiswitching used rows of batteries separated into a pack that supply various voltages. For example, if we look at a pack with a total of 120 V, it could be wired in four separated sections. Each section would yield a separate voltage of 30 V. On startup, one string of batteries is engaged, yielding 30 V, thus limiting the voltage and current on the start. As the vehicle begins to move, another battery string is switched on. With a battery pack with four rows each at 30 V, the vehicle essentially had four speeds. Each speed is represented by switching battery strings on and increasing the voltage—30, 60, 90, and 120 V (Figure 9-2).

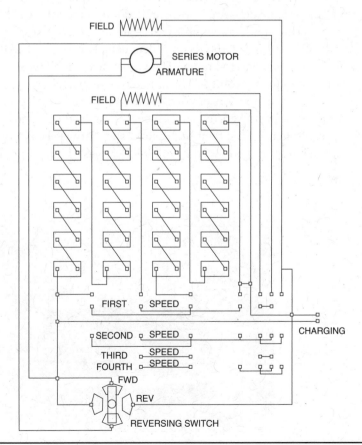

FIGURE 9-2 Early multiswitching device.

Later systems, before electronics, consisted of switches, relays, and contacts wired to rearrange the battery connections to supply different voltages. These often were assisted by very large resistors. Such systems, while capable, often were very jerky and sometimes inefficient and unreliable. These are usually referred to as *series-parallel* or *contactor controllers*.[2]

Solid-State Controllers

As time went on, controller technology made advancements. Now enter late 1960s, when silicon-controlled rectifier (SCR) pulse-width controllers were developed. These used electronics to rapidly switch power on and off to vary motor speed. By controlling the duration of on-off pulses of power, the controller "tricks" the motor into seeing a lower voltage or current. SCR controllers were a huge improvement over the older contactor units, but they operated at low switching frequency, usually around 400 Hz, which created an audible sound. They are easily recognized by the controller's distinctive growl.

In the late 1970s, the modern pulse-width modulated (PWM) controllers, primarily metal-oxide-semiconductor field-effect transistor (MOSFET) units, became available. This finally gave the EVer a smooth, efficient way to control the motor. Unlike SCR controllers, these controllers usually operate at 15,000–18,000 Hz, well above the human hearing range. The higher switching frequency creates smoother motor operation and control. This makes them effectively silent. Motor controllers usually include some sort of current-limiting capability to protect the motor from damage. Some past EVers may remember the distinctive sound of the Curtis 1221/31 series controllers by the faint high-pitch tone that was heard at low speeds. It was not loud, but when you heard it, you knew it was a Curtis (Figure 9-3).

FIGURE 9-3 Curtis controller.

Modern Electronic Controllers

Today, the PWM controller is typical in most EVs. You can think of the controller as a switch. It switches on and off at very high speeds to control how fast you want to go. It is a solid-state device that uses a pulse-width modulator that sends short bursts of current to the motor. It pulses at a rate of 15 kHz. Most controllers will monitor themselves for overcurrent and overheating conditions, cutting back on power or even shutting down temporarily if needed. There are also safety interlocks to make sure that everything is hooked up right, and some controllers will even monitor other aspects of the motor. Most important, the system lockouts keep your vehicle from taking off when it is not supposed to. This feature looks to see that the accelerator is in an "off" condition or not depressed before it will turn the controller on. If the controller senses that something is not correct, it will not turn on. Just think, without this feature, if your accelerator were stuck and you turned the power on, your vehicle would just take off at full power (Figure 9-4).

Undervoltage Cutback

Most motor controllers today have this feature built in. If you discharge a lead-acid battery or most batteries too much, you permanently shorten battery life. The undervoltage cutback monitors the supply voltage from the battery pack and will start cutting back current output. If the battery voltage falls too low, the controller

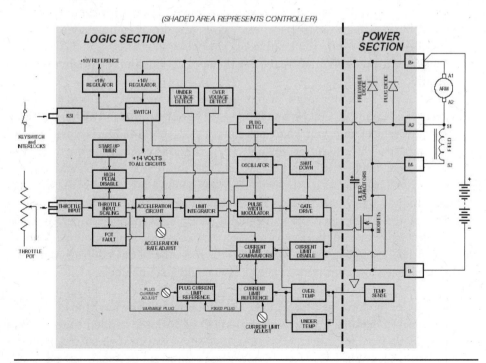

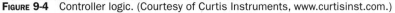

FIGURE 9-4   Controller logic. (Courtesy of Curtis Instruments, www.curtisinst.com.)

may completely cut back all power to the motor, shutting your vehicle down. On some controllers, this feature is programmable so that you can set the limits of the low-voltage cutback. If you are in a situation where your controller starts to cut back, quickly find a safe place to stop and maybe get a charge. If you are in an emergency situation and your vehicle does stop, you are in luck: Most batteries, if you let them sit 15–20 minutes, will come back to life just enough that you can squeeze a few more miles out and get someplace safe or to an outlet to charge.

Overtemperature Cutback

This is another feature all controllers have as a safety measure so that you don't burn your controller out or, even worse, cause an electrical fire. If a controller is overworked, you draw too many amps for too long, or there is inadequate cooling, it will heat up. This is a protective measure. Some controllers have a feature to monitor the temperature of the electric motor and will cut back power when the motor temperature rises. Most controllers will slowly cut back motor current proportionally as the internal temperature of the controller rises past its threshold. At the reduced performance level, the vehicle can be maneuvered out of the way and parked. The controller shifts frequency during overtemperature from its normal 15 kHz to 1 (B models) or 1.5 kHz (C models), providing an audible tone alerting the operator to the overtemperature. By doing this, the controller cuts power, reducing the heat buildup until it reaches normal operating limits again. If the temperature keeps rising owing to inadequate cooling or cooling loss and the controller reaches an extreme limit, it will shut down completely as a feature of self-preservation. If thermal cutback occurs often in normal vehicle operation, the controller is probably undersized for the application, and a higher-current model should be used.

I have a perfect example of this involving my motorcycle, and it shows why gearing, planning, operating revolutions per minute (rpm), and all the things that go into the vehicle and your knowledge are very important. During the first days of filming of the Electra Cruiser after delivery to the *Coolfuel Roadtrip* crew, the motorcycle was cutting back power, and they could not figure out why. For the Zapi motor controller, I had installed extra heat sinks and cooling fans. I knew that with the bike traveling all over the United States, it would encounter temperatures over 100°F. Even with all the extra cooling, the motor controller went overtemperature, past the set threshold, and cut back power. I was very concerned and could not understand why. I had just delivered the bike, it was not more then 2 days into a 9-month 16,000-mile journey, and the bike was failing. You could just imagine my fears.

What I found out was that the bike had been operated in the high gears at low speeds for too long, resulting in very low motor rpm. The low rpm of the motor in high gear generated a very high current draw for an extended time, resulting in overheating of the controller. Even with all the extra heat sinks and cooling fans, the controller still overheated. Under these same conditions, if left unchecked, it could have resulted in overheating of the electric motor and eventual motor failure. When this happened, the controller built up excessive heat from sustained high current draw, resulting in current cutback. This feature also saved the motor from overheating and burning out. To rectify the situation, I instructed Shaun, the rider, about the correct rpm range and gear selections. Most important, I instructed him to watch the amperage gauge for high current draw for extended periods. If he were to see the amperage rising past the controller's peak rating and the rpm dropping, he was to switch gears and get the rpm back up. With this said, always keep in mind the importance of cooling and overloading.

AC Controller

Ac controllers have many advantages over dc types, including increased reliability, wider speed range, increased efficiency, and a range of programmable features. Today's ac systems achieve an efficiency of up to 94 percent; this is 6 percent or more over the dc system. Ac controllers allow more accurate control and full regeneration capability. With the recent advancements in microprocessors and power switching devices, highly efficient ac induction motor controllers are attractive for modern EV designs (Figure 9-5).

Compared with dc controllers, ac controllers exhibit natural regenerative braking without extra hardware, relays, or wires. Regenerative capabilities are all part of the controller and ac motor. Deceleration during regenerative breaking can be the same as acceleration; you can supply to the batteries as much current as you take out of them. It should be mentioned that a small number of dc systems, with the exception of a few controllers, do not offer this feature.

Ac controllers coupled with an ac motor provide a constant torque for a wide range of rpm. This supplies constant acceleration regardless of speed (within certain limits) and often allows your vehicle to use one gear ratio. The maximum shaft rpm

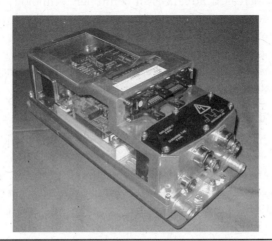

FIGURE 9-5 Siemens ac controller. (Courtesy of Metric Mind, www.metricmind.com.)

of a typical dc motor remains about twice as low as for an ac motor, requiring shifting gears in some cases, thus losing torque at the wheels. Normally, vehicles using dc systems have a higher gear ratio, gaining top-end speed but losing low-speed acceleration.

If your EV is heavy or you feel the need for reverse, this is accomplished easily with an ac controller. With a flip of a switch, the ac controller simply reverses the sequence of the motor phase, and your motor spins in reverse. Since having full power in reverse is unsafe, a simple programming change limits the speed and power in reverse. A dc system requires reversing contactors, not to mention that the brush advance is far from optimal when a dc motor runs in reverse if you have advanced the brush timing. At low speeds, however, it is not that critical for a dc drive; nevertheless, commutator and brush damage has been known to occur while driving a dc motor in reverse when its brushes are set in the advanced position for forward rotation (see Chapter 8).

Most ac controllers operate at elevated voltages, up to 400 V dc. The range of operating voltages varies from 24–450 V dc and above.[3] With high battery pack voltages, battery wiring becomes more flexible, and wire gauge size is reduced. This actually applies to high-voltage ac systems (typically using higher voltage and lower current than dc systems of the same power). Since resistive power losses are lower with high-voltage and low-current applications, vehicle efficiency increases. Typically, with a lower-voltage, higher-current system, you are forced to use heavy-gauge wire to carry the increased amperage. The heavier cable weighs more, needs larger connections, takes up more space, and costs more. Dc high-amperage systems require heavy and more costly welding cable and large, expansive relays and fuses.

Controllers on the Market Today

Today, with increased advances in controller technology, a vast array of motor controller types is available to consumers. In this section I will describe some of the controllers on the market. This is only a small list of what is out there for you. There are many more units to come. Use Chapter 14 to see the extent of various examples. In addition, use the online resource guide at vogelbilt.com for additional information and up-to-date releases as the EV world advances.

Series-Wound DC Controller

Still today, the most popular motor controllers are the series-wound dc motor controllers. They provide many features, are programmable, produce plenty of power, and are cost-effective. Even more important, the array of electric motors you can choose from to couple with your controller selection is huge. You will find a significant number of controllers offering features such as regenerative braking, programmability, and much more. I will briefly describe a few companies and controllers.

Curtis Instruments

When most people talk about motor controllers, Curtis is the first controller maker that comes to mind. Curtis Instruments, established in 1960 in Mt. Kisco, New York, has been a leader and at the forefront of developing clean transportation alternatives and EV technology. NASA used Curtis products for its lunar rover EV on Apollo missions and on experiments aboard the MIR space station. For almost 50 years, Curtis has manufactured an array of products from dc and ac controllers, to management systems, to gauges, to dc/dc converters, to battery chargers and much more. I personally worked for Curtis during 2001–2003 in Mt. Kisco. Curtis was a pleasure to work for, and my job filled me with pride. I worked alongside very talented people, such as George Mugno, in the battery-charger design and testing division, and Joe Mezzone, in the corporate building.

The very first prototype electric motorcycle I built, dubbed the "Electric Hog," used a Curtis 1231C controller. This bike was built in 2001 and became the basic design for the second prototype, now called the Electra Cruiser. The Curtis 1231 series controller worked great and provided plenty of power.

Basic Curtis Series-Wound Controller

This is Curtis' basic high-amperage, high-voltage series-wound dc motor controller (Models 1231C/1221C). This model (Figures 9-6 and 9-7) is the most popular among EV conversions. Curtis also offers similar models with lower operating voltages and amperage output.

FIGURE 9-6   Curtis Model 1231C 15-kHz PWM controller.

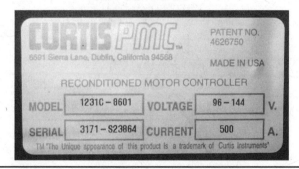

FIGURE 9-7   Curtis controller tag specifications for the Model 1231C.

Curtis Basic Series-Wound DC Specifications

Tables 9-1 and 9-2 list just some of the specifications for a few of the models offered by Curtis. Unit operating voltages range from 24 V dc all the way up to 144 V dc, with peak current output of 700 A on some models. Remember, this is only a fraction of the models offered by Curtis. Chapter 14 lists a few distributors and locations. Check the Curtis Web site or your local Curtis distributor for more models and information.

Installation and hookup are very simple. If you look closely at the controller's terminals (Figure 9-8), you will notice the markings M–, B–, B+, and A2. These correspond to the connections, M– for negative connection on the motor, B– and B+ for battery positive and negative connections, and A2 for motor armature (optional connection, not used on no-road vehicles).

Reduced-Speed Operation

With current-limit adjustment, vehicle top speed can be easily limited for safety or other reasons. A single resistor connected in parallel with the throttle pot will reduce maximum speed based on its resistance value. Use of a variable resistor makes adjustment of maximum speed easier. With a switch, speed can be limited in reverse only, or the speed reduction can be switched off, for example, to allow authorized personnel to run the vehicle or a valet switch to cut power back (Figure 9-9).

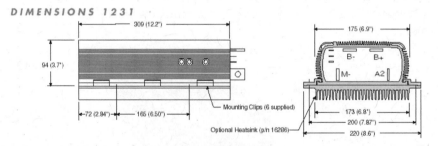

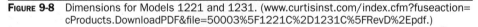

FIGURE 9-8   Dimensions for Models 1221 and 1231. (www.curtisinst.com/index.cfm?fuseaction=cProducts.DownloadPDF&file=50003%5F1221C%2D1231C%5FRevD%2Epdf.)

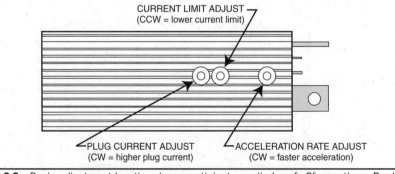

FIGURE 9-9   Basic adjustment location. (www.curtisinst.com/index.cfm?fuseaction=cProducts.DownloadPDF&file=50003%5F1221C%2D1231C%5FRevD%2Epdf.)

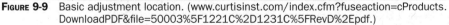

TABLE 9-1 Curtis 72- to 144-V Models 1221 and 1231

Curtis PMC Models	Voltage (Volts)	Current (Amps)	2 Min Rating (Amps)	5 Min Rating (Amps)	1 Hour Rating (Amps)	Voltage Drop @ 100 A	Undervolt Cutback (Volts)
1231C-86XX	96–144	500	500	375	225	.30	64
1231C-77XX	72–120	550	220	375	225	.30	43
1221C-74XX	72–120	400	400	250	150	.50	43

curtisinst.com/index.cfm?fuseaction=cProducts.dspProductCategory&catID=11

TABLE 9-2 Curtis 12- to 48-V Model 1204 and 1205

Curtis PMC Models	Voltage (Volts)	Current (Amps)	2 Min Rating (Amps)	5 Min Rating (Amps)	1 Hour Rating (Amps)	Voltage Drop @ 100 A	Undervolt Cutback (Volts)
1204-0xx	24–36	275	275	200	125	0.35	16
1204-1xx	24–36	175	175	130	75	0.50	16
1204-4xx	36–48	275	275	200	125	0.35	21
1204S-54xx	36–48	450	450 (30 sec)	300	150	0.25	21
1204-6xx	12	275	275	200	125	0.35	9
1205-1xx	24–36	400	400	275	175	0.25	16

curtisinst.com/index.cfm?fuseaction=cProducts.dspProductCategory&catID=11

Throttle Ramp Shaping

Throttle ramp shaping affects the PWM output response relative to the throttle position. The more ramp shaping the throttle circuitry has, the more control the operator has over low speed (see Figure 9-9).

Plug Braking

This feature uses the dc electric motor to slow the vehicle down, much like regenerative braking, but without placing energy back in the batteries. The current is routed back into the dc motor armature, creating a braking force. *Note:* Plug braking is not recommended for on-road EVs. The plug-braking feature is intended for materials handling and low-speed, low-load applications only. Plug braking can be completely eliminated by not attaching a power cable to the A2 terminal on the controller and the A2 terminal on the dc motor (see Figure 9-9).

Basic DC Motor Controller Circuitry Layout

Figure 9-12 provides you with a glimpse at the basic working and functional controls contained within the controller. Speed control is achieved by what is called the *throttle potbox* (Figures 9-10 and 9-11). The potbox has a standard variable 0- to 5-kΩ resistance.

The 0- to 5-kΩ resistance is standard for most motor controller throttle controls (a 5-kΩ pot wired as a two-terminal rheostat). A Curtis PMC potbox or any 5-kΩ pot will work fine. For controllers with other input options, you can use other optional throttles for the vehicle. See Chapter 11 for accessories.

Basic DC Controller Vehicle Wiring Layout

Figures 9-13 through 9-16 display the most basic of wiring and layout of components for your EV conversion. This is only a sample, and your wiring may differ depending

FIGURE 9-10 Potbox (Curtis PB-6). (www.curtisinst.com.)

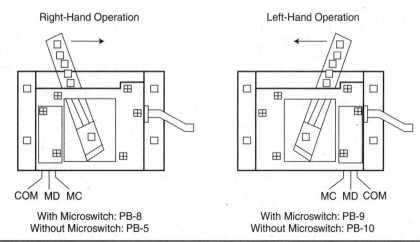

Right-Hand Operation

Left-Hand Operation

COM MD MC

MC MD COM

With Microswitch: PB-8
Without Microswitch: PB-5

With Microswitch: PB-9
Without Microswitch: PB-10

FIGURE 9-11 Curtis potbox showing micro switch and left or right hand operation. (www.curtisinst.com.)

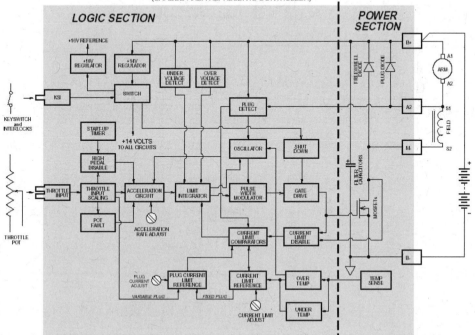

FIGURE 9-12 Typical block diagram for Curtis Model 1209B/1221B/1221C/1231C controllers. (www.curtisinst.com)

on your vehicle, motor, and controller type. This example is a good place to start and is the most basic of all conversion wiring. In this diagram, the cable from the A2 terminal on the motor controller, connecting to the A2 lug on the dc motor, would be removed on most on-road EVs. This connection controls the plug-braking capability of the controller, which you will not need. In Chapter 12 I will explain in more detail the wiring for your EV and important safety precautions.

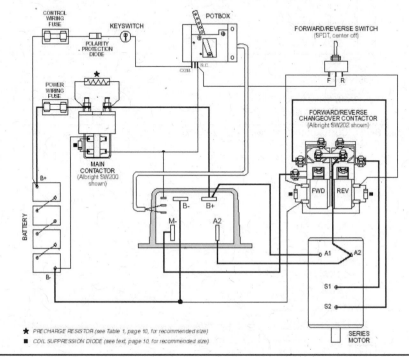

★ *PRECHARGE RESISTOR (see Table 1, page 10, for recommended size)*
■ *COIL SUPPRESSION DIODE (see text, page 10, for recommended size)*

FIGURE 9-13   Typical wiring diagram using a Curtis series dc controller. (www.curtisinst.com/index.cfm?fuseaction=cProducts.DownloadPDF&file=50003%5F1221C%2D1231C%5FRevD%2Epdf.)

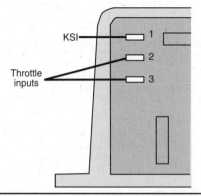

FIGURE 9-14   Curtis Model 1221/1231 series potbox connections. (www.curtisinst.com/index.cfm?fuseaction=cProducts.DownloadPDF&file=50003%5F1221C%2D1231C%5FRevD%2Epdf.)

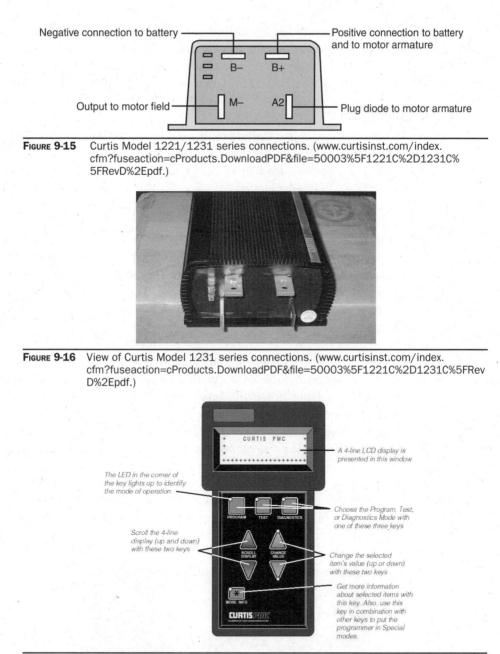

Negative connection to battery

Positive connection to battery and to motor armature

B−   B+

Output to motor field

M−   A2

Plug diode to motor armature

FIGURE 9-15   Curtis Model 1221/1231 series connections. (www.curtisinst.com/index. cfm?fuseaction=cProducts.DownloadPDF&file=50003%5F1221C%2D1231C% 5FRevD%2Epdf.)

FIGURE 9-16   View of Curtis Model 1231 series connections. (www.curtisinst.com/index. cfm?fuseaction=cProducts.DownloadPDF&file=50003%5F1221C%2D1231C%5FRev D%2Epdf.)

CURTIS PMC

A 4-line LCD display is presented in this window

The LED in the corner of the key lights up to identify the mode of operation

Choose the Program, Test, or Diagnostics Mode with one of these three keys

Scroll the 4-line display (up and down) with these two keys

Change the selected item's value (up or down) with these two keys

Get more information about selected items with this key. Also, use this key in combination with other keys to put the programmer in Special modes.

FIGURE 9-17   Curtis programmer. (www.curtisinst.com/index.cfm?fuseaction=cProducts. dspProductCategory&catID=7.)

You will find that Curtis Instruments has an array of motor controllers in many sizes and power ratings to suit your needs. These are just a few of the lineup offered to you and the most popular models used for EV conversions. This is not to say that other models are not as popular in the Curtis lineup. For your vehicle conversion, smaller motor controller models are available with more programmable features. Curtis offers a programming module to vary and control the parameters of other models (Figure 9-17). You also will find that Curtis offers controllers for permanent-magnet motors separately excited (shunt) motors, as well as many ac controllers.

ZAPI Controllers

ZAPI, an Italian company, began manufacturing electronic controls in 1975.[4] ZAPI's early product offerings included permanent-magnet and dc series controllers, and soon the company began to lead in technological advancements in controller design. Since 1995, ZAPI has developed an entire range of ac controllers from 24–96 V. ZAPI currently offers a large product line of all types of controllers ranging from 24–144 V and much more.

I have personally used a Zapi H2 controller designed for dc series-wound motors since 2003 on the Electra Cruiser (Figure 9-18). The H2 controller has functioned flawlessly for 5 years without a hiccup. This controller operates on 120 V dc and puts out about 450–500 A to the dc motor. There were many reasons I chose this motor controller for the new motorcycle. The main reason was its regenerative-braking feature.

While riding with the ZAPI controller on the Electra Cruiser, the bike was able to freewheel as long as the throttle was just barely on. With release of the throttle controller, it enters regen mode similar to that of compression on an internal combustion engine, slowing down the bike. Then, with use of the brake, the stoplight switch, connected to another input on the controller, creates a second mode, further reducing speed by increasing the amount of regenerative current back into the battery pack. The regenerative braking was a big factor and worked very well. The other reasons were price, reputation, size, and the many programmable features included standard with the controller. This controller has more features than I could list in this chapter. The manual takes some reading to grasp all the features. I was very pleased with the smooth throttle control and response, dependability, and smooth regenerative braking.

Figure 9-18   ZAPI dc series motor controller.

ZAPI DC Series Motor Controller

The ZAPI H2 dc controller series is very similar to the Curtis controller in basic functions, PWM, and switching frequency of 15 kHz, but that is where the comparison stops. I chose the ZAPI mainly for the regenerative-braking feature, a rarity at the time, and for the power output. The ZAPI controller came with numerous features and programming options. I even bought the digital programming console to take full advantage of every feature. The programmer plugs into the front of the controller through a serial connection (Figure 9-19).

You will need to read the manual for the ZAPI controller thoroughly. There, you will find a lot of information about how to operate and program it properly. Wiring for the ZAPI is the similar to, if not the same as, the Curtis wiring ciagram in Figure 9-13. Always refer to the manufacturer's manual and specifications because all things may appear similar, but some specifications and wiring possibly will change. ZAPI offers a line of motor controllers for permanent-magnet motors and separately excited (shunt) motors, as well as many ac controllers. The company also offers other accessories designed for all the motor controllers and products it manufactures.

Figure 9-19   ZAPI digital programming console. (www.zapi.co.za/zapi/images/ programmingconsole.jpg.)

Navitas Technologies

Navitas Technologies manufactures a line of series-wound, brushed permanent-magnet, and separately excited motor controllers.[5] The controllers combine the power of high-efficiency MOSFETs with microprocessor technology to provide flexible and adjustable control in a compact design. Some controllers use a 20-kHz switching frequency for smoother operation; other controllers use frequencies of 15–18 kHz. Certain controllers in the Navitas line offer regenerative-braking capabilities and do not require the use of directional contactors. The TPM series of controllers is user-configurable through a Controller Area Network (CAN) interface. See the company Web site for more information.

The TPM 400 series is designed for use with brushed permanent-magnet motors with a drive capacity of up to 400 A peak at 24–48 V dc (Figures 9-20 and 9-21). TPM controllers offer regenerative-braking capabilities and do not require the use of directional contactors. TPM controllers are also user-configurable through a CAN

FIGURE 9-20   Navitas Technologies TPM400 series permanent-magnet motor controller. (www.navitastechnologies.com.)

FIGURE 9-21   Navitas Technologies TPM400 series motor controller. (www.navitastechnologies.com.)

interface. They are fully programmable with the Navitas PC Probit programming package.

The TSE series of series-wound controllers offers

- Up to 1,000 A peak armature current
- Up to 325 A continuous armature current
- Safe sequencing and power-up diagnostics
- Full programmability with the Navitas Probit hand-held programming pendant technology to provide smooth, flexible, and reliable control (Table 9-3)

TABLE 9-3 Navitas Technologies Series-Wound Controller Specifications

Model	System Voltage	Peak Armature Rating	Continuous Rating	Throttle Types
TSE1000-48	24–48	1,000 amps	325 amps	Resistive/Voltage
TSE550-48	24–48	550 amps	175 amps	Resistive/Voltage
TSE600-96	60–96	600 amps	260 amps	Resistive/Voltage

http://www.navitastechnologies.com/wound.html

Alltrax DC Motor Controllers

Alltrax manufactures a line of controllers with an impressive number of features. The founders of Alltrax are dedicated to EVs and their advancement. The company founders, Damon Crockett (a power electronics engineer of 26 years from Klamath Falls, Oregon) and Jeff Bradley, have developed high-power motor controllers for electric racing vehicles and many other applications. A few of these powerful electric race cars had the capability of dumping 750,000 W of power into two motors during an 8-second ¼-mile run down the race track (Figure 9-22). Obviously, this requires controllers that can handle the extremes!

FIGURE 9-22 Corbin Sparrow with a high-performance Alltrax controller. (www.alltraxinc.com/images/sparrow.jpg.)

Following is a timeline of developments:

1996: Mr. Damon Crockett formed a company called DCP, with a focus on providing the EV racing market with an alternative to compete against the gasoline engine's counterparts.

1996: DCP race car controllers:
- Raptor 600 A
- Raptor 1,200 A
- Operating voltages of 48–156 V dc

1997: DCP race car controllers:
- T-Rex 600 A
- T-Rex 1,000 A
- Operating voltages of 96–240 V dc

Alltrax controllers are fully encapsulated, waterproof, and corrosion-resistant, and some models are fully user-programmable (Figure 9-23). Spanning 12–72 V dc from 150–650 A, series-wound, permanent-magnet, and separately excited wound motors should satisfy many of your requirements. These products come with a 2-year warranty and tons of support materials.[6]

The AXE product line is used with series-wound and brushed permanent-magnet motors. These units power golf carts, scissors lifts, boom trucks, neighborhood electric vehicles, and a number of other applications. Their design, compact size, and capabilities are perfect for a motorcycle. Features include

- Programmability via an RS232 communications port using a PC or laptop
- Integrated anodized heat sink with multibolt pattern for flexibility
- Fully encapsulated epoxy-fill environmentally rugged design
- Available in 300- to 650-A performance versions

Figure 9-23   Alltrax controller. (www.alltraxinc.com/images/AXE042-s.jpg.)

- Advanced MOSFET power transistor design for excellent efficiency and power transfer
- Half-speed reverse option and plug-brake options available

The Alltrax controller uses standard connections similar to other major manufacturers of motor controllers (Figure 9-24). What I like very much about Alltrax is the company's dedication to the customer and customer support. First off, on the company Web site you can find many documents, technical information, and just all the things you want and expect to find. If this were not enough, customer support, as Alltrax states, "is the most important aspect of our business, and we are committed to provide the best-possible customer support with a live voice at the other end."

LED Status Indicator

The light-emitting diode (LED) located on the front of the unit indicates the status of the units and is used for easy visible troubleshooting (Figure 9-25).

The LED blink codes occur at power-up; the number of green blinks indicates the throttle configuration:

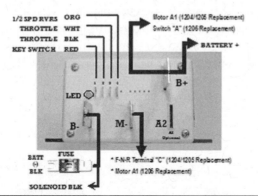

FIGURE 9-24 Typical Alltrax wiring layout. (www.alltraxinc.com/images/AXE-Wire-Diagram.gif.)

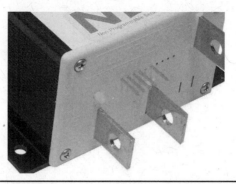

FIGURE 9-25 Alltrax LED status indicator. (www.alltraxinc.com/sitebuilder/images/NCX-LED2-150x107.jpg.)

- 1 green LED flash = 0–5 kΩ resistive
- 2 green LED flashes = 5–0 kΩ resisitive
- 3 green LED flashes = 0–5 V
- 4 green LED flashes = EZ-GO inductive (ITS)
- 5 green LED flashes = Yamaha 0–1 kΩ resistive
- 6 green LED flashes = Taylor-Dunn 6–10.5 V
- 7 green LED flashes = ClubCar 5–0 kΩ, three-wire throttle

Normal display status shows

- Solid green: Controller ready to run
- Solid red: Controller in programming mode (using Controller Pro)
- Solid yellow: Controller throttle is wide open and controller is supplying maximum output and is not in current limit

Programmability

Programmable Alltrax electric motor controllers such as the AXE (series-wound motors) and the DCX (shunt-wound motors) include an RS232 communications port. This port can be used to adjust user settings such as throttle type, power settings, and speed settings. It also can be used to monitor operation of the controller in real time. Alltrax has an added benefit to the customer supplies: All the software is downloadable for free from the Web site (Figure 9-26).

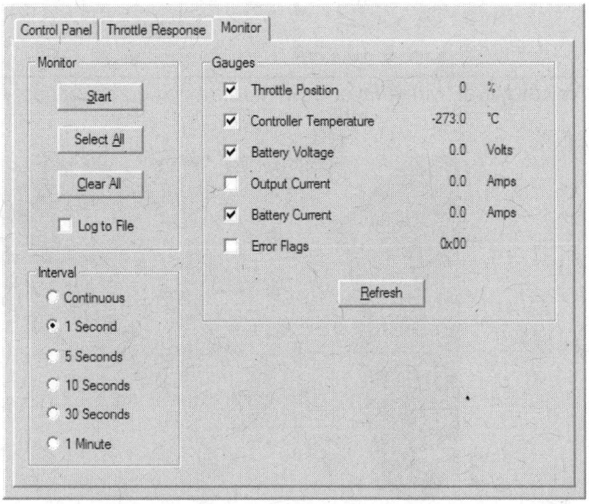

FIGURE 9-26   Alltrax Controller-Pro software. (www.alltraxinc.com/images/Controller-Pro-Screen-Control.gif.)

AC Controllers

With recent advancements in technology, ac controllers are now available in many sizes and types (Figure 9-27). This is great news for the EV enthusiast.

New ac induction motor speed controllers represent the next level in drive systems for all types of EVs, offering lower maintenance, higher performance, and greater flexibility. The ac controllers are compact in size and have fully sealed, waterproof housings. The ac controllers combine many advanced features with programmable logic controllers to provide users with more flexibility and advanced motor controller technology.[7]

For many years, the ac controller was a large, expensive system available or usable only for exotic high-performance EVs. Most were designed for use with very high voltages, with some units bearing a price tag in excess of $25,000. This has all changed. New designs in ac controllers are compact in size, from 6–10 in. long, 4 in. high, and 9 in. wide; some are even smaller (Figure 9-28).

FIGURE 9-27 Curtis Model 1230 basic ac controller.

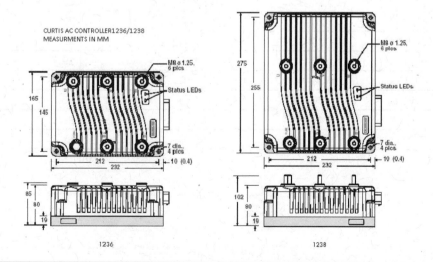

FIGURE 9-28   Curtis Model 1236/38AC controller dimensions. (www.curtisinst.com/index.cfm?fuseaction=cProducts.DownloadPDF&file=50095%5F1236%2D1238%5FRevG1%2E pdf.)

The new ac controllers can operate at lower voltages, ranging from 24–80 V dc and up. These same controllers have peak current outputs in the range of 150–650 V ac or more. An ac controller converts the dc battery power into low-voltage three-phase ac power while simultaneously controlling motor torque speed and direction. As an added bonus, you no longer need costly direction contactors and additional wiring. This is all handled within the motor controller. The vector-controlled algorithms provide high-torque startup conditions with both four- and six-pole three-phase induction motors. In many applications, the performance exceeds that of conventional dc systems.

Curtis Instruments AC Controllers

Curtis instruments has a full line of ac controllers for many applications. They include advanced motor-drive software to provide smooth control over full speed and torque in all modes. The ac controllers include full regenerative-braking capabilities, zero speed, and torque control. The controllers, depending on the model, have an operating voltage of 24–80 V dc and a maximum peak current output of up to 650 A ac. These controllers are fully programmable through Curtis's optional 1311 hand-held programmer or 1314 PC programming station. Table 9-4 lists the chart specifications for Curtis ac controller models. The programmer provides diagnostic and test capability in addition to configuration flexibility (Figure 9-30).

Table 9-4   Curtis AC Controller Chart Specifications

Model	Battery Voltage (V)	2 Min RMS Current Rating Arms (A)	2 Min RMS Power Rating (kWA)
1236-44-XX	24–36	400	16.6
1236-45-XX	24–36	500	20.9
1238-46-XX	24–36	650	25.4
1236-53-XX	36–48	350	19.7
1238-54-XX	36–48	450	25.5
1238-56-XX	36–48	650	36.3
1236-63-XX	48–80	300	28.1
1238-65-XX	48–80	550	51.3

http://curtisinst.com/index.cfm?fuseaction=cProducts.dspProductCategory&catID=8

The Curtis Model 840 LCD Multifunction display contains 8 large, easy to read characters to provide display of battery discharge (BDI), hour meter and error messages. Built-in back-light is also available.

The Curtis Model 1311 Handheld Programmer is ideal for setting parameters and performing diagnostic functions.

Figure 9-29 Curtis controller accessories. (www.curtisinst.com/index.cfm?fuseaction=cProducts. dspProductCategory&catID=25.)

These controllers show major performance, operational, and system advancements over dc, such as

- High-frequency silent operation from 0–300 Hz
- 24- to 80-V battery systems with 350–650 A rms 2-minute current ratings
- Powerful operating system that allows parallel processing of vehicle control tasks, motor control tasks, and user-configurable programmable logic
- Advanced PWM technology that provides efficient use of battery voltage, low motor harmonics, low torque ripple, and minimized switching losses
- Tunability to any ac motor and full programmability for optimal match to individual ac motor characteristics
- Built-in battery state-of-charge algorithms and hour meter
- Field-programmability with Flash downloadable main operating code

Superb Drive Control

- Field-oriented vector control in conjunction with Curtis tuned algorithms, providing peak torque and optimal efficiency across the entire operating range
- Extremely wide torque/speed range, including full regeneration capability
- Internal closed-loop speed and torque control modes that allow for optimized performance—without an additional control box
- Peak performance mapping technology that lets you tune the maximum performance envelope in both "driving" and "braking" to your specific application through the use of original equipment manufacturers (OEM) programmable parameters
- A torque control mode that offers unique features and provides seamless transition and positive response under all conditions

If you look closely at the wiring and controller diagram (Figure 9-30), you will notice many other functions. The controller incorporates internal and external watchdog circuits to ensure proper operation. There is a serial interface for multifunction display to work with the Curtis 840 Spyglass display for hour meter, battery discharge monitoring, and fault messages. Several inputs and outputs monitor other functions, including safety interlocks (Figure 9-30). You will find an additional input to monitor motor temperature. In the manual, there are just too many features to list. With that said, you can do a lot more with ac controllers than with dc controllers.

ZAPI AC Motor Controllers

ZAPI manufactures high-quality ac motor controllers for many applications. Because of the great success I experienced with the Zapi dc controller and the good reviews on all the company's other products, it was only fitting that I include the ac

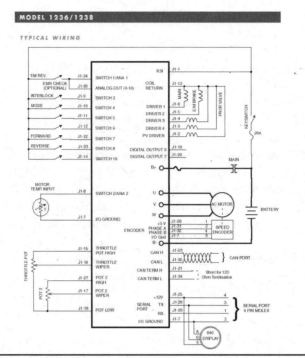

FIGURE 9-30   Curtis Model 1236/38 controller functions. (www.curtisinst.com/index. cfm?fuseaction=cProducts.DownloadPDF&file=50095%5F1236%2D1238%5FRevG1 %2Epdf.)

controller. ZAPI controllers are offered in voltages ranging from 24–96 V dc in various sizes. Amperage output ranges from 150 A on smaller units up to 550 A on the largest units.

The AC3 and the AC4 asynchronous motor controllers represent the latest state of the art technology (e.g., IMS power module, Flash memory, microprocessor logic, and CAN bus). Both the AC3 and the AC4 are very similar accept the AC4 and have a larger power output (Figure 9-31).

The AC3 and the AC4 are rated for asynchronous motors up to 16 and 20 kW, respectively. Depending on the model, operating voltages are 36, 48, 72, 80, and 96 V dc. These controllers have a number of features, as you can see below:

FIGURE 9-31   ZAPI AC3 ac controller.

Power Section ZAPI AC4

- Power supply: 36, 48, 72, 80, 96 V
- Maximum current:
  - (36, 48 V) 750 A
  - (72, 80 V) 650 A
  - (96 V) 450 A
- Continuous output power:
  - (48 V) 12,000 W
  - (80 V) 16,000 W
- Switching frequency: 8 kHz
- Ambient temperature range: –40 to +40°C
- Maximum heat-sink temperature: 75°C (starts to reduce current)

Mechanics

- Dimensions: 264 × 352 × 111 mm (Figure 9-32)
- Connector: Molex Minifit/Amp Saab/Amp Ampseal
- Protection: IP65 (IP54)
- Available with Al baseplate or with finned heat sink

Input/Output

- 9 digital inputs (input range: –Batt to +Batt)
- 3 analog inputs (input range: 0–12 V)
- 1 incremental encoder port
- 2 outputs driving to –Batt
- LC driver 1.5 A continuous
- EB driver 1.5 A continuous

FIGURE 9-32   ZAPI AC3 ac controller size compared with the Curtis 1231.

Other Features

- 16-bit microcontroller
- Flash memory
- CAN interface
- Serial link

This is just a small list of the ac controllers on the market. Many more styles and types are available. This should serve as a good starting point for general information on a few different units.

Metric Mind Engineering

In addition to these units, you can find high-end ac controllers and motors at Metric Mind Engineering. Metric Mind Engineering offers an array of great high-end ac controllers and motors made in Germany and Switzerland. These are some of the best units on the market, and their prices reflect the quality. Some of these units are reasonably priced for the quality you are receiving.

Many of the systems are liquid-cooled synchronous and induction three-phase ac motors. These motors have a power rating of up to 82 kW and peak power ratings two to four times that, often limited only by the inverter. These same ac motors have an rpm range hitting 11,000 rpm or more. The ac motor controller systems are even more impressive. The ac controllers, depending on the model, have an operating voltage of 80–960 V dc with a maximum peak-power output of 212 kW (~162 hp) or more. These systems are manufactured by BRUSA (of Switzerland) and MES-DEA. Some earlier systems supplied by Metric Mind Engineering were made by Siemens.

In the summer of 2004, I drove out to Portland, Oregon, along with my Electra Cruiser in tow to visit Victor Tikhonov, president of Metric Mind Engineering. Victor was very helpful when I was putting together a high-end ac system originally designated for the second-generation Electra Cruiser. I bought from Victor a 100-hp, 10,000-rpm, 400-V ac motor and system ready to go into the newly designed Cruiser. I was excited! Along with that, I bought 100 lithium batteries. Unfortunately, I was way ahead of my time with the lithium batteries. I realized not long into designing the new electric motorcycle (I had not built it yet) that there were no BMSs on the market to handle 100 batteries. The manufacturer of the batteries had said that a system was available. After checking, the only one I could find had a quoted price of $30,000 in 2004. That was not an option, so I went back to the old tried and true dc power system for this build.

Below you will find some example of the BRUSA and MES-DEA systems. I am truly impressed with the quality, durability, and options of these units. You can rest assured that the next build and third-generation Electra Cruiser will have one of these high-powered ac units in it.

All the inverters listed below from MES-DEA and BRUSA are liquid-cooled and provide regenerative-braking recuperating energy back to the traction battery. The output power stage is implemented with insulated gate bipolar transistors (IGBTs), either discrete for older designs or as highly integrated modules with thermal management and driver built in. Currently, several MES-DEA and BRUSA models are offered.

MES-DEA TIM Series

The MES-DEA series of ac controllers offers ac power output ratings from 30–200 kW peak power.[8] Maximum input voltage is 400 V dc with a lower limit of 80 V dc. Note that at the lower input voltage, the inverter will function at a reduced maximum output power rating. Input battery current is limited to 550 A for the larger TIM Model 900. The maximum ac current output is 500/700 A ac for the TIM 900 (Figure 9-33). Looking at the dimensions of these units, and it is apparent that they are really not that big given all the options packed inside (Figure 9-34). For a larger motorcycle build, you just might be able to fit one of these powerhouses in. I know that the Electra Cruiser had just enough to fit a similar Siemens ac system in the plastic tank.

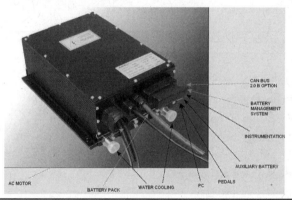

FIGURE 9-33   MES-DEA TIM Series TIM 300 (30 kW), TIM 400 (50 kW), TIM 600 (100 kW), and TIM 900 (200 kW) view and connection description. (www.metricmind.com.)

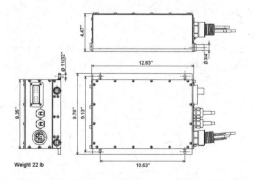

FIGURE 9-34   MES-DEA TIM series ac motor controller dimensions. (www.metricmind.com.)

BRUSA Series DMC514

The DMC514 is one of BRUSA's lower power output models in comparison with the lineup of other units. A unit such as this would make for an insane-performing motorcycle. The smaller unit is offered with 53 kW of output power. The three-phase power inverter operates on 120–460 V dc input voltage with a nominal power 40-kW output (Figure 9-35; see also Table 9-5).

FIGURE 9.35   BRUSA DMC size: 10 × 9.5 × 3.5 in (255 × 240 × 88 mm), 14.3 lb (6.5 kg) (with coolant). (www.brusa.biz/assets/downloads/manuals/DMC524_04.pdf.)

TABLE 9-5   Technical Characteristics of the BRUSA DMC514 (Carl Vogel– www.metricmind.com)

Power	53	kW
Input dc voltage (including HV supply voltage)		
Typical input dc under voltage shown	100	V
Minimum input dc voltage for operation	120	V
Minimum input dc voltage for full current capability	200	V
Maximum input dc voltage for operation	460	V
Typical input dc over-voltage shutdown	480	V
Maximum input dc surviving voltage	520	V
Three phase ac output		
Continuus RMS current	112	A
Repetitive maximum RMS current 30 seconds 100%, 90 seconds 50%	150	A
Peak RMS current derating vs. T coolant >65°	−8	A/°C
Continuous power (V dc = 75%; V dc maximum; IAC = IAC cont, cos phi = 0.9)	40	kW
Maximum power (V dc = 75%; V dc maximum; IAC = IAC maximum, cos phi = 0.9)	53	kW
PWM frequency (symmetrical modulation)	24	kHz
Efficiency (V dc = 75%; V dc maximum, PAC = PAC cont, cos 0.97 phi = 0.9)		

Conclusion

The list of controllers, both dc and ac, is just a small glimpse of the options available to convert your vehicle to all-electric. This chapter packed in a lot of selections and options. Even with all that I covered, there are a lot more controllers and information out there. If you look at Chapter 14, you will discover many more companies and options. With this information, you should have enough knowledge to find the additional resources needed to choose the right controller for you.

CHAPTER 10

The Charger and Battery Management System

The charger is the one component often overlooked in terms of the real importance it plays in your electric vehicle (EV). As you learned back in Chapter 7, the charger plays a significant part in keeping your vehicle performing well. In most cases, EV batteries are damaged not just by improper usage but also by bad charging techniques above all other causes combined.

Your batteries are one of the core components of your EV that need proper care for longevity and performance. You would not place a brand-new motor in your vehicle and use the cheapest low-grade motor oil in it; it would not last for the long haul and would be a waste of time and money. The same goes here. You invest a considerable amount of money in a great battery system, and thus you should use a proper charger and charging technique. Otherwise, you risk losing on the long-term investment in your batteries. Think of the charger as the lifeline of your EV. Each day you bring your batteries to the brink of death. Your charger is the one component that will breathe life, longevity, and performance back into your EV, ensuring your investment and your EV's continued performance.

In this chapter you will learn about the different types of chargers and how they interact with your batteries. I will supply you with the basic knowledge you need to select the right charger for your application. We will look at the charging infrastructure and what may be available in our future. Additionally, we will look at battery management systems (BMSs) and the roll they play. At the time of this writing, the United States elected a new forward-thinking president, has enacted new policies, and is providing money for advancing green energy and technology. I hope that we can look back one day with pride at all the great changes.

Charger Overview

In Chapter 7 we learned all about the batteries. Now it's time to dive into the charger. The charger is worth investing a little time and money into if you plan to keep your EV for any period of time. You may replace your battery pack a few times before you replace your charger, so you may as well invest in a charger that will perform well now and for years to come.

Today, your choice of battery chargers is far greater than what was available to EV owners in the past. You have greater opportunities, choices, and selections. I will guide you through and help you to make the best choice of a charger that is right for your system. Today, chargers are not the large, heavy units of the past with transformers and huge coils of wire. Most chargers now are compact units that use solid-state electronics. They are referred to as *smart chargers*, and many are fully programmable with software tailored specifically to your EV.

Charger Checklist

I cannot overemphasize the importance of matching the correct charger with your batteries and battery technology. All battery chargers are not alike. Use of an inappropriate charger will shorten your batteries' life or even kill them outright. In specifying a charger for your EV, we will examine many important factors.

Fundamentals

- An important requirement for your charger is that it should be the correct one for your battery chemistry and battery pack. If you have lead-acid or advanced technology batteries such as lithium batteries, the charger needs to be capable of charging them properly.
- If possible, look for a charger that is programmable or one for which you have control of the charging profile. Some chargers can be changed or programmed right from the distributor or manufacturer for your batteries with a charging profile to match. Others allow you to control and change the charging profile via a link to your computer.
- There should be some system to protect against overcharging. This is not a mandatory item, and most chargers cut back or shut down when they reach a threshold voltage. Some advanced chargers have inputs to read battery temperature and will adjust the charging accordingly. This is something you may want on advanced battery systems.
- What is your power source? Are you using 110 V ac or 220 V dc?
- Will you have more than one charger?
- Will you have an onboard charger and a stationary charger? You will need to identify the requirements for both.
- Will you want opportunity charging or short charging periods during lunch or other stops. Will this be normal charging or fast charging? Remember, every charging cycle, whether 1 hour or overnight for 8 hours, counts as 1 cycle and takes away from the cycle life of your batteries. This is much like an ATM charge; no matter how much money you take out, you are still

getting charged the fee. You might want to make that charging cycle count when you can.

- You may opt to be totally off the grid and use solar or wind sources or a combination of these.

Your charger has three main functions:

- Getting the charge into the battery in a safe manner and in a specific time (charging)
- Monitoring and optimizing the charging rate (stabilizing)
- Knowing when to stop charging to prevent over- or undercharging (terminating)

Charging Times

During rapid charging, energy is pumped into the battery faster than the chemical process can react to it. This can have damaging results in many ways. First, the chemical action in the battery, as you learned in Chapter 7, cannot take place instantaneously. The electrolyte closest to the electrodes in the battery is being converted, or "charged," before the electrolyte and electrode further away. Excessively high rates of charging create heat, gassing, and internal pressure. In a controlled manner, some heat is tolerable and will hasten the chemical conversion process in the battery. Charging times and rate of current need to be tailored to the capacity of the battery to receive a charge.

Charging and Optimization

During the normal charging sequence, the charger may follow a charging program and monitor charging voltage and/or temperature. Under normal circumstances, the charger will bring the battery to its charging voltage and cut back at a predetermined point to a finishing charging profile until complete. If for any reason there is a risk of overcharging the battery, either from errors or from abuse, this normally would be accompanied by a rise in temperature. This condition within the battery or high ambient temperatures also can take a battery beyond its safe operating temperature limits or cell voltage. Elevated temperatures advance the grim reaper of death for batteries. Monitoring the cell temperature is a good way to detect early signs of trouble. The temperature signal or other warning device can be used to turn off or cut back the charger when danger signs appear. This is particularly important when using exotic or high-power batteries, where the consequences of failure can be both serious and expensive.

End of Charge Cycle (Termination)

The most important job of the charger is to detect and determine when to cut back and finish the charging cycle. Detecting this cutoff point and terminating the charge are critical in preserving battery life. Once the battery reaches a fully charged state, the charging current has to be dissipated somehow. The result of continued charging is the generation of heat and gases, both of which are bad for batteries. The sign of a good charger is the ability to detect when charging is complete and stop the charging process before any damage is done. In the basics of many chargers, this is when a predetermined upper voltage limit is reached, often called the *termination voltage*. This is particularly important with fast chargers, where the danger of overcharging is greater.

Charge Efficiency

Charge acceptance and charge time are considerably influenced by temperature, as just noted. Lower temperature increases charge time and reduces charge acceptance. Note that at low temperatures the battery will not necessarily receive a full charge, even though the terminal voltage may indicate a full charge.

Charging Methods

Next, we will review some of the basic charging methods used by different chargers.[1] Some charging methods have certain advantages depending on battery type. Given your battery chemistry, you may need a particular charging profile. When selecting your charger, make sure that you know the requirements and charging profile of your batteries so that you can match the two. This will ensure extended performance, battery cycles, and the life of your battery, let alone provide worry-free charging and safety.

Constant-current chargers vary the voltage they apply to the battery to maintain a constant current flow, switching off when the voltage reaches the level of a full charge. This design is usually used for nickel-cadmium and nickel–metal hydride cells or batteries.

Constant-voltage chargers are basically dc power supplies, which in their simplest form may consist of a stepdown transformer from the mains with a rectifier to provide the dc voltage to charge the battery. Such simple designs are often found in cheap car battery chargers. The lead-acid cells used for cars and backup power systems typically use constant-voltage chargers. In addition, lithium-ion cells often use constant-voltage systems, although these usually are more complex with added circuitry to protect both the batteries and the user.

Taper-current chargers supply a crude, unregulated constant-voltage source. This is not a controlled charge. The current diminishes as the cell voltage builds up. With these systems, there is a serious danger of damaging the cells through overcharging. To avoid this, the charging rate and duration should be limited. This type of charging is suitable for large industrial lead-acid batteries only.

Pulsed chargers feed current to the battery in pulses. During the charging process, short rest periods of 20–30 ms between pulses allow the chemical action in the battery to stabilize by equalizing the reaction throughout the bulk of the electrode before recommencing the charge. This enables the chemical reaction to keep pace with the rate of inputting of electrical energy. It is also claimed that this method can reduce unwanted chemical reactions at the electrode surface, such as gas formation and crystal growth.

IUI charging is a recently developed charging profile used in many new chargers. This type of charging is used for fast charging standard flooded lead-acid batteries. It is not suitable for all lead-acid batteries, though. Initially, the battery is charged at a constant (*I*) rate until the cell voltage reaches a preset value near the voltage at which gassing occurs. This first part of the charging cycle is known as the *bulk-charge phase*. When the preset voltage has been reached, the charger switches into the constant-voltage (*U*) phase, and the current drawn by the battery will drop gradually until it reaches another preset level. This second part of the cycle completes the normal charging of the battery at a slowly diminishing rate. Finally, the charger switches again into the constant-current mode (*I*), and the voltage continues to rise up to a new, higher preset limit, when the charger is switched off. This last phase is used to equalize the charge on the individual cells in the battery to maximize battery life.

Trickle chargers are designed to keep a battery fully charged while not being used. It is a way to compensate for the self-discharge of the battery. This type of charging is not suitable for some batteries, such as NiMH and lithium batteries, which can be damaged from overcharging. In some charger applications, the charger is programmed to switch to trickle charging when the battery is fully charged.

Opportunity Charging

Another possibility for charging or type of charging is opportunity charging. I have read and heard two different sides to the argument for this type of charging. It sounds like a good concept, if used properly. *Opportunity charging* is charging a battery during break time, lunchtime, or any opportunity that presents itself during the work day. This appears to be a great concept and a way to add a little more charge to your batteries to increase your range and keep your batteries way above the lower depth of discharge. I see this as a great opportunity for anyone who has to go shopping or just wants to stop somewhere for a short period.

What we have learned about charging and batteries is that we can place a large amount of charge in them during the initial charging phase as long as we stay below 80 percent of full charge. Owing to frequent charging and to limit battery gas generation, opportunity chargers normally are set to charge batteries up to 80–85 percent charge throughout the day and back to 100 percent once a day when you finish with the vehicle. For this to take place, special control electronics are needed to protect the batteries from overvoltage. Safeguards also need to be in place to protect the batteries from excessive heat. By avoiding complete discharge of the battery, cycle life can be increased.

Now this is one theory, but another theory says that opportunity charging adds abnormal heat during the charge cycle and one more cycle to the battery, reducing its life. Opportunity charging not only decreases the cycles of the battery life, but the heat added while charging causes additional damage to the plates, further accelerating battery death and reducing the expected cycles.

I believe that this needs more research to support or refute either theory. I would surmise that if a battery were near 80 percent depth of discharge (DOD) and opportunity charging was used, then yes, maybe we could count that as one cycle. But what if your DOD were only 30–40 percent and you topped the battery off to a DOD of only 20 percent? I would surmise that maybe we helped extend the life of the battery by keeping it from the lower DOD, where life and cycles are robbed from your battery.

Charge Efficiency

The *efficiency* of a charger refers to the actual energy available or the losses from input to output. Generally, chargers average 95–80 percent efficient. Newer solid-state chargers are much more efficient, reaching the 95 percent range. Older models with transformers and step-up and step-down transformers lose energy through heat loss and other inefficiencies. Also remember that you also will have losses in your battery from heat and resistance.

Charge acceptance and charge time are considerably influenced by temperature. Lower temperature increases charge time and reduces charge acceptance from your battery. At low temperatures during charging, the battery will not necessarily receive a full charge, even though the terminal voltage may indicate a full charge.

Battery Discharging Cycle

Let's observe the discharge cycle first to contrast what is happening to the parameters during charging. Capacity, cell voltage, and specific gravity all decrease with time as you discharge a battery. Figure 10-1 shows how these key parameters change (a standard temperature of 78°F is presumed):

- *Ampere-hours.* The measure of a battery's capacity and percent state of charge (the area under the line in this case) are shown decreasing linearly versus time from its full charge to its full discharge value.
- *Cell voltage.* Cell voltage predictably declines from its nominal 2.1-V fully charged value to its fully discharged value of 1.75 V.
- *Specific gravity.* Specific gravity decreases linearly (directly with the battery's discharging ampere-hour rate) from its full charge to its full discharge value.

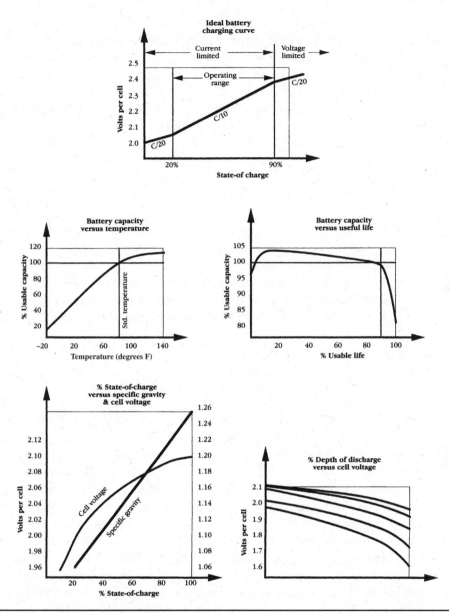

FIGURE 10-1   Graphic summary of battery discharging and charging cycles. (From *Build Your Own Electric Vehicle*, Table 9-1, p. 216.)

Battery Charging Cycle

Battery charging is the reverse of discharging. Figure 10-1 again shows you how the key parameters change:

- *Ampere-hours.* This is the opposite of the discharging case, except that you have to put back slightly more than you took out (typically 105–115 percent more) because of losses, heating, etc. The area under the line increases linearly versus time from its fully discharged value to its fully charged value.
- *Specific gravity.* Specific gravity increases wildly over time as a battery is charging, so making specific gravity measurements during the charging cycle is not a good idea. At the early part of the charging cycle, specific gravity increases slowly because the charging chemical reaction process is just starting. Specific gravity increases rapidly as the sulfuric acid concentration builds, and gassing near the end of the cycle contributes to its rise.
- *Cell voltage.* Voltage also increases wildly over time as a battery is charging, so making voltage measurements during the charging cycle is not a good idea either. Notice that cell voltage jumps up immediately to its natural 2.1-V value, slowly increases until 80 percent state of charge (approximately 2.35 V), increases rapidly until 90 percent state of charge (approximately 2.5 V), and then builds slowly to its full charging value of 2.58 V.

The Ideal Battery Charger

Battery charging is the reverse of discharging, but the rate at which you do it is crucial in determining battery lifetime. The basic rule is: Charge the battery as soon as it is discharged, and fill it all the way up. The charging-rate rule: Charge the battery slower at the beginning and end of the charging cycle (below 20 percent and above 90 percent). When a lead-acid battery is almost empty or almost full, its ability to store energy is reduced owing to changes in the cell's internal resistance. Attempting to charge it too rapidly during these periods causes gassing and increased heating within the battery, significantly reducing its life. Ideally, you limit battery current during the first 90 percent of the charging cycle and limit battery voltage during the last 10 percent of the charging cycle. Either method by itself doesn't do the job. The graph at the upper right in Figure 10-2 illustrates constant-voltage charging in the ideal case. The constant voltage is usually set at a level where gassing causes a decrease in current flow through the battery with time as the battery charges. Unfortunately, with no restrictions on current, this method allows far too much current to flow into an empty battery. Feeding 100 A or more of charging current into a fully discharged battery can damage it or severely reduce its life. Let's look at the ideal approach during all four state-of-charge (SOC) phases: 0–20 percent, 20–90 percent, 90–100 percent, and above 100 percent. Figure 10-2 shows the results.

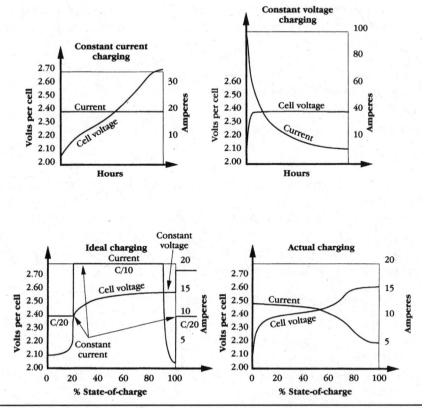

FIGURE 10-2   Graphic summary of battery discharging and charging cycles. (From *Build Your Own Electric Vehicle*, Figure 9-3, p. 211.)

Charging between 0 and 20 Percent

The first 20 percent of a fully discharged battery's charging cycle is a critical phase, and you want to treat it kindly.[2] You learned in Chapter 7 that all batteries have a standardized 20-hour capacity rating. Every battery is rated to deliver 100 percent of its rated capacity at the C/20 rate. During the first 20 percent of the charging cycle, you preferably want to charge a battery at no more than this constant-current C/20 rate. To determine the first 20 percent charging current, use the following equation:

$$\text{Charging current} = \text{battery capacity}/\text{time} - C/20$$

For a 200-Ah capacity battery, charging current would be

$$\text{Charging current} - 200/20 = 10 \text{ A}$$

In other words, you would limit this battery's preliminary charging current to 10 A. You can force your battery with 200 A and try to charge it in 1 hour, but you will reduce the cycle life and kill the battery—it will not deliver its full useful life cycles. The graph at the lower left in Figure 10-2 shows the result of current-limited C/20 rate charging during the first 20 percent part of the charging cycle. The voltage rises gently, and your battery sustains a simple, easy charge.

Charging between 20 and 90 Percent

In the middle of the charging cycle, you can charge at up to the C/10 rate. This is the fastest rate that efficiently charges a lead-acid battery. This rate is not as efficient as the C/20 rate—more energy is wasted in heat, but the battery charges faster. At even less efficiency (with more risk to your batteries), you can bump up the charging to the C/5 or C/3 rate during this period of recharging if time is essential to you and if you closely monitor the battery's temperature so that its operating limits are not exceeded and you don't wind up "cooking," or gassing, the battery. Charging current would be 20 A at the C/10 rate for a 200 Ah battery. Figure 10-2 shows that voltage, after a step increase when current settings were changed, rises slowly to its 90 percent SOC value of approximately 2.50 V.

Charging between 90 and 100 Percent

At this point, you want to drop back to the C/20 rate or, ideally, switch to a constant-voltage method. If you switch to constant voltage, set at the deep-cycle battery's full charging value of 2.58 V, Figure 10-2 shows the result—current provided to the battery drops rapidly during this last 10 percent of charging, and your battery is very happy while receiving its full charge.

Charging above 100 Percent (Equalizing Charging)

You learned about equalizing charging in Chapter 7. Equalizing is used to restore all cells to an equal SOC (to "equalize" the characteristics of the cells) to keep the battery operating at peak efficiency, to restore some capacity to aging batteries, to restore float-charged or shallow-charged batteries to regular service, and to eliminate the effects of sulfation in idle or discharged batteries. Equalizing charging is a controlled overcharging at a constant-current C/20 rate with the charging voltage limit raised to 2.75 V. Equalization is performed after the battery is fully charged and maintained at this level for 6–10 hours. Equalizing charging should not be done at rates greater than C/20. Also, equalizing charging should be done every 5–10 cycles or monthly (whichever comes first), but it should be done only in well-ventilated areas (with no sparks or smoking) because it produces substantial gassing. In addition, it should be done only while close attention is being paid to electrolyte level because water consumption is substantial during rapid gassing periods. Remember, gassing of a battery produces hydrogen, and it only takes a 4 percent concentration in the air to become explosive. Keep the batteries well ventilated. Figure 10-2 shows the step increase in voltage to 2.75 V and the increase in current back to the C/20 level.

Now let's look at the time involved in using the ideal approach to charge our hypothetical 200-Ah capacity battery:

10 A (C/20) for 5 hours = 50 Ah
20 A (C/10) for 7 hours = 140 Ah
10 A (C/20) for 1 hour = 10 Ah
Total: 13 hours = 200 Ah

This approach requires 13 hours to charge a 200-Ah capacity battery. Provided that you do not exceed battery temperature, you could charge at the C/5 rate during the middle of the cycle (40 A for 3.5 hours) and reduce total time to 9.5 hours.

Battery Chargers Today

Battery chargers today have come a long way since the days of early batteries. The days of large, noisy, heavy devices are long gone. New chargers are intelligent, programmable, and very efficient. They are robust in power, light in weight, and compact in design. Now that you have learned some of the basics, it is time to size the right charger for your application and battery pack.

If we look at the X pattern in the graph at the lower right, Figure 10-2 shows what most actual battery chargers deliver. Using a variation or combination of constant current, constant voltage, tapering, and end-of-charge voltage versus time methods, all battery chargers arrive at a method of current reduction during the charging cycle as the cell voltage rises. Fortunately, you can buy something off the shelf to take care of your needs. But you have to investigate before buying to make sure that a given battery charger does what you want it to do.

Battery chargers are sized using the formula

Charging current = battery capacity × 115 percent/time + dc load

In this equation—very similar to the equation presented earlier in this chapter—the charging current determines the size charger you need, the 115 percent is an efficiency factor to take losses into account, and the dc load is whatever else is attached to the battery (this is zero if you disconnect your batteries from your EV's electrical system while recharging). You're already familiar with battery capacity and time. You can plug chargers up to15–20 A into your standard household 120-V ac outlet. Just verify the circuit you have. Many household 120-V outlets are only rated for 15 A. Higher current capacity chargers require a dedicated 220/240-V ac circuit—the kind that drives your household electric range or clothes dryer. Your home or shop probably has 220/240 V ac already. Your best options are several different types of off-the-shelf chargers you can buy.

Whether to have an onboard or an offboard charger is another consideration. An onboard charger gives your vehicle the convenience of charging whenever you like, but you might be limited on space. The Zivan charger I use was just the right size to fit in a backpack and did not weigh a lot. Some other models are even smaller; they could be mounted right on your vehicle. An offboard charger is fairly simple if you have the space. With an offboard charger, you are not limited to space and can take advantage of its high power capability, which translates to minimum charging time. With a charger in a permanent charging location or station, you can take advantage of many additional features.

Below I will go through some of the popular chargers on the market today. They are standard for the industry and have many great features.

Zivan Charger

The Zivan charger is one of my favorites (Figure 10-3). I use this charger exclusively for the Electra Cruiser. These chargers can charge with an output voltage from 12–312 V dc up to 100 A depending on the model. Input voltages are 120/230 V (Table 10-1). In addition, the charger has an optional plug that can sense battery temperature and adjust charging accordingly too. Figure 10-4 shows the location of this accessory plug for optional battery temperature sensing. I have to say that these chargers take a beating. They have been left in the rain, had chemicals and fuels spilled on them, been dropped and dragged on the ground, hit with power surges, and much more.

FIGURE 10-3   Zivan NG3 charger.

Thermal Sensor and/or External Indicator

Thermal Sensor and External Indicator are Options that have to be connected to the 5 poles socket 180°.

Unless otherwise stated, the compensation of the Battery Voltage in function of the temperature of the Thermal Sensor is of -5mV/°C for battery cell.
The control range of the Thermal Sensor goes from -20°C to +50°C.

The External Indicator reflects exactly the LED Indicator which is placed on the equipment.
Further information can be found in the description of the Charging Curve.

FIGURE 10-4   Optional Zivan outlet for a temperature sensor. (www.zivanusa.com/pdf/NG3.pdf.)

TABLE 10-1   Zivan NG3 Charger Profile

Code	Type	Nominal Battery Voltage	Output Current	Output Current wt-lb	Recommended Batteries Capabilities
F7 AV	NG3 12-100	12 V	100 A	120	500-1000 AH
F7 BQ	NG3 24-50	24 V	50 A	60	250-500 AH
F7BT	NG3 24-80	24 V	80 A	95	400-800 AH
F7 CR	NG3 36-60	36 V	60 A	70	300-600 AH
F7 EQ	NG3 48-50	48 V	50 A	60	250-500 AH
F7 GN	NG3 60-35	60 V	35 A	40	175-350 AH
F7 HM	NG3 72-30	72 V	30 A	35	150-300 AH
F7 IL	NG3 80-27	80 V	27 A	30	135-270 AH
F7 LL	NG3 84-25	84 V	25 A	30	125-250 AH
F7 MI	NG3 96-22	96 V	22 A	26	110-220 AH
F7 NH	NG3 108-20	108 V	20 A	25	100-200 AH
F7 PH	NG3 120-18	120 V	18 A	22	90-180 AH
F7 QG	NG3 132-16	132 V	16 A	19	80-160 AH
F7 RG	NG3 144-15	144 V	15 A	18	75-150 AH
F7 WG	NG3 156-14	156 V	14 A	17	70-140 AH
F7 SF	NG3 168-13	168 V	13 A	16	65-130 AH
F7 TF	NF3 180-12	180 V	12 A	14	60-120 AH
F7 UE	NG3 192-11	192 V	11 A	13	55-110 AH
F7 VE	NG3 216-10	216 V	10 A	12	50-100 AH
F7 XC	NG3 240-9	240 V	9 A	11	50-100 AH
F7 YB	NG3 288-8	288 V	8 A	10	50-100 AH
F7 YB	NG3 312-7	312 V	7.5 A	9	50-100 AH

From *Build Your Own Electric Vehicle*, Table 9-1, p. 216.

They have been beaten up and just keep working. The batteries in the Cruiser lasted over 5 years, and I will attribute this in large part to the charger. I do know for a fact that the batteries have been fully abused during the whole cross-country trip, which was a good thing and a test to the whole system. I am sure that the quality of the Trojan batteries helped too.

One of the many features I like about the Zivan is the programming option. I actually bought three Zivan (NG3) chargers for the Cruiser. One was a 220-V input voltage charger, putting out about 19–22 A at 120 V dc. The second was the same charger but with a 120-V ac input voltage and about 11 A 120-V dc output. Both these chargers were programmed the same to my specifications for the ten 12-V Group 27 Trojan batteries in the frame. The Zivan controller uses an IUI charging profile, as described earlier. If you look at Figures 10-5 through 10-7, you can see the actual charging profiles. Figure 10-5 shows you the initial charging curves T_1, where the charger starts out with the maximum amperage until a voltage limit is reached

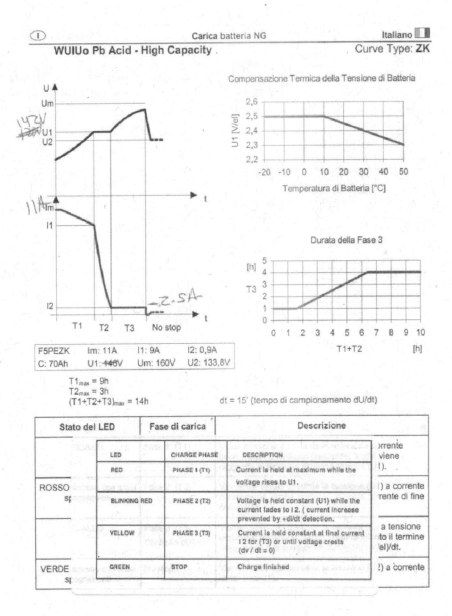

FIGURE 10-5   Charging profile for NG3 110-V ac/120-V dc unit.

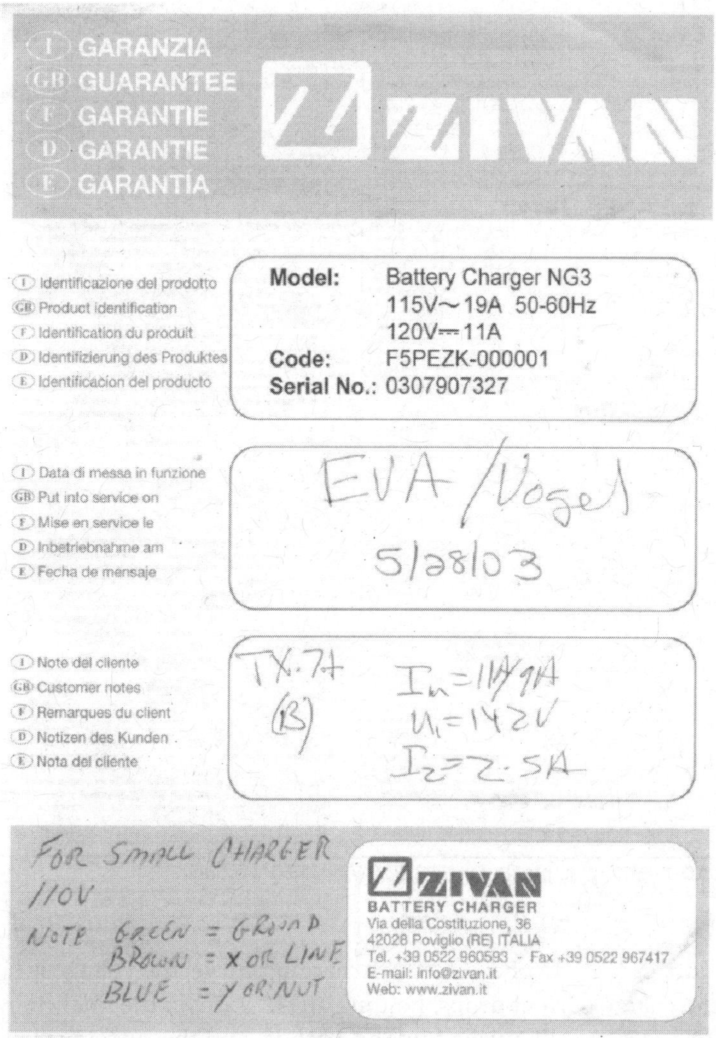

(I) GARANZIA
(GB) GUARANTEE
(F) GARANTIE
(D) GARANTIE
(E) GARANTIA

ZIVAN

(I) Identificazione del prodotto
(GB) Product identification
(F) Identification du produit
(D) Identifizierung des Produktes
(E) Identificacion del producto

Model: Battery Charger NG3
115V~19A 50-60Hz
120V⎓11A
Code: F5PEZK-000001
Serial No.: 0307907327

(I) Data di messa in funzione
(GB) Put into service on
(F) Mise en service le
(D) Inbetriebnahme am
(E) Fecha de mensaje

EVA / Vogel
5/28/03

(I) Note del cliente
(GB) Customer notes
(F) Remarques du client
(D) Notizen des Kunden
(E) Nota del cliente

TX.74 (B)
$I_n = 11A/9A$
$U_1 = 142V$
$I_2 = 2.5A$

FOR SMALL CHARGER
110V
NOTE GREEN = GROUND
BROWN = X OR LINE
BLUE = Y OR NUT

ZIVAN
BATTERY CHARGER
Via della Costituzione, 36
42028 Poviglio (RE) ITALIA
Tel. +39 0522 960593 - Fax +39 0522 967417
E-mail: info@zivan.it
Web: www.zivan.it

FIGURE 10-6 Charger info for NG3 110-V ac/120-V dc unit.

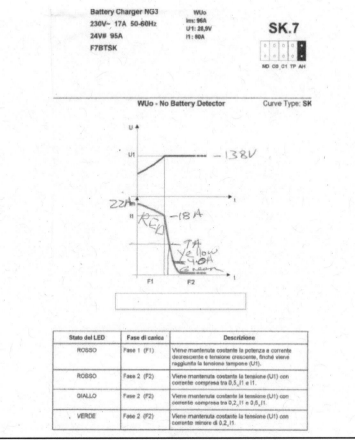

FIGURE 10-7 Charging profile for NG3 220-V ac/120 V dc unit.

of about 142 V dc. In phase T_2 of the charging curve, the voltage is held at 142 V dc, and the charge current drops, holding at 142 V dc. In the final charging profile T_3, the voltage is usually pushed up to 148 V dc, and the current is held at 2.5 A until that time; then the charger turns off.

The third charger that I mentioned I programmed differently. The Cruiser has a sidecar with a 4,500-W 220-V ac diesel generator in the back. The charger is programmed to charge all the time in relation to the voltage. As the voltage goes down under load, the charger kicks in 100 percent, providing full power from the generator. As the voltage goes back up, the charger cuts back charging until it reaches the upper voltage limit and trickle charges.

Manzanita Micro PFC-20

The PFC series offers three models. Figure 10-8 shows the PFC-20, which is designed to operate from a 20-A, 240-V outlet. The company also offers the PFC-30, which is designed to operate from a 30-A, 240-V dryer outlet, and the PFC-50, which is

FIGURE 10-8   Manzanita Micro PFC-20, an extremely versatile battery charger. (From *Build Your Own Electric Vehicle*, Figure 9-4, p. 219.)

designed to operate from a 50-A, 240-V range outlet. They will operate at half power (same line current) from a 120-V ac source.

Here are some of the specifications of the PFC-20:

- It is designed to charge any battery pack from 12–360 V nominal (14.4–450 V peak).
- It is power factor–corrected and designed either to put out 20 A (if the battery voltage is lower than the input voltage) or draw 20 A from the line (if the line voltage is lower than the battery voltage).
- The buck enhancement option will increase the output to 30 A.
- There is a programmable timer to shut off the charger after a period of time set by the user.
- For installation instructions, go to www.manzanitamicro.com/installpfc 20revC_nophotos.doc.

Curtis Instruments

Among the many other products Curtis instruments manufactures, the company also designs and builds battery chargers. Curtis has a whole line of chargers to choose from, and they are compact high-frequency chargers that are perfect for smaller vehicles and motorcycles (Figures 10-9 and 10-10). The company's units

FIGURE 10-9 Curtis Model 1621 high-frequency battery charger. (www.curtisinst.com/index. cfm?fuseaction=cProducts.BatteryChargers.)

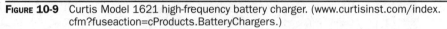

MODEL 1621

DIMENSIONS mm

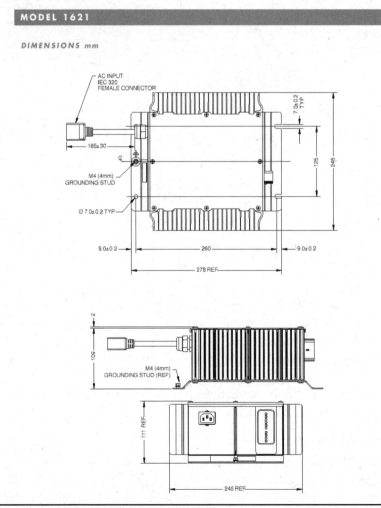

FIGURE 10-10 Curtis Model 1621 battery charger dimensions. (www.curtisinst.com/index. cfm?fuseaction=cProducts.BatteryChargers.)

can be powered with an input voltage of 85–265 V ac. The output dc charging voltage ranges from 24–96 V dc with charging current from 9–25 A. Here are some features:

- Advanced high-frequency switch-mode design allows more efficient (90 percent) and faster charging and optimal charging independent of battery type or condition.
- Power factor of greater than 0.99 minimizes utility surcharges and optimizes the use of ac line power.
- There is an extensive list of approved charge algorithms (e.g., default I1, I2, U, I3a).
- The chargers can store 10 separate algorithms that can be selected to match the specific batteries in use, thereby eliminating the need for multiple models and resulting in lower operating costs.
- The chargers are lightweight and compact, and this allows onboard use and offers space advantages over ferroresonant chargers in traditional off board installations.
- Extensive safety features such as reverse polarity and short-circuit protection ensure safe operation for both the operator and the charger itself.
- Light-emitting diodes (LEDs) allow at-a-glance charge status determination.
- Battery temperature monitoring via an optional temperature-sensor input allows more accurate measurement and charging.

Brusa

I have saved the best for last. In my opinion, Brusa makes one of the best chargers on the market (the company makes plenty of other great things too). The NLG5 can charge any battery in the voltage range of 100–720 V dc (Figures 10-11 and 10-12). Owing to the design, programmability (i.e., automatic/CAN/booster operation), and scalability, these chargers are able to charge at 3.3/6.7/10 kW while being universally adaptable. They can handle any new battery or charging parameters or control strategy at any time with a software update or new programming. Brusa has an amazing list of features and a price that backs that up. In the scheme of chargers, though, a Brusa charger is truly a safe investment because you would never have to buy another one. This is the top end of chargers.

The NLG5 is a universal 3.3-kW charger for all kinds of batteries with a nominal voltage range of 100–720 V. The charger comes in both air- and liquid-cooled versions. Owing to its compact design, durable construction, and light weight, it is ideal for mobile applications such as electric and hybrid vehicles. In the case of an electric motorcycle, this charger would be best for stationary applications. The charger includes a standard CAN interface that allows simple control and date acquisition from the charger by a PC or laptop. Through the PC, the charging profile

FIGURE 10-11   Brusa charger. (Courtesy of Metric Mind Engineering, www.metricmind.com/images/ta1.jpg.)

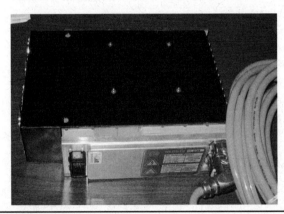

FIGURE 10-12   Brusa NLG5 charger.

is fully programmable or free charging profiles can be downloaded. By using an external current sensor (BCM98-mess), you can interface a BMS with the charger. Up to three chargers can be connected in parallel without using external connections.

Below is a list of just some of the many features. There are just so many that I could only list some of them.

Power specifications
- Isolation between mains and battery by high-frequency transformer
- Input voltage: 230 V ± 10 percent, 48–62 Hz (400 V optional)
- Maximum mains current: 16 A, sinusoidal
- Efficiency: 90–93 percent

- Power factor > 0.99
- Maximum charging current: up to 25 A (NLG511)
- Maximum charging voltage: up to 720 V (NLG514)
- Accuracy of charging voltage: ±1 percent
- Short-circuit- and open-circuit-proof
- Overtemperature protection by linear derating
- Reverse-polarity protection by internal fuse
- Switches off at mains with overvoltage
- Battery temperature monitoring

Additional Functions and Interfaces

- Power multiplying can be done by connecting multiple chargers together.
- Control pilot enables accelerated charging (mode 3, according to SAE 1772) using the dedicated infrastructure.
- All types of charging profiles can be programmed by PC via a serial RS232 interface.
- Charging voltage is temperature-compensated.
- Actual firmware can be downloaded by PC.
- A CAN interface is included.
- There is a built-in status display (five LEDs).
- There are four analog inputs (three temperature sensors, one power control).
- There are four digital inputs (charging profile control and battery current sensor for internal Ah counter).
- There are four open collector outputs (three programmable) that can drive relays, lamps, fans, etc.

Battery Management Systems and Battery Balancers

The battery management system (BMS) and battery balancers are a few other ways to monitor and/or control your batteries. I feel that this is an important topic to touch on. It could have been placed in Chapter 7, but I think it better suited here. Below I will explain and give a few examples of these two basic systems. For the most part, your EV will not need a BMS; rather battery balancers would work just fine. A BMS may be needed only if you choose to use an exotic battery pack with multiple batteries. For my purposes, I will stick with balancers.

Battery Balancers

Since one or more batteries in a series string of batteries can discharge lower than the other batteries, it is important to ensure that this weaker battery receives extra charging. This will ensure increased life of the pack because a weaker battery will drag the pack down and shorten the life of the other batteries in the string. In the worst case, you could kill the pack early. Virtually any type of battery can be damaged by excessively high or low voltage, and in some cases, the results can be catastrophic.

In any battery pack or string of batteries, you will find that no two cells are created equal. When batteries are connected in series and being cycled as one group, the cells will gradually drift out of balance. Lower-capacity cells charge and discharge quicker, so their terminal voltage may be higher or lower than the average; the temperature gradient across the battery pack results in further imbalance. Battery balancers, also referred to as *equalizers*, attempt to adjust the charge going into the batteries.

There are several types of battery balancers, each with its own technique:

- Circuits that monitor the batteries (battery monitors)
- Circuits that monitor the batteries and somehow adjust the charge going into a battery (battery balancers)

PowerCheq Battery Equalizer

These are small units that are connected to each pair of batteries to equalize the batteries continuously. The PowerCheq modules interconnect batteries in a series string, creating a bidirectional energy-transfer path between neighboring batteries and enabling the entire battery string to be equalized. The system equalizes and maintains batteries during charging, discharge, and while sitting idle. PowerCheq is adaptable to all battery systems and configurations and can be easily installed in new and existing battery systems. Figure 10-13 shows you how simple the installation is. Figures 10-14 and 10-15 provide two graphs showing the capacity and power in relation to cycle life. This comparison was performed with two identical electric scooters, one with the balancing system and one without. As you can see, balancing the batteries increases their performance and cycle life by more than half.[3]

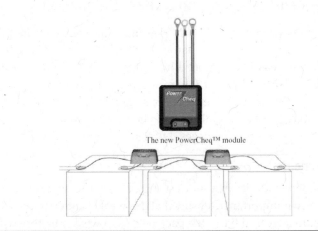

The new PowerCheq™ module

FIGURE 10-13   PowerCheq battery equalizer. (Courtesy of Power Designers USA, http://powerdesignersusa.com/powercheq_faq.htm.)

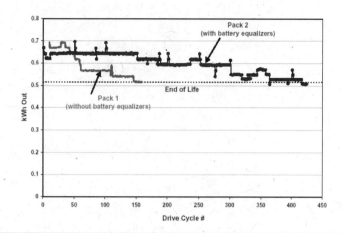

FIGURE 10-14 PowerCheq cycle life with balancing module. (Courtesy of Power Designers USA, http://powerdesignersusa.com/powercheq_faq.htm.)

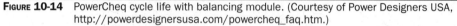

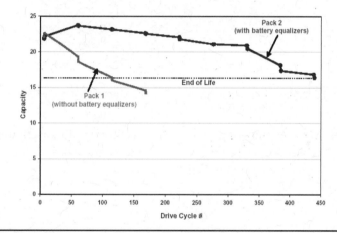

FIGURE 10-15 PowerCheq capacity life with balancing module. (Courtesy of Power Designers USA, http://powerdesignersusa.com/powercheq_faq.htm.)

Battery Management Systems

A BMS is a whole step further than a balancing system and handles more activities. In practice, a BMS also may be coupled with other vehicle systems that communicate with the BMS via a CAN bus. Such systems could include a thermal management system, an antitheft device that disables the battery, or a number of other systems on your EV. In addition, a BMS can provide battery charge protection, discharge protection, state-of-charge monitoring, and much more.

With the onset of alternative battery technologies such as lithium and NiMH batteries, the batteries are more sensitive to overcharging and overdischarging on a cell-by-cell basis. When the cells are used in a series, these battery technologies are generally protected with a BMS.

FIGURE 10-16   Battery management system. (Courtesy of Metric Mind Engineering, www. metricmind.com/bms.htm.)

Metric Mind Engineering has developed a great BMS for lithium batteries over the past few years. The system was designed for use on a lithium battery called Thunder Sky manufactured in China (Figure 10-16).

Conclusion

You should now have a good grasp of battery chargers and how they relate to your batteries and the longevity of your battery pack. The charger and batteries work hand in hand as a team. To help this team along, the battery balance system or BMS maintains battery balance and function much longer. Keep your batteries in good health, and the pack should last a long time.

CHAPTER 11

Accessories and Converters

You learned from the previous chapters all about the various components that make up your electric vehicle (EV) and how each component plays an important role in the conversion. Now we will examine many of the components that help you to monitor your EV to extend the life and to keep you informed of system status and state of charge (SOC). How better to know your EV than to have it talk back to you. These components will enable you to view real-time information to make decisions on how to extend the life of the battery pack and how much energy you have left. When you get to Chapter 13, I will show you how to take all the components you have learned about and bring them together—from your batteries and motor controller to all the other components we have looked at.

This chapter will review dc-to-dc converters. These are not necessarily an accessory, but not every EV uses one, so they are sort of an add-on item. They are important for your EV in maintaining your standard 12-V system for lights and other functions separate from the high-voltage power system. The object of this chapter is to look at a few of the different accessories, components, and communications systems that keep you in touch with your vehicle. As you plan your EV conversion, think about these accessories and how they will best suit you as you integrate them into your vehicle. There are plenty more I will cover in Chapter 12, where I show you how to bring all the components together.

Communications

The key to getting the most out of your EV is knowing what is going on. The real thing is that you want to get the most out of your EV—the best range, the greatest performance—without being stuck someplace. To do this, you need feedback from your systems. You need to know what is happening, how much energy are you using at any time, and how much energy you have left. What condition are your batteries in? What is the voltage? In Chapter 7, you studied all about the importance of maintaining your batteries and the life of the batteries. We know that as a battery approaches certain states of charge or discharge, critical actions need to happen or not happen. If you want to keep your batteries in good health and not go past 80 percent of discharge, how are you going to do that? Your batteries are not going to tap you on the shoulder and say, "Hey, getting a little empty here." However, your batteries, if not managed properly, *will* punch you in your wallet when they fail prematurely.

Having all the gauges in the world is only as good as the person paying attention to them. Case in point: I fell victim to operating the first Electra Cruiser one night and not paying attention to my gauges until it was too late. On a summer evening, I accompanied my long-time friend Brian Lima to a concert in New York at the famous Jones Beach Theater. Brian was riding a traditional gas-powered Harley-Davidson, and I had my Electric Cruiser. Not to be outdone by the Harley, I flexed the Cruiser's muscles, showing that it was no wimp and giving the Harley a run for its money. By doing so, I zapped too much juice from the batteries and did not watch my gauges. On the ride back that night, the Cruiser was fine for three-quarters of the trip home, and then suddenly the bike started to lose speed. Alarmed, I now looked at my gauges and viewed the volt gauge dropping fast and my e-meter flashing red (Figure 11-1). Not good! The Cruiser kept losing power fast until it almost came to a stop 2 miles from home. Now, if I had looked at my gauges earlier and budgeted my power, I would not have had a problem. The nice thing about this is that I learned two lessons: First, watch your gauges and budget your power consumption. Second, after I pulled over to the side of the road and waited 15 minutes, the Cruiser came back to life with plenty of power to get me home. This proved the statement in Chapter 7 that lead-acid batteries will come back to life.

Figure 11-1   Electra Cruiser prototype 1 tank gauge layout.

Battery "Fuel Gauge" and Monitoring

Your batteries are your fuel tank, just like the fuel tank in your car. In your car, you have a fuel gauge that tells you the amount of fuel (energy) you have left, which relates to how much farther you can travel. On some vehicles, you have electronics that tell you instantly how much fuel you are using at any time—miles per gallon or, on some, gallons per minute. For your EV, fuel usage at any instant would equate to amperage consumed at any given time. In your liquid-fueled vehicle, you also have an alarm in most cases, a bell, a chime, or a light alerting you to low fuel. Well, that is the same thing you want to achieve for your EV. There are many products on the market that can do just what you need. They monitor your batteries and calculate state of charge, charge remaining, charge received, and much more.

Battery Indicator

Battery indicators are devices or instruments that indicate the state of charge (SOC) of your batteries from your last charge. Some are wired directly into your main battery pack, monitoring voltage, amperage used, and charge replaced. The gauges with these data calculate remaining charge and battery state; some even monitor temperature and log data that are downloadable through a port on the back. Xantrex and Curtis Instruments both manufacture high-quality state-of-the-art battery monitors.

Xantrex Link 10

Xantrex produces many electronic devices throughout the world. One device that is very popular is the Link 10. This device uses sophisticated microprocessor technology to provide complete battery status information. It uses a simple multicolor digital display showing volts, amperes, ampere-hours consumed, and operating time remaining. The Link 10 has the ability to capture real-time data and store them for download through a port on the back. The gauge can display key historical battery information such as charge efficiency, deepest discharge, and average discharge.

Output Format

Time, kilowatt-hours, amperes, volts, ampere-hours, Peukert ampere-hours, Peukert amperes, time remaining, bar-graph SOC, and temperature (°C) are all available with the Link 10 (Figures 11-2 and 11-3).

Link 10 Product Features

- Digital numeric display, an LED display, showing numeric readout of volts, amperes, ampere-hours, and time remaining
- Easy-to-read multicolor LED bar graph

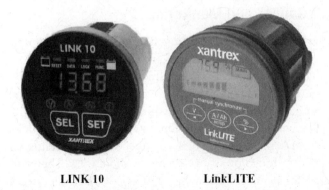

LINK 10   LinkLITE

FIGURE 11-2 Xantrex Link 10 e-meter and LinkLITE. (www.xantrex.com/web/id/273/p/1/pt/7/ product.asp.)

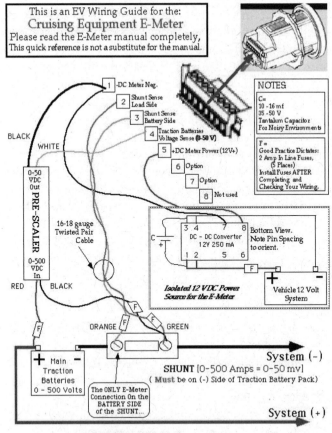

FIGURE 11-3   Link 10 wiring. (www.xantrex.com.)

- Splash-proof panels that allow for outdoor mounting and hands-free operation
- Display of key historical battery information, such as charge efficiency, deepest discharge, and average discharge
- Compatible with 12- and 24-V dc systems
- Works with any battery type
- Includes dc shunt (part no. 84-2010-00)
- Low-battery alarm contacts
- One-year warranty

Accessories

- Color-coded twisted-pair cable (eases installation), available in 25-ft (part no. 84-2014-00) and 50-ft lengths (part no. 84-2015-00)
- Prescalers (0–100 or 0–500 V) to extend voltage range covered by your meter (see Table 11-1)

Optional Serial Port (RS-232)

The Link 10 may be equipped to transmit serial communications data to a personal computer or data-logging device. When equipped with the optional RS-232 port, the Link 10 will transmit a data message once a second. The structure of this data is as follows:

Data rate: 9,600 b/s
Data bits: 8
Stop bits: 1
Parity bits: None

LinkLITE

The LinkLITE battery monitor can measure currents up to 1,000 A. It selectively displays voltage, charge and discharge current, consumed ampere-hours, and remaining battery capacity. It is equipped with an internal programmable alarm relay to run a generator when needed or to turn off devices when the battery voltage exceeds programmable boundaries.

Curtis Series 800 and 900 Battery SOC Instrumentation

Curtis Instruments, in addition to manufacturing motor controllers and a host of other EV equipment, makes few lines of battery "fuel gauges" and SOC monitors. One of the nice features about their gauges is that most of them interface with and plug right into Curtis motor controllers. This makes your job a lot easier and keeps the wiring simple. Many also are programmable with multifunctions.

The Curtis Model 900R battery gauge is an example of an inexpensive and easy-to-install gauge (Figures 11-4 and 11-5). It is a single-piece package that installs via

TABLE 11-1   Link 10 Specifications

Electrical Specifications	
Voltage Measurement (standard model auto range)	0–19.95 VDC (0.05 V resolution) 20.0–50.0 VDC (0.1 V resolution)
Voltage Measurement (optional prescalers)	0–100 V (used with standard models) 0–500 V (used with standard models)
Amperage Measurement	Low range ± 0–40 A (0.1 A resolution) High range ± 500 A (1.0 A resolution)
Amp-hour Measurement	Low range ± 0–199 Ah (0.1 hour resolution) High range ± 200–1,999 Ah (1 hour resolution)
Time Remaining Measurement	Low range 0-199.9 hours (0.1 hour resolution) High range 0-255 hours (1 hour resolution)
Power Requirements	9.5–40 V dc (dc power supply voltage)
Power Consumption	50–225 mA (display auto dims with ambient light) 28 mA (sleep mode—bar graph display only)
Shunt Type	500 A/50 mV (included)
Accuracy	Voltage ± 0.6% of reading + 1 least count of resolution Amperage ± 0.8% of reading + 1 least count of resolution
General Specifications	
Installation	Flush mount
Front Panel	Splash resistant
Outer bezel diameter (face)	2.5" (63.5 cm)
Barrel diameter	1.95" (50 mm)
Depth	3.15" (80 mm)
Hole cut size	2.25" (52 mm) diameter
Weight (not including shunt)	4.6 oz (130.4 g)
Warranty	1 year

Part numbers	84-2016-01 (Link 10 Standard)
	84-2010-00 (Shunt)
	84-2024-00 (Link 10 temperature sensor)
	84-2014-00 (Twisted Pair 25'—
	    recommended for Link installations)
	84-2015-00 (Twisted Pair 50'—
	    recommended for Link installations)
	84-6000-00 (100v—prescaler)
	84-6000-05 (500v—prescaler)

FIGURE 11-4 Curtis Model 900R battery gauge. (www.curtisinst.com/index. cfm?fuseaction=cProducts.DownloadPDF&file=500_46%.)

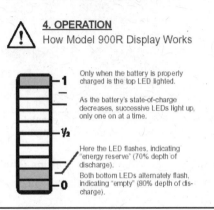

FIGURE 11-5 Curtis Model 900R battery gauge operation. (www.curtisinst.com/index. cfm?fuseaction=cProducts.DownloadPDF&file=500_46%.)

a simple two-wire connection. This is a great basic instrument to monitor your batteries. It is ideally suited for lead-acid battery–powered vehicles that require a display of SOC only.

Features

- Double flashing red LEDs signal "empty" alarm at 80 percent discharge.
- It recognizes an improperly charged battery.
- It is available in single voltages of 12, 24, 36, 48, 72, and 80 V dc.
- A multicolored 10-bar (5 green, 3 yellow, 2 red) LED displays SOC.

Curtis enGage II

enGage II is a dual-function microprocessor-based instrument that can be factory or user defined to monitor various and multiple functions. Gauge options include fuel, temperature, pressure, voltage, tachometer, battery SOC, hour meter, settable hour meter, and field-programmable maintenance monitor. Figures 11-6 and 11-7

FIGURE 11-6   Curtis enGage II battery and dual-function microprocessor-based instrument. (www. curtisinst.com/index.cfm?fuseaction=cProducts.dspInstrumentation.)

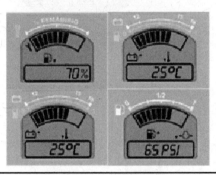

FIGURE 11-7   Curtis enGage II dual-function display examples. (www.curtisinst.com/index. cfm?fuseaction=cProducts.dspInstrumentation.)

show the gauge and the various display options. This gauge can cover a multitude of functions all in one package.

Voltmeter

The voltmeter is one of the top instruments every EV should have. There are many volt gauges on the market to choose from. The volt gauge acts as a simple form of a battery SOC indicator. In Chapter 7 we learned that a battery's SOC is reflected by the voltage; as a battery's capacity goes down, so does the voltage. The gauge is also handy to monitor voltage during charging. Figure 11-8 shows a volt gauge used on the Electra Cruiser that was manufactured by Westberg Manufacturing, Inc. This company has manufactured many types of gauges for all industries since 1944. You can find company information in Chapter 14.

Ammeter

The ammeter is one of the most important gauges you can have on your EV. An ammeter displays instantaneous amperage your electric motor is using instantly. The ammeter is your key to extending the range of your EV. The more amperage you are drawing, the less range you will achieve. The gauge is a great tool for monitoring current draw when you are going up a hill or under acceleration. The

FIGURE 11-8   Voltmeter used on the Electra Cruiser. (www.westach.com/gauge_images/2C6-30. gif.)

amperage usage is an early sign that your motor may have too much load on it at too low a speed. If you have gears, this is a good indicator that you need to switch to a lower gear to reduce the load. Remember from Chapter 8 that an increased load (amperes) and high current draw, coupled with low motor rpm, mean increased heating and early motor failure. The ammeter is your first insight to any overload in your EV electrical system. Figure 11-9 shows a few gauges offered by Westburg. There are a number of other manufacturers in the marketplace, including Curtis and Xantex, with multipurpose gauges.

These are just a sample of some of the gauges you can use for your EV conversion; there are many more. I just want to give you an idea of what you can do and the items available to you. You are by no means limited; the bike market has an array of gauges you can use for other purposes. Figures 11-10 through 11-12 show a few gauges from the second prototype Electra Cruiser.

DC-to-DC Converter

In your EV conversion, once you remove all the internal combustion engine components, you will still be left with the 12-V dc electrical system. This system still will need power from a 12-V dc source. You could use a small 12-V battery to keep this system operating, but that battery would soon run out of charge because without the engine, you now have no alternator. You could run the system off one battery of the battery pack, which will work but is not advisable to do. As we discussed in Chapters 7 and 10, you do not want to discharge one battery more than any other and create an unbalanced pack. This would only lead to an early failure of the battery as opposed to the other batteries. So what do you do? Simple. Use a dc-to-dc converter.

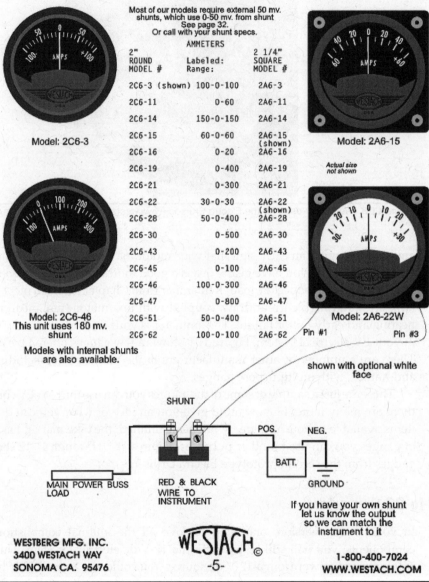

AMMETERS
2" & 2 1/4"

Most of our models require external 50 mv.
shunts, which use 0-50 mv. from shunt
See page 32.
Or call with your shunt specs.

Model: 2C6-3

Model: 2C6-46
This unit uses 180 mv.
shunt

Models with internal shunts
are also available.

Model: 2A6-15

*Actual size
not shown*

Model: 2A6-22W

Pin #1   Pin #3

shown with optional white
face

2" ROUND MODEL #	Labeled: Range:	2 1/4" SQUARE MODEL #
2C6-3 (shown)	100-0-100	2A6-3
2C6-11	0-60	2A6-11
2C6-14	150-0-150	2A6-14
2C6-15	60-0-60	2A6-15 (shown)
2C6-16	0-20	2A6-16
2C6-19	0-400	2A6-19
2C6-21	0-300	2A6-21
2C6-22	30-0-30	2A6-22 (shown)
2C6-28	50-0-400	2A6-28
2C6-30	0-500	2A6-30
2C6-43	0-200	2A6-43
2C6-45	0-100	2A6-45
2C6-46	100-0-300	2A6-46
2C6-47	0-800	2A6-47
2C6-51	50-0-400	2A6-51
2C6-62	100-0-100	2A6-62

SHUNT

POS.   NEG.

BATT.

MAIN POWER BUSS
LOAD

RED & BLACK
WIRE TO
INSTRUMENT

GROUND

If you have your own shunt
let us know the output
so we can match the
instrument to it

WESTBERG MFG. INC.
3400 WESTACH WAY
SONOMA CA. 95476

WESTACH ©
-5-

1-800-400-7024
WWW.WESTACH.COM

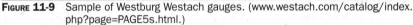

FIGURE 11-9   Sample of Westburg Westach gauges. (www.westach.com/catalog/index.
php?page=PAGE5s.html.)

Figure 11-10   Electra Cruiser prototype 2 tachometer and speedometer.

Figure 11-11   Electra Cruiser prototype 3 tachometer for use with 10,000-rpm ac motor.

Figure 11-12   Electra Cruiser prototype 2 tank and gauges.

A dc-to-dc converter is similar to an alternator. It charges the 12-V battery by chopping voltage from the main battery pack down to 13.5 V. When you drive a combustion engine, the alternator recharges the battery and kicks in extra current when you have lots of electrical items running (e.g., fan, radio, lights). The dc-to-dc converter takes power from your bank of batteries, the main pack, and gives some to the auxiliary battery as needed to keep it charged.

On your conversion, since you are not running any large loads, you also could opt not to use a 12-V auxiliary battery at all. A dc-to-dc converter can run alone without a 12-V dc battery as long as you size the converter to match the power needed for your vehicle. To do this, you just need power from the main battery pack. The dc-to-dc converter should have a separate main power switch to turn it on or off when the vehicle is not in use.

Another reason to use a dc-to-dc converter is isolation of the main battery pack from the 12-V frame or chassis ground. The main battery pack always should be isolated from every other system and should *not* be grounded to the frame with the 12-V system. The main battery pack always should be isolated. I will go into this in more detail in Chapter 12. What's nice about most dc-to-dc converters is that they isolate the high-voltage pack from the low-voltage 12-V system.

For motorcycles and other smaller vehicles, you do not need a lot of current to operate the standard 12-V circuitry. If you look at an EV car conversion, you would need to run a fan, possibly other auxiliary drives, a radio, a heater, twice as many lights, and much more. But, for your conversion, you are only running a few items that use little current. The largest power consumer in your conversion will be the front head lamp. Below are a few examples of dc-to-dc converters.

Vicor DC-to-DC Converter

Vicor has a great line of converters for many applications. You can easily choose the model and specifications online and place your order. The company has great online support with plenty of documentation. I used a Vicor dc-to-dc converter in both Electra Cruisers, and they have worked flawlessly for over 6 years. What I liked about the Vicor converter was the size, flexibility, power output, cost, and quality. The company has a few models to choose from. I used the BatMod (Figure 11-13).

The BatMod current-source modules are ideal for use with equipment that requires a controlled current output, such as battery chargers. They are compatible with all major battery types used in applications for vehicles such as golf carts, fork lifts, automated guide vehicles, and electric cars. Each module offers output currents up to 14.5 A with input voltages in the range of 48–300 V dc. Output voltages are 12, 24, and 48 V.

The BatMod allows the user to independently program a constant output current and a maximum float voltage. The float voltage is the point at which the BatMod transitions from constant current to constant voltage. These features make

FIGURE 11-13 Vicor BatMod dc-to-dc converter.

the BatMod an ideal candidate for battery charging and controlled-current source. Table 11-2 shows the basic specifications. What is also nice is that you can use the online resources from the Vicor Web site to tailor the output on your unit (Figure 11-14). You can set the float voltage and the charge current with the simple addition of a resistor. The online resource will tell you exactly what you need.

TABLE 11-2 Vicor BatMod Specifications

Parameter	Rating	Notes
Nominal input voltage	48 V dc, 150 V dc, 300 V dc	42–60 V, 100–200 V, 200–400 V
Output current	0–14.5A 1–7.25A 0–3.6A	12 V battery system, 24 V battery system, 48 V battery system
Current control input	1–5 V	Zero to maximum current
Current monitor output	1–5 V	Zero to full load
Voltage control input	0–2.5 V	Zero to FS output
Output voltage setpoint Trimmable +10%, −25%	15 V, 30 V, 60 V, ± 1%	12 V, 24 V, 48 V Output respectively
Dynamic characteristics	V-Mode: 300 µsec typ. I-Mode: 250 µsec typ.	V_{NOM} for 50–100% load changes

Dielectric withstand
   Input to output
   Output to baseplate
   Input to baseplate
	3,000 V_{RMS} 500 V_{RMS} 1,500 V_{RMS}	

www.cdn.vicorpower.com/documents/datasheets/ds_batmod.pdf.

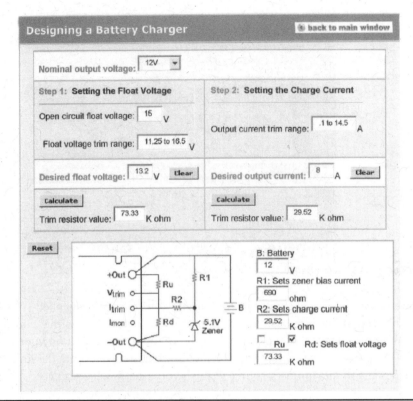

FIGURE 11-14   BatMod online self-help calculations for voltage and current settings. (www.vicr. com/products/dc-dc/converters/bat_mod.)

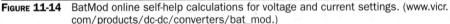

Curtis DC-to-DC Converter

The Curtis 1400 high-efficiency series dc-to-dc converter is configured specifically for EVs. Available in 250- and 375-W models, the devices provide regulated output of 13.5 or 28.0 V for driving lamps and charging auxiliary batteries (Figures 11-15 and 11-16).

FIGURE 11-15   Curtis dc-to-dc converter. (www.vicr.com/products/dc-dc/converters/bat_mod.)

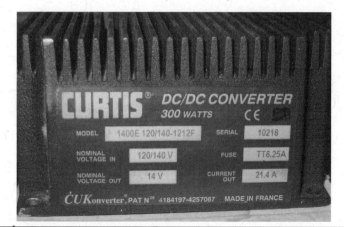

FIGURE 11-16   Curtis dc-to-dc converter back panel.

1400 Series DC-to-DC Converters

These converters are available in both 250-W peak (Model 1410) and 375-W peak (Model 1400) ratings.

- Volt input: 24–96 V
- Volt output: 12, 13.5, 24, or 28 V
- Input and output are dielectrically isolated for maximum safety

Conclusion

Communication with your EV and its systems is a vital part of owning an EV. The EV does have a limited supply of power, and you must budget energy as best as possible. If you look at or equate the amount of energy in your battery pack to a gasoline equivalent, you are lucky if the total energy equals half a gallon of gasoline. This puts things in perspective in terms of how efficient an EV really is. Your gauges will help you with that task. After using your EV over time, you will get to know the signs and what to look for. In addition, your dc-to-dc converter will help to power your accessories and keep you moving.

CHAPTER 12

Electrical System and Wiring

The electrical system of your electric vehicle (EV) is at the heart of what an EV is all about. After all your reading and learning about each system, you now can take that knowledge and bring it all together. By this time, maybe you have found your donor vehicle or are building from scratch. You have removed and discarded the dirty internal combustion engine, and you are getting ready to dig in and get a plan going.

This chapter is very important; you will essentially take all the various components and bring them together. Even if you are not sure of the exact controller, the electric motor, or a few other components you will use, the basic wiring and the interconnections remain the same. If you do not know the item you will use, that is okay; you can add it later.

In this chapter you will learn all you need to know about wiring for your EV—the dos and don'ts. You will integrate all the systems into a simple wiring schematic. I will go through all the components and parts you need to consider first. Then I will provide a discussion of wire size and how it relates to your wiring.

Electrical Safety

One of the things that I cannot stress enough is safety. Dealing with electricity is no joke; it will kill you in a flash. A 12-V battery can kill or hurt you just the same as a high-voltage system. As I mentioned in Chapter 7, it is not the voltage but the amperes or current and the path it takes through your body that will kill you. The amount of current it takes to kill a person is very little and varies with the path the current takes. All it takes is 50 mA to kill a human. To put this into perspective, 50 mA is 0.05 A. Not much at all, is it? Now, let's look at the big picture. You have a battery pack using, for example, 48 V for your system, and your batteries can crank out 1,000 A (48,000 W or 48 kW) or more for a short burst. I think you get the picture: If you get blasted with that kind of power, you are dead! If you are lucky and the path does not follow a vital organ (e.g., heart) or your brain, you will have one hell of a burn, if you don't lose a limb. Now take that a step further, and let's look at the battery pack from the Electra Cruiser. The Cruiser operates on 120 V dc with ten 115-Ah batteries. Under a shorting condition, the batteries can easily put out 1,200 A in a short burst. Do the math: That's a 144,000-W burst, or 144 kW, or 193 hp.

EV Electrical System Components

In this section we will look at and go through all the different components that make up the EV electrical system. You can pick and choose what items you will use for your build. We will look mostly at the high-voltage side of the wiring; the 12-V dc system that originally wired your vehicle should remain mostly intact.

Take particular care in this section, and plan out your wiring carefully. Try to adhere to all wiring codes for wire capacity. Lay out a basic schematic of how you want things to connect. This is actually not that hard at all, but it allows you to learn the components and the process involved in putting all the pieces together. To make it even simpler, you can just follow or copy the basic EV wiring diagrams I will supply for you in this book. Most important is to do your wiring in a clean, neat manner. Take your time, and do a nice job. In the end, it will pay off greatly. Do a sloppy job, and you will have problems, short circuits, and an even harder time troubleshooting. If you plan the wiring out now and do a simple diagram, it will save you problems in the future.

Main Circuit Breaker or Quick Disconnect

For safety, every EV should have a main circuit breaker or a quick disconnect to separate the batteries from the rest of the system. In essence, you want to be able to disconnect the main battery pack in an emergency. On some vehicles, a sign or plate is mounted near the main disconnect to alert any emergency personnel in an extreme situation (Figure 12-1). Figure 12-2 shows the quick disconnect on the

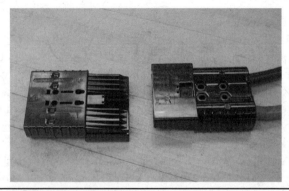

FIGURE 12-1 Anderson 350-A quick disconnect.

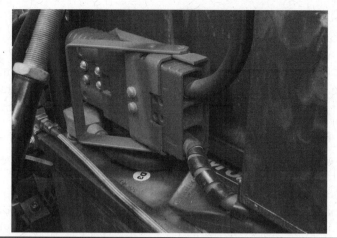

Figure 12-2   Quick disconnect on the Electra Cruiser.

Electra Cruiser with a handle release. It may be a little hard to see, but in an emergency, pull that lever, and you unplug the entire pack.

Main Contactor

The main contactor is basically a big relay. This is a single-pole normally open contactor. What this means is the contactor must be energized by the 12-V circuit to activate and complete the main circuit. This kind of contactor is rated anywhere from 100–300 A. Other manufacturers have contactors that are rated for over 500 A. This relay is normally energized when the key switch is turned on, activating the main high-voltage source to the motor controller (Figure 12-3).

Figure 12-3   Albright SW 200 main contactor. (From *Build Your Own Electric Vehicle*, Figure 9-8, p. 219.)

Reversing Relay

You may not use this contactor in your EV conversion because you are building a lighter vehicle. On the chance that you build a heavier vehicle, this may come in handy. This contactor is very similar to the main contactor but uses two relays (Figure 12-4). By using two relays, you can mechanically reverse the polarity of current flow to the electric motor and achieve reverse in your vehicle.

Safety Fuse

This is a fuse to interrupt the current flow from the main battery pack in the event of a failure, short-circuit, or accident. This is the first line of safety in the worst-case scenario. These fuses are normally placed in-line with the battery pack in two places. If you had two levels of batteries, you would place one on the upper lever and another on the lower level. This provides a better level of protection. Figure 12-5 shows a basic high-amperage fuse that you would use in-line with the battery pack.

Figure 12-4   Albright SW 202 reversing contactor (double pole). (From *Build Your Own Electric Vehicle*, Figure 9-8, p. 220.)

Figure 12-5   500 amp in-line fuse.

Low-Voltage, Low-Current System

Your low-voltage 12-V system remains pretty much the same as it was before. You may want to clean it up and use a new fuse panel. Remember, this low-voltage system must be isolated from you high-voltage battery pack. If you do not do so, you risk the chance of shock and leaking currents. When using a dc-to-dc converter, confirm that the converter has a dielectrically isolated output, meaning no interconection between the high-voltage and low-voltage systems. If you use a dc-to-dc converter, calculate the power needed to run the existing 12-V load, and size your converter accordingly.

Throttle Potentiometer

The throttle potentiometer is essentially your throttle, linked to your handlebar twist grip through a cable. The one shown in Figure 12-6 is a Curtis PB-6 5-kΩ potentiometer. The Curtis PB-6 is a universal throttle control that works with most motor controllers. Curtis and a few other companies make other models and styles. The PB-6 has a small switch activated by the control lever that works in conjunction with the controller. The controller looks for an ohm reading that is in the full nonactivated position. If the controller does not sense that the throttle is in the right position, it will not activate.

Shunts

Shunts are precisely calibrated resistors that enable current flow in a circuit to be determined by measuring the voltage drop across them. They come in varying sizes. Depending on the current you feel your EV will draw, you need to size the shunt for the amperage used. From the shunt you can connect an ammeter or other device designed to measure the voltage drop. From the voltage drop, the meter will equate it to a meter for amperage (Figure 12-7).

FIGURE 12-6 Curtis PB-6 5-kΩ potentiometer.

Figure 12-7   A 500-A, 50-mV shunt.

Wiring Your System Together

In this section we will look at sample wiring diagrams and try to bring the rest of the electrical system together. Table 12-1 is a sample wire gauge chart. One important thing to remember is to know how may amperes you will be drawing and size the wire.

Table 12-1   Wire and Cable AWG

AWG	Amps (140°F)	Amps (167°F)	Amps (194°F)
4/0	300	360	405
3/0	260	310	350
2/0	225	265	300
1/0	195	230	260
1	165	195	220
2	140	170	190
3	120	145	165
4	105	125	140
6	80	95	105
8	60	70	80
10	40	50	55
12	30	35	40
14	25	30	35
16	15	20	24
20	10	12	18

Wire

Wire size is very important. You need to know exactly how much current you will use and size the wire accordingly. Use too small wire gauge, and the wire will heat up from resistance in the wire (Figure 12-8). You can think of it as if you are trying to force too much of something into a place it does not fit. Therefore, if you try to force too much current through a wire not properly sized, it will get hot, possibly melt the wire coating, and then short out. This is the time hopefully that you used the right fuses in your battery pack and they save your system.

Minimal resistance depends on how well the connectors are attached to the wire cable ends. This is equally important to the overall result. Poor connections will result in heat and wires burning up. You can have the largest cable, but it is only as good as the connections. Crimp the connectors to the wire using the proper crimping tool. For large wires such as 2/0, you can rent a heavy-duty crimping tool to do the job (Figure 12-9).

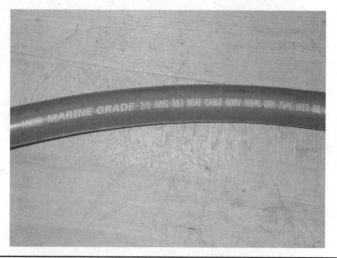

FIGURE 12-8   2/0 copper cable.

FIGURE 12-9   Heavy-duty crimping tool.

Cable Connectors

Any connectors going to the cables, batteries, or any other wiring must be sized correctly. When connecting any wires, make sure that the connections are clean and free of dirt, grease, or anything else. On any connections using a stud with a nut, make sure to use a lock washer or a star washer that will bite into the metal and ensure a good connection (Figures 12-10 through 12-12).

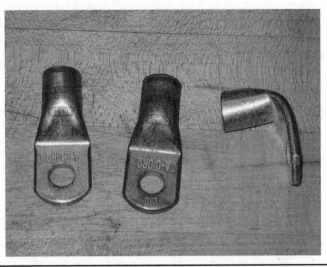

FIGURE 12-10   2/0 terminal ends used to connect to the controller or motor.

FIGURE 12-11   2/0 battery terminal ends.

FIGURE 12-12   Anderson connector used to connect batteries to a charger.

Wire Covers

As you route all your wires and crimp the connectors, take a few extra moments and spend the few extra bucks to protect the bare ends. Nothing is worse than dropping a wrench or having a part come loose that arcs across a bare terminal or wire end. Moreover, this is important from a safety standpoint. In addition, when you are all finished with your great conversion, people are going to want to see it. As we all know, people love to touch things they are not supposed to, especially little people with little hands and fingers, and they can get shocked easily if you don't use covers. Taking this extra step will keep your vehicle safe and will protect the people around you (Figure 12-13).

Routing

Aim for the minimum length of routing for most of your wiring, but leave a little room for installation. For certain wires, you want to leave a little more room. When

FIGURE 12-13   2/0 wire terminal covers.

you start dealing with heavy-gauge wires, they cost more and add weight to your EV. On the instrument side and the 12-V circuit, try to keep the wiring as neat and as organized as possible. If you created a simple written diagram, keep it handy to follow as well as to note any changes; also keep a notepad handy to jot down reminders. If you really want to track things, take a picture; this will be a big help in the future in tracking any changes.

As you route your wire, take particular care that the wires do not rub on anything or that anything will not rub on them. If this is even a question, secure the wire or place a protector around it to guard against any damage.

Grounding

When you hear about grounding on an EV, it takes on a whole different meaning from what you would expect. Some grounding on an EV is bad.

Floating Propulsion System Ground

On any EV main battery pack, no part of the high-voltage system is to be grounded (i.e., batteries, relays, controller, etc) to any part of the vehicle frame in any way. The pack should be completely isolated from the frame and the 12-V system. This minimizes the possibility of shock and ghost voltages.

Accessory 12-V System Grounded to Frame

The 12-V system stays grounded to the frame in most cases, just as it was in with the internal combustion engine machine. Since the frame is not connected to the high-voltage propulsion system, this is not a concern.

Frame Grounded to AC Neutral When Charging

The body of your EV should be grounded to the ac ground wire (green wire) when charging; this will prevent any electric shock and current leaks from finding the wrong path. If you do not have an onboard charger, attach an external ground when charging.

Electrical Wiring Diagrams

Figures 12-14 through 12-16 contain sample wiring diagrams for you to follow or just to examine. For your particular motor and controller setup, you will need to consult with the manufacturer for the correct wiring. There are far too many variations to ever list in just one chapter.

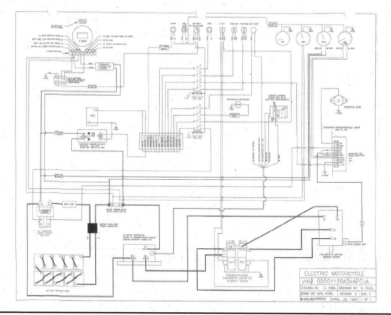

FIGURE 12-14 Electra Cruiser 120-V dc wiring schematic.

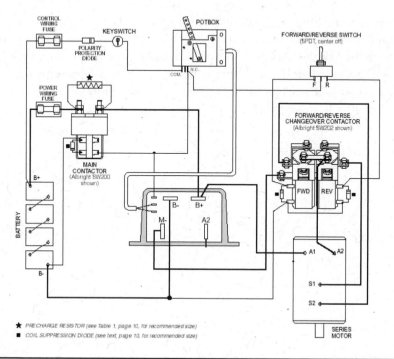

FIGURE 12-15 Typical wiring for a series-wound motor. (Courtesy of Curtis Instruments, www. curtisinst.com/index.cfm?fuseaction=Products.DownloadPDF&file=1209%2Epdf.)

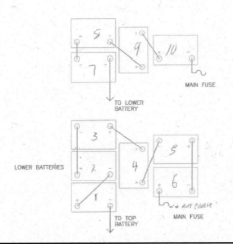

FIGURE 12-16   Battery layout for 10 batteries in series with two fuses.

Conclusion

The wiring of your EV is very important, so make sure that you take your time and do an exceptional job. This is one area where you do not want to rush or skimp. If there is something you are still not sure about, ask someone. It is better to ask a dumb question than to make a costly or dangerous mistake. Check with your local EV clubs. Ask the manufacturer of the products you are using; they will support you to some extent. To accompany this book, I will supply some additional online help on my Web site to answer any questions. Sometimes it is just the little question or that simple answer that can mean so much.

CHAPTER 13

The Build

This is finally the chapter that tells you how to put it all together. Previous chapters brought you through each system or component, giving you a basic knowledge of each subject. You have learned about electric motors, motor controllers, batteries, wiring, and many other subjects. I have tried to give you a little insight from my experience and the builds that I did so that you can learn from my mistakes and not have to repeat them. When I started years ago to build an electric motorcycle, people thought I was crazy. I was told that it could not be done. Now I sit here writing a book on the very subject, having proven that it can be done and done very well. Not many people can say that their electric motorcycle was a TV star on Discovery Science in the *Coolfuel Roadtrip*, traveling cross-county on clean energy (Figure 13-1). I proved that with a little ingenuity and determination, anything can happen. I hope that this helps to inspire you.

In this chapter I will take you through the conversion process step by step. I will point out the most important steps and what to look for. Since we are not using a known vehicle, and there are many variations, some of the information will be general. I think the best way to start is to keep it simple and plan your conversion wisely. After figuring out your first build, you will soon be an expert.

Conversion Overview

Where do we start? Well, at this point, you have an idea of the components you are going to use or you have acquired most of them. Your biggest piece of the puzzle is the frame you are using. This is the biggest deciding factor and sets the stage for the complete build.

Depending on the frame and the size bike you want to build, you will need to define many factors. You may need to scratch your head and go back to the drawing board and try to figure a new way to do something. Keep in mind that I am talking

FIGURE 13-1   Electra Cruiser during filming of the *Coolfuel Roadtrip* for Discover Science in New Jersey. Pictured are Shaun Murphy and Sparky. (Courtesy of Shaun Murphy and Gus Roxburgh, Balance Vector Productions, www.balancevector.com.)

about a systematic (step-by-step) process, part of which you will have to define yourself as you go along.

The object of this book is to get you up and running on your own electric vehicle (EV) as quickly and easily as possible. Figures 13-2 and 13-3 show some EVs. You will have some challenges, but a little planning will go a long way. Keep it simple. The actual process of your conversion is straightforward. Here are a few things to consider as you plan your build:

- Before your conversion, plan out your build so as to find as many answers as possible.
- During your build, stick to the plan; if changes arise, modify the plan and keep moving forward.
- After your conversion, complete all safety tests and do plenty of system testing and checking.

Before the Conversion

Before your actual conversion, gather all the information you can, just as you did with the motors, controllers, and batteries. This is an important step; the more planning that goes into the build, the better off you will be. If you are not sure about something, ask someone in the business or in the field for help. If you belong to a local EV group chapter, meet with them for as much help as you can get.

FIGURE 13-2   EVT electric scooter. (www.evtamerica.com/images/R-30blueleft.jpg.)

FIGURE 13-3   ZERO electric motorcycle. (www.zeromotorcycles.com/gallery.php.)

Help on Your Project

Make a list of all the types of help you might need, who you know that could help you, and who has expertise in what area. Maybe you know someone who can weld or another person who is good with wiring or electronics. Seek all the talent you can find.

Inside Help

Schedule, if possible, an extra hand or an extra set of eyes to help you through the process. Sometimes a fresh or different point of view is all you need. Frequently, you can get so focused on one thing that you forget to look outside the box for new answers.

Outside Help

Outside help involves people and professionals who have more knowledge in a subject than you. You might be able to figure something out, but sometimes another person can do it 10 times faster. If you need welding performed, subcontract that part out. If you are not a good welder, it is not worth your safety and the risk to you and your vehicle.

Arrange for Space

Not everyone has a garage, workshop, or large space in which to work. This is where you can enlist a friend who might have some space or a business such as a shop where you could work on your conversion. This may work to your advantage because now you have interested people around you who can help and perhaps tools other than your own available to you.

Arrange for Tools

Not everyone is a mechanic or has specialty cutting or machining tools. For some of your tasks, you can send the work out to a local machine shop. Maybe there are other tools you need? See if a friend can help and lend the proper tools; at the same time, enlist the help of that friend.

Arrange for Purchases and Deliveries

This actually falls in two areas. Planning is key, so knowing when a part or multiple parts will arrive is key to the planning of your build. Second, not everyone is always home to receive a special package in the mail or to have it delivered. You might want to make special arrangements to have certain items shipped to another address where they can be received. How horrible would it be if the local delivery person left your $1,500 motor controller on the steps of your house and someone stole it?

Conversion

Proper planning will pay off in the end. Do your build stage by stage; plan each piece one at a time. Take careful notes, pictures if you can. I found that as well as I planned, something would change, and I would have to work around it. I did find it useful to write things down as the design changed. I have done this myself—made a change and then forgot what I did months later.

Things to Keep in Mind

- *Frame.* Purchase, modify, and prepare

- *Mechanical.* Motor mount fabrication and drivetrain
- *Electrical.* High current, low current, and charging system
- *Battery.* Purchase and install the batteries

Frame

For the frame, you either decided to convert an existing motorcycle or you opted to purchase a complete frame, maybe a rolling frame, saving you the work of modifying the suspension and removing the engine. Or maybe you are adventurous and started completely from scratch.

Purchasing the Frame

The first step is selection of the frame and the complete suspension. Hopefully, you have a complete vehicle or a what is referred to as a *rolling frame* complete with suspension, tires ready for a transmission, and a motor. As stated earlier, take your time, and plan well.

Frame purchase details were covered in Chapter 6. Try to get the best vehicle to work with for the least amount of time and money. Ideally, if you bought a complete motorcycle, you don't need the engine, so you can do a tradeout, selling off what you don't need, and put that money back into the vehicle. Or maybe you want to do your friends a favor; keep the money for pizza and beer, and your friends are sure to keep coming back to help. Too much beer, however, and you may not get much work done. In the removal process, keep what you need, making sure that you do not sell off something you might require in the future. Figure 13-4 shows the finished Cruiser frame ready to receive batteries. You also could start like this with a clean frame and just build into the frame the battery support.

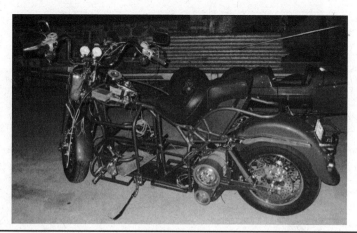

FIGURE 13-4 Prototype 2 Electra Cruiser ready for batteries.

Purchase of Other Components

Once you pick your frame, you can make other part decisions based on your overall performance goals: high mileage, quick acceleration, or general-purpose cruiser style bike. Expected vehicle range and acceleration can be calculated from vehicle's total weight, tire rolling resistance, aerodynamics, and the amount of energy and power available from the motor and batteries. This is accomplished with all the calculations found in Chapter 6.

One of the easiest and quickest ways to do your conversion is to order some of the parts you need from an EV distributor (see Chapter 14). Unlike EV cars, there are no real kits at this time that you could just call for and buy. This is one of the reasons creating your own vehicle will be such a unique experience. It would be nice if you could just call up and purchase a prepackaged kit, which would greatly simplify your conversion. Maybe that day will come in the very near future.

All the parts will be available from either one person or a few different vendors. You will have to decide who is the best and who has the better prices. The other items you want to order at this time can be found in your local motorcycle shop (Figure 13-5). You also may want to look for a service manual to cover basic wiring schematics to integrate the gasoline-powered bike's wiring into your EV circuitry.

Prepare the Chassis

The next step is to clean the frame and make some measurements. The first frame cleaning, if needed, will give you a good view and a clean canvas with which to work (Figure 13-6). After all the cleaning, you might want to paint the frame or

FIGURE 13-5 Loads of parts for the Electra Cruiser prototype 1.

FIGURE 13-6   Prepping the Cruiser frame for cleaning and more welding.

keep it clean and prepped for painting in the future. At this step, you still may opt for more modifications to fit batteries and battery mounts. Depending on what is needed, you may want to wait on the paint.

The measuring step involves determining the position of the transmission/ drivetrain or chain drive in relation to where the electric motor will be placed. This will take a little figuring out and maybe some actual placements of the motor in the frame. Keep in mind during all your measuring and fitting the optimal placement of your batteries and other components. Try to keep the weight as low as possible. You want to use all the space as best you can.

If you are dismantling an existing bike, the parts-removal process starts with draining all fluids: oil, transmission fluid, and gasoline. Remember to dispose of your fluids in an environmentally sound manner or recycle them. Draining gasoline from the tank is particularly dangerous and tricky. Drain as much as you can before you physically remove the tank. If the fuel is still good or marginal, you can use it in your car or lawnmower in a diluted mixture. Disposing of waste gasoline is expensive. If it is still usable, you might as well save the money. Next, carefully disconnect the throttle linkage—you will need it later—and set it aside, out of harm's way. Then remove everything that might interfere with the engine-removal process. Once the engine is removed, a shop or individual may purchase the engine and parts from you if they are still usable.

Mechanical

The mechanical part involves all the steps necessary to mount the motor and install the battery mounts and any other mechanical parts. In other words, next, do all the mechanical steps necessary for conversion. You follow this sequence because you want to have all the heavy drilling, banging, and welding—along with any associated metal shavings or scrap—done well and cleaned up before you tackle the more delicate electrical components and tasks. Let us take a closer look at the steps.

Mounting Your Electric Motor

Your mission here is to attach the new electric motor to the remaining mechanical drivetrain. The motor-to-drivetrain interface is your contact point. Depending on what type of system you are using, you may need to do some modifications. Try to figure out the best position for the motor that gives you as much room as possible. Leave some room for adjustments and error.

Four elements are involved:

- The critical distance between the motor and drive wheel
- Supports and mounts for the electric motor
- Front support-motor-to-transmission adapter plate
- Motor shaft–drive wheel connection

I will cover what's involved in each of these four areas in sequence. Understand that this discussion needs be generalized because there are at least a dozen good solutions for any given vehicle. So I'm going to talk in general terms here. You'll have to translate them to your own unique case. If your skills do not include precision machining of metal parts, this is another good area where you should enlist the services of a professional such as a l ocal machine shop.

The Critical Distance—Motor Interface with Wheel

Knowing that your goal here is how you are going to connect the motor to the drive wheel makes it easier to navigate toward it. In Chapter 5 we looked at a few different rear suspension configurations. As an example, in my build, I placed the transmission right on the rear swingarm, removing it from the frame and allowing more room (Figures 13-7 and 13-8). Pay particular attention to the movement of the swingarm if you are using a chain or a belt. As the swingarm moves, the distance between the motor and the back wheel can change, causing the chain or belt to loosen or tighten and bind. Try to place the motor as close to the center of the pivot point as possible. Figure 13-9 provides an example of a chain-drive system by ZERO electric motorcycles.

Support for the Electric Motor

This is a fairly straightforward area. Figure 13-10 shows the main mounting plate for mounting the motor to the rear swing arm. The mount uses four bolt holes that attach to the face of the motor. The two halves of a curved steel strap go around the

FIGURE 13-7 Fitting the transmission to the swingarm.

FIGURE 13-8 Transmission placed on prototype 1 swingarm.

rear of the motor and hold it securely in place. Always keep in mind that in some cases you may need to shim or just tweak things a little. This was the case on the Electra Cruiser. Once the motor and transmission were assembled, I had to make changes. Under load, the electric motor had so much torque that it pulled down on the transmission, slightly flexing the input shaft. This caused a slight misalignment in the 3-in-wide belt, making it shift and rub on the flange. To rectify this, I had to disassemble the drivetrain and create an input shaft-bearing support to compensate for the extra torque.

FIGURE 13-9   ZERO electric motorcycle chain drive. (www.zeromotorcycles.com/gallery.php.)

FIGURE 13-10   Modifying the motor mount on the rear swingarm.

Figure 13-11 shows the Harley-style 1948 transmission mounted to the rear swingarm. This picture is of the prototype 1 Electra Cruiser, which used a chain drive on both the primary and the secondary drives. Because of the high torque generated by this configuration, the prototype 1 would break drive chains under heavy acceleration. The last time the bike broke a chain was on the West Side Highway in New York City during the Tour de Sol. I heard a loud bang and watched three pieces of my chain fly past me and skid down the road. You will notice in the prototype 2 design that both the primary and secondary chains were replaced—the primary with a 3-in-wide belt and the secondary with a 1.5-in Kevlar belt. Prototype 2 managed to break a belt during a burnout.

FIGURE 13-11   Fitting the transmission to the swingarm, early prototype 1 chain drive.

In Figure 13-12, the transmission is removed, showing the mounting of the electric motor to the swingarm and the transmission mounting plate. Figure 13-13 shows the rear mounting bracket for the dc motor. Notice the 3-in-wide pulley on the motor shaft.

Figure 13-14 shows you how the clutch basket interfaces with the transmission and the electric motor on the rear swingarm.

Figure 13-15 shows the 1.5-in Harley-style Kevlar belt used to transfer power from the five-speed transmission to the rear wheel.

FIGURE 13-12   Fitting the motor to the swingarm.

FIGURE 13-13   Rear mounting bracket for the dc motor.

FIGURE 13-14   Clutch basket and belt configuration.

Creating Battery Mounts

For the two Electra Cruisers, the battery configurations were very similar. The big difference in the frame design was in how the batteries were loaded on the frame. Each frame I designed and built to accommodate 10 Trojan Group 27 lead-acid batteries. The total weight was just under 600 lb in batteries alone, so the frame had to be strong. Additionally, the weight had to be as low as possible. Therefore, in the layout I kept the lower level loaded more with batteries to keep the center of gravity low.

Figure 13-16 shows how all 10 batteries fit in the massive frame. This frame was solid steel. The batteries were slid from the lower front and fitted from front to rear. Then brackets were bolted in place. Figure 13-17 shows just the bottom row in place.

FIGURE 13-15 Cruiser swingarm and drive belt.

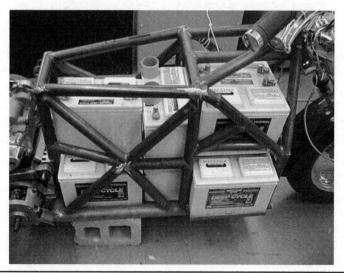

FIGURE 13-16 Fitting 10 Group 27 batteries in prototype 1.

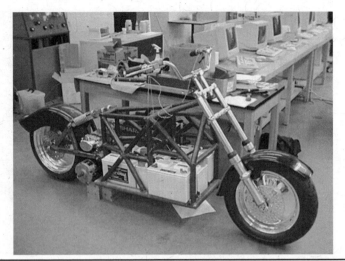

Figure 13-17   Bottom battery row in place (six batteries total in the lower level).

Electrical

The electrical part involves mounting the high-current, low-voltage, and charger connectors. Because I do not have a charger on board, we will just make a connector for one. Doing the electrical wiring requires knowledge of your EV's grounding plan: The high-current system is floating, and the low-voltage system is grounded to the frame. Doing the electrical wiring also involves knowledge of your EV's safety plan: Appropriate electrical interlocks must be provided in each system to ensure system shutdown in the event of a malfunction and to protect against accidental failure modes. Let us take a closer look at the steps.

High-Current System

First, you attach the high-current components, and then you pull the AWG 2/0 cable to connect them. Look back at Figure 12-15. Notice that there are six components in the high-current line:

- Series dc motor
- Motor controller
- Circuit breaker
- Main contactor
- Safety fuse
- Ammeter shunt

Figure 13-18 shows all the wiring tightly packed under the seat area. Also contained in this area is the Zapi dc motor controller. In this design, no space was left.

FIGURE 13-18   Controller and components packed tightly in the underseat area.

Low-Voltage System

On the low-voltage side, the idea is to blend the existing ignition, lighting, and accessory wiring with the new instrumentation and power wiring. There are six main components on the low-voltage side:

- Key switch
- Throttle potentiometer
- Ammeter, voltmeter, or other instrumentation
- Safety interlock(s)
- Accessory 12-V battery or dc-to-dc converter
- Safety fuse(s)

Every EV conversion should use the already-existing ignition key switch as a starting point. In an EV, the key switch serves as the main on-off switch with the convenience of a key—its starting feature is no longer needed. You should have no problem in locating and wiring this switch.

Figure 13-19 shows the inside of the fake fuel tank. Inside houses all the electronics that make the Cruiser function. You can see the Curtis PB-6 pot box in the front of the picture. Connected to the pot box is a cable from the throttle twist grip.

Figure 13-20 is another view of the inside of the tank from the side so that you can see the 12-V auxiliary gel battery for operating the lights and other 12-V systems. Directly underneath the battery is the Vicor dc-to-dc converter.

FIGURE 13-19   View into the Cruiser plastic mock fuel tank.

FIGURE 13-20   Inside view of mock tank showing gel battery and PB-6 pot box.

Battery Wiring

The most important consideration in battery wiring is to make the connections clean and tight. Figure 13-21 is a drawing of the top and bottom battery packs in their wired-up condition. Check that you have not accidentally reversed the wiring to any battery in the string as you go. Double-check your work when you finish, and use a voltmeter to measure across the completed battery pack to see that it produces the nominal voltage you expect. If not, measure across each battery

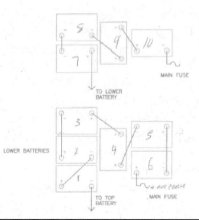

FIGURE 13-21 Battery wiring, top and bottom levels.

separately to determine the problem. If reversed wiring was the culprit, the correctly installed and wired battery should fix it. If a badly discharged or defective battery is the culprit, check to see that it comes up on charging and/or replace it with a good battery from your dealer. A recharged "dead" battery will shorten the life of the entire battery pack. Please be careful to check all the batteries. *Important:* Make sure that the main circuit breaker is off before you connect the last power cable in the battery circuit. Better still, switch the main circuit breaker off, and wait until the system checkout phase before making the final battery connection. Wear gloves, and remove all jewelry.

After Conversion

This is the system check, trial run, and finishing touches stage. First, make sure that everything works, and then find out how well it works. Then, try to make it work even better. When you're satisfied, you can paint, polish, and sign your work. Let's look at the individual areas.

System Checkout on Blocks

Jack up the drive wheel of your EV, and make sure that you are supporting the frame in such a way as to keep the bike from tipping over. The objective is to see that everything works right before you drive it out on the street for a test run. With your vehicle's drive wheel off the ground and the transmission in neutral (if you have a transmission), do the following:

- Before connecting the last battery cable, verify that the proper battery polarity connections have been made to the controller's B+ and B– terminals.
- Obtain a 100- to 200-Ω, 5- or 10-W resistor, and wire it in place across the main contactor's terminals. With the key switch off but the last battery cable

connected and the main circuit breaker on, measure the voltage across the controller's B+ and B– terminals. It should measure approximately 90 percent of the main battery pack voltage with the correct polarity to match the terminals. If this does not happen, troubleshoot the wiring connections. If it does, you're ready to turn the key switch on.

- Turn on the key switch with the accelerator off. If the motor runs without the accelerator pedal depressed, turn off the key switch and troubleshoot your wiring connections. If nothing happens when you turn on the key switch, go to the next step.

- With the transmission in first gear, slowly press the accelerator pedal to see if the wheels turn. If the wheels turn, good. Now look to see which way the wheel is turning. If the wheel is turning in the right direction, this is doubly good. If not, turn off the key switch and main breaker and interchange the dc series motor's field connections. If you are moving in the right direction, go to the next step.

- If you have the high pedal disable option on the Curtis controller, turn off the key switch, depress the accelerator pedal, and turn on the key switch. The motor should not run. Now completely release the accelerator, and slowly reapply it. The motor should run as before. If this does not work correctly, troubleshoot your wiring connections. If it works, you are ready for a road test. Turn off the key switch.

Trial Test Run

- Check the state of charge of your main battery pack. If it is fully charged or nearly full, you can proceed. If it is not charged, recharge it before taking the next step.

- After the batteries are fully charged, remove the jack and/or wheel stands from under your EV, and turn on the key switch. Put it in gear, crack the throttle slowly, and cruise off for a quick spin.

- The vehicle should have smooth acceleration and a good top speed, and it should brake and handle normally. The overwhelming silence should enable you to hear anything out of the ordinary with the drivetrain, motor, or brakes.

Moving Forward

Now that you have completed your EV, you must be full of pride. Riding an EV, especially a motorcycle, is an experience you cannot put into words. Usually the mile-long smile is enough. Take great care of your EV, and it will give you years of exceptional service. Cruise around and show it off. You will be amazed at the attention you will get.

CHAPTER 14

Sources

This chapter is a valuable tool to anyone looking for more information on any related subject. I included as many sources from around the country and the world as possible. I am sure that there are many more that I could have included. In 1996, when I first started the task of building an electric vehicle (EV), finding information was one of the hardest parts. I spent days in libraries, searching books, articles, magazines, and technical publications just trying to find all the information I needed. Sure, I found information eventually, but it was so time-consuming. At that time, trying to find information on how to build an electric motorcycle or similar vehicle was almost impossible. Today, that task is easier with the Internet, but you still have to search for the information. When I finally discovered the original book *Build Your Own Electric Vehicle*, it was like striking gold! This book became my roadmap to the EV world. As good as this book is, I still needed more information. The book was written about and based on full-sized electric cars; I needed more information on smaller vehicles and components. I hoped for information on electric motorcycles, but there was none—nothing at all for smaller EVs.

With this book, I vowed to supply my readers with as much information and resources as possible. Remembering back to all the time I spent and what I searched for, I have tried to include everything possible so that you do not have to spend too much of your valuable time. You will still have to do some reading, searching, and investigation on your own, but now it will be a lot easier. Some of the best places to start are with your local associations, such as the Electric Auto Association (EAA). In this chapter you will find listings for EAA chapters in almost every state and even some locations overseas. If you cannot find one in your state, start your own by contacting the national EAA, and bring other electronic vehicle enthusiasts together in your area.

One of the main goals of this book is to give you, in one place, all the benefits of my experience. I hope I have succeeded in doing so.

More Information over Time

This chapter contains as much information as I can give you today at the time of this printing. Ultimately, more information and technology will become available over time. To address this issue, I have set up a section on the Vogelbilt Web site with additional links, sources, and calculations for your convenience.

The rest of this chapter is divided into four sections:

- Clubs, associations, and organizations
- Manufacturers, converters, and consultants
- Suppliers
- Books, articles, and literature

Clubs, Associations, and Organizations

The original Electric Auto Association has numerous local chapters. There are offshoots from the original and new local entities having no connection with the original. There are also associations and organizations designed to serve corporate and commercial interests rather than individuals. Each one of these has its own meetings, events, and newsletter.

Electric Auto Association—www.eaaev.org

Founded in 1967, this is the oldest, largest organization, and it has consistently been the best source of EV information for individuals (Figure 14-1). The newsletter subscription is well worth the price of the membership dues. Recent newsletters have averaged 16–20 pages and provide information on current EV news and happenings. Becoming a member of the EAA and a local EAA chapter will gain you invaluable knowledge and resources from the members of this organization. The experience level of the EV enthusiasts who have built their own vehicles can shorten your learning curve substantially. Information on and photos of the many conversions done over the years by this organization and many others can be found at http://evalbum.com.

Figure 14-1   The Electric Auto Association's logo says it all. Registered trademark of the Electric Auto Association.

The following list contains all the current EAA chapters I could find at this time. Hopefully, one is near you, or if not, start your own!

Alaska

Alaska EAA
Web site: www.alaskaEVA.org
Contact: Mike Willmon <electrabishi@ak.net>
(907) 868-5710
Mailing: Attn: Mike Willmon, 2550 Denali Suite 1, Anchorage, AK 99503
Meetings: 8:00–9:00 p.m., third Friday of the month

Arizona

Flagstaff EAA
Contact: Barkley Coggin <cbcoggin@yahoo.com>
(928) 637-4444
Mailing: 6215 Rinker Circle, Flagstaff, AZ 86004
Meetings: 7:00–9:00 p.m., first Wednesday of the month

Phoenix EAA
Web site: www.phoenixeaa.com
Contact: Jim Stack <jstackeaa@yahoo.com>
(480) 659-5513
Mailing: Attn: Sam DiMarco, 1070 E. Jupiter Place, Chandler, AZ 85225
Meetings: 9:00 a.m., fourth Saturday of the month

Tucson EVA II
Web site: www.teva2.com
Contact: John Barnes <johnjab@cox.net>
(520) 293-3500
Mailing: Attn: John Barnes, 4207 N. Limberlost Place, Tucson, AZ 85705
Meetings: 9:00 a.m., second Saturday of the month

California

Central Coast EAA
Web site: www.eaacc.org
Contact: Will Beckett <will@becketts.ws>
(831) 688-8669
Mailing: 323 Los Altos Drive, Aptos, CA 95003
Meetings: Call or see Web site for meeting information.

Chico EAA
Web site: geocities.com/chicoeaa
Contact: Chuck Alldrin <chicoeaa@sunset.net>
(530) 899-1835
Mailing: 39 Lakewood Way, Chico, CA 95926
Meetings: 11:00 a.m.–1:00 p.m., second Saturday of the month

East (SF) Bay EAA
Web site: www.ebeaa.org
Contact: Ed Thorpe <EAA-contact@excite.com>
(510) 864-0662
Mailing: 2 Smith Court, Alameda, CA 94502-7786
Meetings: 10:00 a.m.–12:00 noon, fourth Saturday of the month

Education Chapter: San Diego State University, College of Engineering
Contact: James S. Burns, PhD <jburns@mail.sdsu.edu>
(619) 933-6058
Mailing: 6161 El Cajon Boulevard, San Diego, CA 92115
Meetings: Fourth Tuesday of each month during the academic year, except for December

EVA of Southern California
Contact: Leo Galcher <leo4marg@mac.com>
(949) 492-8115
Mailing: 35 Maracay, San Clemente, CA 92672
Meetings: 10:00 a.m., third Saturday of the month

Greater Sacramento EAA
Contact: Tim Hastrup <tim.hastrup@surewest.net>
(916) 791-1902
Mailing: 8392 West Granite Drive, Granite Bay, CA 95746
Meetings: 12:00 noon, third Tuesday of February, May, August, and November

Konocti EAA
Web site: www.konoctieaa.org
Contact: Dr. Randy Sun <rsun@mchsi.com>
(707) 263-3030
Mailing: 800 S. Main Street, Lakeport, CA 95453
Meetings: 11:00 a.m., last Friday of the month

North (SF) Bay EAA

Web site: www.nbeaa.org

Contact: Chris Jones <chris_b_jones@prodigy.net>

(707) 577-2391 (weekdays)

Mailing: c/o Agilent Technologies, 1400 Fountaingrove Parkway, Santa Rosa, CA 95403

Meetings: 10:00 a.m.–12:00 noon, second Saturday of the month; check Web site for details

EVA of San Diego

Web site: www.evaosd.com

Contact: Bill Hammons <ncsdca@att.net>

(858) 268-1759

Mailing: 1638 Minden Drive, San Diego, CA 92111

Meetings: 7:00 p.m., fourth Tuesday of the month

San Francisco EVA

Web site: www.sfeva.org

Contact: Sherry Boschert <info2007@sfeva.com>

(415) 681-7716

Mailing: 1484 16th Avenue, San Francisco, CA 94122-3510

Meetings: 11:00 a.m.–1:00 p.m., first Saturday of the month

San Francisco Peninsula EAA

Contact: Bill Carroll <billceaa@yahoo.com>

(650) 589-2491

Mailing: 160 Ramona Avenue, South San Francisco, CA 94080-5936

Meetings: 10:00 a.m., first Saturday of the month

San Jose EAA

Web site: geocities.com/sjeaa

Contact: Terry Wilson <historian@eaaev.org>

(408) 446-9357

Mailing: SJEAA, 20157 Las Ondas, San Jose, CA 95014

Meetings: 10:00 a.m., second Saturday of the month

Silicon Valley EAA

Web site: www.eaasv.org

Contact: Jerry Pohorsky <JerryP819@aol.com>

(408) 464-0711

Mailing: 1691 Berna Street, Santa Clara, CA 95050

Meetings: Third Saturday (January–November)

Ventura County EAA
Web site: geocities.com/vceaa
Contact: Bruce Tucker <tuckerb2@adelphia.net>
(805) 495-1026
Mailing: 283 Bethany Court, Thousand Oaks, CA 91360-2013
Meetings: Please contact Bruce for time and location.

Colorado

Denver Electric Vehicle Council
Contact: Graham Hill <ghill@21wheels.com>
(303) 544-0025
Mailing: 6378 S. Broadway, Boulder, CO 80127
Meetings: Third Saturday monthly; contact Graham for time and location.

Florida

Florida EAA
Web site: www.floridaeaa.org
Contact: Shawn Waggoner <shawn@suncoast.net>
(561) 543-9223
Mailing: 8343 Blue Cypress, Lake Worth, FL 33467
Meetings: 9:30 a.m., second Saturday of the month

Georgia

EV Club of the South
Web site: www.evclubsouth.org
Contact: Stephen Taylor <sparrow262@yahoo.com>
(678) 797-5574
Mailing: 750 West Sandtown Road, Marietta, GA 30064
Meetings: 6:00 p.m., first Wednesday every even-numbered month

Illinois

Fox Valley EAA
Web site: www.fveaa.org
Contact: Ted Lowe <ted.lowe@fveaa.org>
(630) 260-0424
Mailing: P.O. Box 214, Wheaton, IL 60189-0214
Meetings: 7:30 p.m., third Friday of the month

Kansas/Missouri

Mid-America EAA
Web site: maeaa.org
Contact: Mike Chancey <eaa@maeaa.org>
(816) 822-8079
Mailing: 1700 East 80th Street, Kansas City, MO 64131-2361
Meetings: 1:30 p.m., second Saturday of the month

Massachusetts

New England EAA
Web site: www.neeaa.org/
Contact: Bob Rice <bobrice@snet.net>
(203) 530-4942
Mailing: 29 Lovers Lane, Killingworth, CT 06419
Meetings: 2:00 p.m.–5:00 p.m., second Saturday of the month

Pioneer Valley EAA
Web site: www.pveaa.org
Contact: Karen Jones <PVEAA@comcast.com>
Mailing: P.O. Box 153, Amherst, MA 01004-0153
Meetings: 2:00 p.m., third Saturday of the month (January–June; September–November)

Minnesota

Minnesota EAA
Web site: mn.eaaev.org
Contact: Craig Mueller <craig.mueller@nwa.com>
(612) 414-1736
Mailing: 4000 Overlook Drive, Bloomington, MN 55437
Meetings: 7:00 p.m.–8:30 p.m. CDT

Nevada

Alternative Transportation Club, EAA
Web site: www.electricnevada.org
Contact: Bob Tregilus <lakeport104@yahoo.com>
(775) 826-4514
Mailing: 2805 W. Pinenut Court, Reno, NV 89509
Meetings: 6:00 p.m., monthly; see Web site or call for details

Las Vegas Electric Vehicle Association
Web site: www.lveva.org
Contact: William Kuehl <bill2k2000@yahoo.com>
(702) 636-0304
Mailing: 2816 El Campo Grande Avenue, North Las Vegas, NV 89031-1176
Meetings: 10:00 a.m.–12:00 noon, third Saturday of the month

New York

Long Island Electric Auto Association
Web site: www.LIEAA.org
Contact: Carl Vogel, president
Mailing: See Web site
Meetings: 6:00 p.m. the first Wednesday of the month. Normally, meetings are held on the campus of Farmingdale State College in Lupton Hall, Room T100. See Web site for details. Contact the LIEAA for more information and location because we change our location from time to time.

North Carolina

Coastal Carolinas Wilmington EEA
Contact: Page Paterson <pagepaterson@mac.com>
(910) 686-9129
Mailing: 1317 Middle Sound, Wilmington, NC 28411
Meetings: Please contact us for time and date.

Piedmont Carolina Electric Vehicle Association
Web site: www.opecthis.info
Contact: Todd W. Garner <tgarnercgarner@yahoo.com>
(704) 849-9648
Mailing: 1021 Timber Wood Court, Matthews, NC 28105
Meetings: Please contact us for time and date.

Electric Cars of Roanoke Valley
Contact: Harold Miller <EV@schoollink.net>
(252) 534-1258
Mailing: 567 Miller Trail, Jackson, NC 27845
Meetings: Please contact us for time and date.

Triad Electric Vehicle Association
Web site: www.localaction.biz/TEVA
Contact: Jack Martin <jmartin@hotmail.com>
(336) 213-5225
Mailing: 2053 Willow Spring Lane, Burlington, NC 27215
Meetings: 9:00 a.m., first Saturday of the month

Triangle EAA

Web site: www.rtpnet.org/teaa
Contact: Peter Eckhoff <teaa@rtpnet.org>
(919) 477-9697
Mailing: 9 Sedley Place, Durham, NC 27705-2191
Meetings: Third Saturday of the month

Oregon

Oregon Electric Vehicle Association

Web site: www.oeva.org
Contact: Rick Barnes <barnes.rick@verizon.net>
Mailing: 19100 SW Vista Street, Aloha, OR 97006
Meetings: 7:30 p.m., second Thursday of the month

Pennsylvania

Eastern Electric Vehicle Club

Web site: www.eevc.info
Contact: Peter G. Cleaveland <easternev@aol.com>
(610) 828-7630
Mailing: P.O. Box 134, Valley Forge, PA 19482-0134
Meetings: 7:00 p.m., second Wednesday of the month

Texas

Alamo City EAA

Web site: www.aceaa.org
Contact: Alfonzo Ranjel <acranjel@sbcglobal.net>
(210) 389-2339
Mailing: 9211 Autumn Bran, San Antonio, TX 78254
Meetings: 3:00 p.m. CST, third Sunday of the month

AustinEV: The Austin Area EAA

Web site: www.austinev.org
Contact: Aaron Choate <austinev-info@austinev.org>
(512) 453-2890
Mailing: P.O.Box 49153, Austin, TX 78765
Meetings: Please see our Web site.

Houston EAA

Web site: www.heaa.org
Contact: Dale Brooks <brooksdale@usa.net>
(713) 218-6785
Mailing: 8541 Hatton Street, Houston, TX 77025-3807
Meetings: 6:30 p.m., third Thursday of the month

North Texas EAA

Web site: www.nteaa.org/
Contact: John L. Brecher <jlbrecher@verizon.net>
(214) 703-5975
Mailing: 1128 Rock Creek Drive, Garland, TX 75040
Meetings: Second Saturday of the month

Utah

Utah EV Coalition

Web site: www.saltflats.com
Contact: Kent Singleton <kent@saltflats.com>
(801) 644-0903
Mailing: 325 E. 2550 N #83, North Ogden, UT 84414
Meetings: 7:00 p.m., first Wednesday of the month

You'll meet the BYU Electric Team, the WSU-EV Design Team, and other land speed racing celebrities. Always a great turnout.

Washington

Seattle Electric Vehicle Association

Web site: www.seattleeva.org
Contact: Steven S. Lough <stevenslough@comcast.net>
(206) 524-1351
Mailing: 6021 32nd Avenue NE, Seattle, WA 98115-7230
Meetings: 7:00 p.m., second Tuesday of the month

Washington, DC

EVA of Washington, DC

Web site: www.evadc.org
Contact: David Goldstein <goldie.ev1@juno.com>
(301) 869-4954
Mailing: 9140 Centerway Road, Gaithersburg, MD 20879-1882
Meetings: 7:00 p.m., second or third Tuesday of the month

Electric Vehicle Association of Greater Washington, DC, has an excellent overview, "Build an EV," at www.evadc.org/build_an_ev.html. Much of the material presented herein comes from this Web site.

Wisconsin

Southern Wisconsin EV Proliferation

Web site: www.emissionsfreecars.com
Contact: Mike Turner <mike.turner@emissionsfreecars.co>
(920) 261-7057
Mailing: 808 Fieldcrest Court, Watertown, WI 53511
Meetings: Please contact us for date and location.

Canada

Durham Electric Vehicle Association

Web site: www.durhamelectricvehicles.com
Contact: J. P. Fernback <mail@durhamelectricvehicles.com>
(905) 706-6647
Mailing: P.O. Box 212, Whitby, ON L1N 5S1, Canada
Meetings: First Thursday of the month from September to June

Electric Vehicle Council of Ottawa

Web site: evco.ca
Contact: Alan Poulsen <info@evco.ca>
(613) 271-0940
Mailing: P.O. Box 4044, Ottawa, ON K1S5B1, Canada
Meetings: 7:30 p.m.–10:00 p.m., last Monday of the month

Electric Vehicle Society of Canada—Toronto

Web site: www.evsociety.ca
Contact: Neil Gover <neil@ontarioev.ca>
(416) 255-9723
Mailing: 88 Lake Promenade, Etobicoke, ON M8W-1A3, Canada
Meetings: 7:30 p.m., third Thursday of the month (except July and August)

Vancouver Electric Vehicle Association

Web site: www.veva.bc.ca
Contact: Haakon MacCallum <info@veva.bc.ca>
(604) 527-4288
Mailing: 4053 West 32nd Avenue, Vancouver, BC V65 1Z5, Canada
Meetings: 7:30 p.m., third Wednesday of the month (please check Web site for details)

Europe

European Chapter
Web site: www.eaaeurope.org
Contact: Rüdiger Hild, chairman
Mailing: Forststrasse 14, D-66538 Neunkirchen, Saarland, Germany
The EAA Europe was formed in 2008 in Germany as the European Chapter.

EAA Special-Interest Chapters

AltWheels
WebSite: www.altwheels.org
Contact: Alison Sander <info@altwheels.org>
(617) 868-1582

California Cars Initiative
Web site: calcars.org
Contact: Felix Kramer <info@calcars.org>
(650) 520-5555
Mailing: P.O. Box 61045, Palo Alto, CA 94306

Electric Drive Transportation Association (EDTA)
Web site: www.electricdrive.org
(202) 408-0774
Mailing: 1101 Vermont Avenue, NW, Suite 401, Washington, DC 20005
EDTA is the preeminent industry association dedicated to advancing electric drive as a core technology on the road to sustainable mobility. As an advocate for the adoption of electric drive technologies, EDTA serves as the unified voice for the industry and is the primary source of information and education related to electric drive. Our membership includes a diverse representation of vehicle and equipment manufacturers, energy providers, component suppliers and end users.

EV Album
Web site: www.evalbum.com
A great site to view other custom vehicles in all types and sizes.

Helping People Get Rid of Gas since 1995
Web site: www.evconvert.com
Online forum with lots of information, a great EV calculator page, and a battery page.

MAEAA Web Links
Web site: www.geocities.com/mideaa/links.html
From this site you will find an array of different links for components, batteries, user groups, plans, events, and much more. Some of the links might be out of date, but most are current.

Northeast Sustainable Energy Association (NESEA)

(413) 774-6051

Mailing: 23 Ames Street, Greenfield, MA 01301

Organized the annual American Tour de Sol and an electric vehicle symposium from 1989 to 2006. As of 2007, The 21st Century Automotive Challenge takes over for the American Tour de Sol (see below).

Plug In America

Web site: www.pluginamerica.com

Contact: Linda Nicholes <Linda@pluginamerica.com>

(714) 974-5647

Mailing: 6261 East Fox Glen, Anaheim, CA 92807

Meetings: Please contact us for details.

Solar and Electric Racing Association

(602) 953-6672

Mailing: 11811 N. Tatum Boulevard, Suite 301, Phoenix, AZ 85028

Organizes annual Solar and Electric 500 in Phoenix and promotes electric vehicles.

Solar Energy Expo and Rally (SEER)

(707) 459-1256

Mailing: 239 S. Main Street, Willits, CA 95490

Host for annual Tour de Mendo, when Willets temporarily becomes the solar capital of the world.

The EV Tradin' Post

Web site: www.austinev.org/evtradingpost

This site offers an array of resources for electric vehicles. You can find want ads, parts, accessories, events, manuals, and services.

21st Century Automotive Challenge

Web site: www.eevc.info

Contact: Oliver H. Perry

(609) 268-0944

Organized by the Eastern Electric Vehicle Club, a chapter of the U.S. EAA. The competition showcases cutting-edge approaches to energy-saving vehicle transportation, including hybrid vehicles, biofuel vehicles, electric vehicles, and any other non–fossil fuel vehicle or energy-saving vehicle.

V is for Voltage

Web site: http://visforvoltage.org/

EV Racing

National Electric Drag Racing Association (NEDRA)

Web site: www.nedra.com

Mailing: 3200 Dutton Avenue, No. 220, Santa Rosa, CA 95407

NEDRA exists to increase public awareness of electric vehicle performance and to encourage, through competition, advances in electric vehicle technology. NEDRA achieves this by organizing and sanctioning safe, silent, and exciting electric vehicle drag racing events.

Plasma Boy EV Racing

Web site: www.plasmaboyracing.com

We blow things up, so you don't have to!

ProEV

Web site: ProEV.com

(305) 610-6412

Mailing: 7735 NE 8th Avenue, Miami, FL 33138

ProEV is a professional race team that offers electric vehicle and components testing and development. They develop and promote electric vehicles through competition. ProEV believes that the electric motor is the tool to replace the internal combustion engine (ICE). We plan to prove it, at the track!

Electric Utilities and Power Associations

Any of the following organizations can provide you with information.

American Public Power Association

(202) 775-8300

Mailing: 2301 M Street, NW, Washington, DC 20202

Arizona Public Service Company

(602) 250-2200

Mailing: P.O. Box 53999, Phoenix, AZ 85072-3999

California Energy Commission

(916) 654-4001

Mailing: 1516 9th Street, Sacramento, CA 95814

Director of Electric Transportation

Department of Water and Power, City of Los Angeles

(213) 481-4725

Mailing: 111 N. Hope Street, Room 1141, Los Angeles, CA 90012-2694

Electric Power Research Institute
(415) 855-2580
Mailing: 412 Hillview Avenue, P.O. Box 10412, Palo Alto, CA 94303

Public Service Company of Colorado
(303) 571-7511
Mailing: 2701 W. 7th Avenue, Denver, CO 80204

Sacramento Municipal Utility District
(916) 732-6557
Mailing: P.O. Box 15830, Sacramento, CA 95852-1830

Southern California Edison
(818) 302-2255
Mailing: 2244 Walnut Grove Avenue, P.O. Box 800, Rosemead, CA 91770

Government

The following agencies are involved with EVs directly or indirectly at the city, state, or federal government level.

California Air Resources Board (CARB)
(916) 322-2990
Mailing: 1012 Q Street, P.O. Box 2815 Sacramento, CA 95812

Environmental Protection Agency (EPA)
(202) 260-2090
Mailing: 401 M Street SW, Washington, DC 20460

National Highway Traffic Safety Administration
(202) 366-1836
Mailing: 400 7th Street SW, Washington, DC 20590

New York Power Authority
Mailing: 123 Main Street, White Plains, NY 10601

New York State Energy Research and Development Authority (NYSERDA)
Web site: www.nyserda.org
Mailing: 17 Columbia Circle, Albany, New York 12203-6399

Manufacturers, Converters, and Consultants

There is a sudden abundance of people and firms doing EV work. This category is an attempt to present you with the firms and individuals from whom you can expect either a completed EV or assistance with completing one.

Manufacturers

This category includes the household names plus the major independents. When contacting the larger companies, it is best to go through the switchboard or a public affairs person who can direct your call after finding out your specific needs.

Ampmobile Conversions, LLC

Mailing: P.O. Box 5106, Lake Wylie, SC 29710

(803) 831-1082 or toll free 1 (866) 831-1082

E-mail: info@ampmobiles.com

Battery Automated Transportation

Mailing: 2471 S. 2570 W, West Valley City, UT 84119

(801) 977-0119

Best known for its proprietary Ultra Force lead-acid batteries and Ford Ranger pickup truck conversions.

California Electric Cars

Mailing: 1669 Del Monte Boulevard, Seaside, CA 93955

(408) 899-2012

Best known for its Monterey electric vehicle.

Clean Air Transport of North America

Mailing: 23030 Lake Forest Drive, Suite 206, Laguna Hills, CA 92653

(714) 951-3983

Best known for its LA301 electric vehicle.

Cloud Electric Vehicles Battery Powered Systems

Mailing: 102 Ellison St., Unit A, Clarksville, GA 30523

(866) 222-4035

Bob Beaumont

Columbia Auto Sales

Mailing: 9720 Owen Brown Road, Columbia, MD 21045

(301) 799-3550

Bob produced the Renaissance Tropica seen in the late 1990s on the network television show *Nash Bridges*. The sleek two-seater was powered by 72-V lead-acid batteries; only two or three survived.

Cushman

Mailing: 900 North 21st Street, Lincoln, NE 68503

(402) 475-9581

Manufactures three-wheeler industrial and commercial electric carts.

Electric Mobility

Web site: www.icdri.org/Mobility/electric_mobility_corporation.htm
Mailing: 591 Mantua Boulevard, Sewell, NJ 08080
(800) 257-7955
Manufactures electric carts, bicycles, etc.

ElectroAutomotive

Web site: www.electroauto.com
Mailing: P.O. Box 1113-W, Felton, CA 95018-1113
(831) 429-1989
Fax: (831) 429-1907

Electric Motorsport

Web site: www.electricmotorsport.com
Mailing: 2400–2404 Mandela Parkway, Oakland, CA 94607
(510) 839-9376
Supplier of EV parts for cars, trucks, boats, ATVs, motorcycles, and much more.

EV Parts, Inc.

Web site: www.evparts.com
Mailing: 160 Harrison Road, No. 7, Sequim, WA 98382
(360) 582-1271 or toll free at (888) 387-2787
Fax: (360) 582-1272
E-mail: sales@evparts.com

Green Motor Works (also a solar electric dealer)

Mailing: 5228 Vineland, North Hollywood, CA 91601
(818) 766-3800

Metric Mind Engineering

Web site: www.metricmind.com
Mailing: 9808 SE Derek Court, Happy Valley, OR 97806-7250
(503) 680-0026
Fax: (503) 774-4779

Motorworks Clean Vehicles, Inc.

Web site: www.CleanVehiclesNY.com
Contact: Gary Birke <Gary@CleanVehiclesNY.com>
Mailing: 11 Sunrise Highway, Amityville, NY 11701
(866) 527-2669
(631) 608-4380
All-electric and flex-fuel low-speed vehicles.
  Clean vehicles . . . for a cleaner tomorrow! Help us clean New York's air with Clean Air NY! Visit us at www.cleanairny.org/exthome.htm.

Palmer Industries
Web site: www.palmerind.com
Mailing: P.O. Box 707, Endicott, NY 13760
(800) 847-1304
Manufactures an electric bicycle.

Conversion Specialists

In this category, the line between those who provide parts and those who provide completed vehicles is blurred.

Electric Auto Conversions
Bill Kuehl
Mailing: 4504 W. Alexander Road, Las Vegas, NV 89030
(702) 645-2132

CoolGreenCar.net or EvPorsche.com
Web site: coolgreencar.net or ElectricPorsche.net
E-mail: PVL959@bellsouth.net
Mailing: West Palm Beach, FL 33406
(561) 301-2369
Building the finest daily-driver electric vehicle in the world using state-of-the-art components. This company builds an array of high-end EVs, including motorcycles.

Grassroots Electric Vehicles
Mailing: 1918 South 34th St., Fort Pierce, FL 34947
(772) 971-0533

Greenshed Conversions
Contact: Steve Clunn <Steveclunn@gmail.com>
Fax: (206) 202-4171
Mailing: P.O. Box 13077, Fort Pierce, FL 34979
Steve is a pioneer in the EV conversion business.

Vehicles and Components

Electric Motor Cars Sales and Service
Ken Bancroft
Mailing: 4301 Kingfisher, Houston, TX 77035
(713) 729-8668
Vehicles and components.

Electric Transportation Applications
Don Karner
Mailing: P.O. Box 10303, Glendale, AZ 85318
(602) 978-1373
Vehicles and components.

Electric Vehicles, Inc.
Stan Skokan
Mailing: 1020 Parkwood Way, Redwood City, CA 94060
(415) 366-0643

Electric Vehicle Custom Conversion
Larry Foster
Mailing: 1712 Nausika Avenue, Rowland Heights, CA 91748
(818) 913-8579
Vehicles and components.

Hitney Solar Products
Gene Hitney
Mailing: 655 N. Highway 89, Chino Valley, AZ 86323
(602) 636-2201

Interesting Transportation
Frank Kelly
Mailing: 2362 Southridge Drive, Palm Springs, CA 92264-4960
(619) 327-2864

San Diego Electric Auto
Ron Larrea
Mailing: 9011 Los Coches Road, Lakeside, CA 92040
(619) 443-3017

Vicor Corporation
Mailing: 25 Frontage Road, Andover, MA 01810-5413
(800) 735-6200
Fax: (978) 475-6715
dc-dc, dc-ac converters

W. D. Mitchell
Mailing: 20 Victoria Drive, Rowlett, TX 75055
(214) 475-0361

Experienced EV Conversions and Consulting

Eyeball Engineering
Ed Ranberg
Mailing: 16738 Foothill Boulevard, Fontana, CA 92336
(714) 829-2011
Experienced EV conversion professional; components and consulting.

E-Motion
Lon Gillas
Mailing: 515 W. 25th Street, McMinnville, OR 97128
(503) 434-4332

Consultants

Companies and individuals who are more likely to provide advice, literature, or components—rather than completed vehicles—are listed.

Aerovironment
Mailing: P.O. Box 5031, Monrovia, CA 91017-7131
(818) 359-9983
Developers of the GM Impact, Paul McCready and Aerovironment need no further introduction. In September 2007, Paul passed away after a short illness, just after retiring from Aerovironment. His insight initially sparked the concept car that GM made into the EV-1, the subject of the 2006 movie *Who Killed the Electric Car?*

Bob Wing
Mailing: P.O. Box 277, Inverness, CA 94937
(415) 669-7402

Carl Taylor
Mailing: 3871 SW 31st Street, Hollywood, FL 33023
(305) 981-9462
EV maintenance, repair, and troubleshooting.

Earthmind
Mailing: P.O. Box 743, Mariposa, CA 95338
(310) 396-1527

Electro Automotive
Mailing: P.O. Box 1113, Felton, CA 95018-1113
(831) 429-1989
Contacts: Michael Brown and Shari Prange
This organization, an experienced participant in the EV field, offers books, videos, seminars, consulting, and components. Mike and Shari still supply kits for

conversion builders, complete parts, and instruction manuals and are finding that with the high gasoline prices since Hurricane Katrina came ashore in 2005, their business is brisk. They carry ac drive systems from Azure Dynamics (formerly Solectria, founded by MIT students).

EV Consulting, Inc.

Web site: www.evconsultinginc.com
Mailing: 944 West 21st Street, Upland, CA 91784
(909) 949-1818
Performs engineering consulting only. This consulting is confined to conventional dc hardware such as series-wound motors, PWM controllers, and all the other ancillary components that support a dc system.

Howard G. Wilson

Mailing: 2050 Mandeville Canyon Road, Los Angeles, CA 90049
Former Hughes vice president, Howard Wilson was the real "make it happen" factor behind GM's Impact and Sunraycer projects.

Michael Hackleman

Author, editor of *Alternative Transportation News*, experienced EV participant, and a consultant.

Mike Kimball

Mailing: 18820 Roscoe Boulevard, Northridge, CA 91324
(818) 998-1677
EV technician and maintenance mechanic extraordinaire, Mike has probably forgotten more about EVs than most people will ever know.

3E Vehicles

Mailing: Box 19409, San Diego, CA 92119
Another experienced participant in the EV field, 3E offers an outstanding line of conversion booklets that (although somewhat dated today) are highly useful.

Vogelbilt Corp.

Web site: www.vogelbilt.com
Mailing: 656 Wellwood Avenue, C 318, Lindenhurst, NY 11757
Contact: Carl Vogel

Williams Enterprises

Mailing: Box 1548, Cupertino, CA 95015
Contact: Bill Williams
Experienced participant in the EV field, conversion specialist, and consultant, Williams offers an outstanding conversion guide that (although somewhat dated today) is very useful.

Suppliers

This category includes those from whom you can obtain complete conversion kits (all the parts you need to build your own EV after you have the chassis), conversion plans, and suppliers specializing in motors, controllers, batteries, chargers, and other components.

You can find more information about conversions and components at http://eaaev.org/eaalinks.html.

Battery Powered Systems
Web site: www.beepscom.com/
Mailing: 204 Ellison St., Unit A, Clarkesville, GA 30523

Canadian Electric Vehicles, Ltd.
Mailing: P.O. Box 616, 1184 Middlegate Rd., Errington, BC V0R 1V0, Canada
(250) 954-2230
Fax: (250) 954-2235
E-mail: randy@canev.com

Cloud Electric, LLC
Web site: www.cloudelectric.com
Mailing: 204 Ellison St., Clarkesville, GA 30523
(706) 839-1733
(877) 808-0939
Open: 9:00 a.m.–5:00 p.m. Eastern time Monday–Friday
Electrical and electronic products for EVs, home, RVs, and marine, industrial, and other applications.

Datel
Web site: www.datel.com
Manufacturer of dc-dc converters, ac-dc power supplies, high-reliability power supplies, digital panel meters, and much more. See Web site for location of nearest dealer.

ElectroCraft Systems
Web site: www.evcraft.com
Mailing: 23 Paperbirch Drive, Toronto, ON M3C 2E6, Canada
(416) 391-5958
E-mail: sales@evcraft.co

EV Parts, Inc.
Web site: www.evparts.com
Mailing: 160 Harrison Road, No. 7, Sequim, WA 98382
(888) 387-2787
E-mail: sales@evparts.com

EV Source LLC
Mailing: 19 W Center, Suite 201, Logan, UT 84321
(877) 215-6781
E-mail: sales@evsource.com

KTA Services, Inc.
Web site: www.kta-ev.com
Mailing: 20330 Rancho Villa Road, Ramona, CA 92065
(760) 787-0896 or toll free at (877) 465-8238
Fax: (760) 787-9437
E-mail: wistar.rhoads@kta-ev.com
Provides EV components and kits.

Manzanita Micro EV Components
Web site: www.manzanitamicro.com

Metric Mind Corporation
Web site: www.metricmind.com
Mailing: 9808 SE Derek Court, Happy Valley, OR 97086
(503) 680-0026
Fax: (503) 774-4779
Contact: Victor Tikhonov
The main goal of Metric Mind Corporation is to promote EVs and make available high-end EV components manufactured specifically for the EV industry by the world's leading suppliers. Unlike large OEMs, however, MMC provides (imports, sells, and supports) top-end EV ac drive systems as well as other EV components to individual EV enthusiasts and small businesses.

Rich Rudman
Mailing: 5718 Gamblewood Rd., NE, Kingston, WA 98346
Office: (360) 297-7383
Cell: (360) 620-6266
Production shop: (360) 297-1660
Metal shop: (360) 297-3311

ThunderStuck Motors
Mailing: 3200 Dutton Avenue, No. 319, Santa Rosa, CA 95407
(707) 575-0353
Fax: (707) 544-5304
ThunderStruck Motors is a small research, development, and manufacturing company that also retails EVs and components.

Xantrex

Web site: www.xantrex.com

Mailing: 8999 Nelson Way, Burnaby, BC V5A 4B5, Canada

(604) 422-8595

Fax: (604) 420-1591

Supplier of the Link 10 battery monitor.

Conversion Kits

Companies and individuals listed here are those more likely to provide the parts that go into converting or building an EV once you already have the chassis, such as components, advice, literature, etc.

Electric Auto Crafters

John Stockberger

Mailing: 643 Nelson Lake Road, a2S, Batavia, IL 60510

(312) 879-0207

Provides parts, information, and testing for EV builders.

Electric Vehicles of America (EVA)

Bob Batson

Web site: www.ev-america.com

Mailing: Wolfeboro, NH 03894

(603) 569-2100

Provides kits, components, and literature. EVA was founded in 1988 by Bob Batson.

Global Light and Power

Steve van Ronk

Mailing: 55 New Montgomery, Suite 424, San Francisco, CA 94105

(415) 495-0494

Kits and components; promotes annual Clean Air Revival.

King Electric Vehicles

Steve Deckard

Mailing: Box 514, East Syracuse, NY 13057

KTA Services, Inc.

Web site: www.kta-ev.com

Mailing: 20330 Rancho Villa Road, Ramona, CA 92065

(760) 787-0896 or toll free at (877) 465-8238

Fax: (760) 787-9437

E-mail: wistar.rhoads@kta-ev.com

Paul Schutt and Associates
Mailing: 673 Via Del Monte, Palos Verdes Estates, CA 90274
(310) 373-4063
Represents manufacturers who supply EV components. Well known for their prototype vehicles using proprietary technology; offers numerous advanced EV capabilities and components.

Performance Speedway
C. Fetzer
Mailing: 2810 Algonquin Avenue, Jacksonville, FL 32210
(904) 387-9858

Conversion Plans

Listed here are companies and individuals who are more likely to provide vehicle plans, kits, or components rather than completed vehicles.

Doran Motor Company
Rick Doran
Mailing: 1728 Bluehaven Drive, Sparks, NV 89431
(805) 546-9654
(702) 359-6735
Best known for the Doran three-wheeler and its plans.

Dolphin Vehicles
Mailing: P.O. Box 110215, Campbell, CA 95011
(408) 734-2052
Best known for the Vortex three-wheeler and its plans for either internal combustion or electric propulsion.

Motors

A list of the popular motors on the market from dc to ac motors.

Advanced DC Motors, Inc.
Mailing: 219 Lamson St., Syracuse, NY 13206
(315) 434-9303

Aveox, Inc.
Web site: www.aveox.com/Default.aspx
Mailing: 2265A Ward Avenue, Simi Valley, CA 93065
(805) 915-0200

Baldor Electric Co.
Mailing: 5711 South 7th, Ft. Smith, AR 72902
(501) 646-4711

Hi-Torque Electric
Web site: www.hitorqueelectric.com/about
Mailing: 460 NE Hemlock Avenue, Unit C, Redmond, OR 97756
(541) 548-6140
Electric motor sales, repairs, and high-performance modifications.

Lynch Motor Company, Ltd.
Web site: www.lmcltd.net
Mailing: Unit 8, Park Court, Heathpark, Honiton, Devon, EX14 1SW, United
Kingdom
44 (0) 1404 549940
Fax: +44 (0) 1404 549546
E-mail: sales@lmcltd.net
Specialists in the field of low-voltage, high-torque permanent-magnet dc motors
and generators. All their products offer the very best in efficiency and low weight
with maximum power possible in the smallest package possible.

NetGain Technologies, LLC
Web site: www.go-ev.com/
Mailing: 900 North State Street, Suite 101, Lockport, IL 60441
(630) 243-9100
Fax: (630) 685-4054
NetGain Technologies is the exclusive worldwide distributor of WarP, ImPulse and
TransWarP electric motors for use in EVs and EV conversions. These powerful electric
motors also may be used in the conversion of conventional internal combustion
engine vehicles to hybrid gas/electric or electric-assist vehicles. Their motors are
manufactured in Frankfort, Illinois, by Warfield Electric Motor Company.

Sevcon, Inc.
Web site: www.sevcon.com
Mailing: 155 Northboro Rd., Southborough, MA 01772
(508) 281-5500

UQM Technologies
Web site: www.uqm.com
Mailing: 7501 Miller Drive, P.O. Box 439, Frederick, CO 80530
(303) 278-2002
Fax: (303) 278-7007
UQM Technologies is a developer and manufacturer of power-dense, high-
efficiency electric motors, generators, and power electronic controllers for the
automotive, aerospace, medical, military, and industrial markets.

Controllers

A considerable number of companies manufacture controllers; again, this short list is only to get you started.

Alltrax, Inc.

Web site: www.alltraxinc.com
Mailing: 1111 Cheney Creek Road, Grants Pass, OR 97527
(541) 476-3565
E-mail: info@alltraxinc.com

Alltrax is a U.S.-based company that builds rugged electric dc motor controllers using the latest power electronics technology.

Café Electric LLC

Web site: www.cafeelectric.com
(866) 860-6608

Supplier of the Zilla and Baby Zilla dc motor speed controllers. This well-engineered design is proving virtually indestructible compared with some of its predecessors, such as Auburn and DCP controllers. The IGBT-based solid-state controllers are favorites among street and drag race performance EVs. They can handle 2,000 A at peak voltages to 348 V dc and 1,000 A for the baby Zilla.

ElectroCraft Systems

Web site: www.evcraft.com
Mailing: 23 Paperbirch Drive, Toronto, ON M3C 2E6, Canada
(416) 391-5958
E-mail: sales@evcraft.com

Curtis Instruments, Inc.

Mailing: 200 Kisco Avenue, Mount Kisco, NY 10549
(914) 666-2971

Curtis PMC

Web site: www.curtisinst.com
Mailing: 235 East Airway Boulevard, Livermore, CA 94551
(925) 961-1088

Supplies a number of different components for EVs, including motor controllers, gauges, battery chargers, contactors, and more. See Web site for complete listing. Also has offices in Europe and Asia.

Kelly Controls, LLC

Web site: www.kellycontroller.com
(001) 224 637 5092
See Web site for local distributors.

Navitas Technologies, Ltd.

Web site: www.navitastechnologies.com

Mailing: C-855 Trillium Drive, Kitchener, Ontario N2R 1J9, Canada

(519) 725-7871

High-efficiency MOSFET controller with the innovation of microprocessor technology to provide smooth, flexible, and reliable control. Some models have regen capabilities.

P&G Drives Technology

Web site: www.pgdt.com

Mailing: 2532 East Cerritos Avenue, Anaheim, CA 92806-5627

(714) 712-7911

Sevcon, Inc.

Web site: www.sevcon.com

Mailing: 155 Northboro Road, Southborough, MA 01772

(508) 281-5500

Zapi, Inc.

Web site: www.zapiinc.com

Mailing: 210 James Jackson Avenue, Cary, NC 27513

(919) 789-4588

E-mail: info@zapiinc.com

Manufacturer of electronic controllers since 1975. Supplier of motor controllers for both dc and ac systems.

Batteries

AeroBatteries, Inc.

Web site: www.aerobatteries.com

Mailing: 309 Airport Drive, Tyler, TX 75704

(903) 592-2176

Alco Battery Co.

Mailing: 2980 Red Hill Avenue, Costa Mesa, CA 92626

(714) 540-6677

Offers a full line of lead-acid batteries suitable for EVs.

Concorde Battery Corp.

Mailing: 2009 W. San Bernadino Road, West Covina, CA 91760

(818) 962-4006

Offers lead-acid batteries for aircraft use.

Discover Energy Corp.
Mailing: Suite 880-999 West Broadway, Vancouver BC V5Z 1K5, Canada
(604) 730-2877
E-mail: info@discover-energy.com

Eagle-Picher Industries
Mailing: P.O. Box 47, Joplin, MO 64802
(417) 623-8000
Offers a full line of lead-acid batteries suitable for EVs.

East Penn Manufacturing Company, Inc.
Web site: www.eastpenn-deka.com
Mailing: Deka Road, Lyon Station, PA 19536
(610) 682-6361
Customer service: (610) 682-4231

EnerSys
Mailing: 2366 Bernville Road, Reading, PA 19605
(610) 208-1991
Manufacturer of the Odyssey battery and others.

Hawker
Web site: www.hawkerpowersource.com
Mailing: P.O. Box 808, 9404 Ooltewah Industrial Drive, Ooltewah, TN 37363
(423) 238-5700 or (800) 238-VOLT
Fax: (423) 238-6060

Northeast Battery
Web site: www.northeastbattery.com
Mailing: 200 Saw Mill River Road, Hawthorne, NY 10532
(800) 441-8824
Fax: (508) 832-2706

OPTIMA Batteries, Inc.
Web site: www.optimabatteries.com
Mailing: 5757 N. Green Bay Avenue, Milwaukee, WI 53209
(888) 867-8462
E-mail: info@optimabatteries.com

Saft
Web site: www.saftbatteries.com
See Web site for local contacts and suppliers. Saft is the world's leading designer, developer, and manufacturer of advanced technology batteries for industrial and defense applications. You will need to visit the Web site for your local battery dealer and product information. They are a worldwide company.

Storage Battery Systems, Inc.
Web site: www.sbsbattery.com
Mailing: N56 W16665 Ridgewood Drive, Menomonee Falls, WI 53051
(262) 703-5800

SAL
Mailing: 251 Industrial Boulevard, P.O. Box 7366, Greenville, NC 27835-7366
(919) 830-1600
Manufactures nickel-iron and nickel-cadmium batteries suitable for EVs.

Trojan Battery Co.
Mailing: 12380 Clark Street, Santa Fe Springs, CA 90670
(800) 423-6569
(213) 946-8381
(714) 521-8215
Trojan has manufactured deep-cycle lead-acid batteries suitable for EV use longer than most companies and has considerable expertise.

U.S. Battery Manufacturing Co.
Mailing: 1675 Sampson Avenue, Corona, CA 91719
(800) 695-0945
(714) 371-8090
Manufactures deep-cycle lead-acid batteries suitable for EVs. Thriving today with distributors all around.

Yuasa Battery (Europe) GmbH
Mailing: Wanheimer Straße 47, 40472 Düsseldorf, Germany
+49 (0)211 417 90 0
Fax: +49 (0)211 417 90 11
E-mail: info@yuasa-battery.de
Manufactures deep-cycle lead-acid batteries suitable for EVs.

Yuassa-Exide
Mailing: 9728 Alburtis Avenue, P.O. Box 3748, Santa Fe Springs, CA 90670
(800) 423-4667
(213) 949-4266

Valence Technology
Web site: www.valence.com
Mailing: 12303 Technology Boulevard, Suite 950, Austin, TX 78727
(512) 527-2900
Design and manufacture programmable lithium iron magnesium phosphate packs.

Chargers

There are many battery charger manufacturers; this list will get you started.

Avcon Corporation

Mailing: 640 Ironwood Drive, Franklin, WI 53132

(877) 423-8725

Fax: (414) 817-6161

E-mail: powerpak@webcom.com

Curtis Instruments, Inc.

Mailing: 200 Kisco Avenue, Mount Kisco, NY 10549

(914) 666-2971

Curtis PMC

Web site: www.curtisinst.com

Mailing: 235 East Airway Boulevard, Livermore, CA 94551

(925) 961-1088

Supplies a number of different components for EV, including motor controllers, gauges, battery chargers, contactors, and more. See Web site for complete listing. Also has offices in Europe and Asia.

ElectroCraft Systems

Web site: www.evcraft.com

Mailing: 23 Paperbirch Drive, Toronto, ON M3C 2E6, Canada

(416) 391-5958

E-mail: sales@evcraft.com

elcon@jps.net

Excellent compact chargers with 20 years of experience in high-frequency switching applications. Chargers are programmable to your battery type and pack voltage.

K&W Engineering

Mailing: 3298 Country Home Road, Marion, IA 52302

(319) 378-0866

K&W's lightweight, transformerless chargers are designed for onboard use.

Lester Electrical

Web site: www.lesterelectrical.com

Mailing: 625 West A Street, Lincoln, NE 68522

(402) 477-8988

Lester has been manufacturing battery chargers suitable for EV use longer than most companies and has considerable expertise.

Manzanita Micro

Rich Rudman

Web site: www.manzanitamicro.com

Mailing: 5718 Gamblewood Rd. NE, Kingston, WA 98346

(360) 297-7383

Designer Joe Smalley and protégé Rich Rudman make a range of fully powered factor-corrected chargers that deliver 20–50 A dc into traction packs from 48–312 V from any line source (120–240 V).

Zivan USA

Web site: www.zivanusa.com

Mailing: 215 14th Street, Sacramento, CA 95814

(916) 441-4161

Fax: (916) 444-8190

Electric Motorcycle Sales

Electric Cyclery

Web site: www.greenspeed.us/jackal_electric_bicycle.htm

Mailing: 910 North Coast Hwy., Laguna Beach, CA 92651

(949) 715-2345

Electric Motorsport

Mailing: 2400–2404 Mandela Parkway, Oakland, CA 94607

E-mail: sales@electricmotorsport.com

(510) 839-9376

Enertia Bike

Web site: www.enertiabike.com/

EVdeals

Web site: www.evdeals.com

Mailing: 9 South Street, Plainville, MA 02762

(508) 695-3717

Fax: (508) 643-0233

EVTAmerica

Web site: www.evtamerica.com

Mailing: 3515 SW 99 Avenue, Miami, FL 33165

(305) 480-6007

Skype phone number: (305) 767-4406

Fax: (305) 229-8831

ThunderStruck Motors

Web site: www.thunderstruck-ev.com/jackal_home.htm

Mailing: 3200 Dutton Avenue, No. 220, Santa Rosa, CA 95407

(707) 575-0353

Best option for technical questions and direct service if there are any electrical/mechanical issues.

21 Wheels

Web site: www.21wheels.com

Mailing: 637 S. Broadway, Suite 227, Boulder, CO 80305

(303) 544-0025

Vectrix USA

Web site: www.vectrix.com

Mailing: Tech Plaza III, 76 Hammarlund Way, Middletown, RI 02842

(401) 848-9993

Fax: (401) 848-9994

Vectrix Europe

Mailing: Hazeley Enterprise Park, Hazeley Road, Twyford, Hampshire SO21 1QA, United Kingdom

+44 (1962) 777 600

Fax: +44 (1962) 713 113

Vectrix Service

Mailing: 55 Samuel Barnett Boulevard, New Bedford, MA 02745

(508) 992-5300

Fax: (508) 992-6252

Vogelbilt Corp.

Web site: www.vogelbilt.com

Mailing: 656 Welwood Avenue, C 318, Lindenhurst, NY, 11757

E-mail: info@vogelbilt.com

Zero Motorcycles, Inc.

Web site: www.zeromotorcycles.com/

Mailing: 1 Victor Square, Scotts Valley, CA 95066

(888) RUN-ZERO or (888) 786-9376

Other Parts

Here you'll find an assortment of goodies designed to assist your EV enjoyment and pleasure; again, it's not an all-inclusive list—just one to get you started.

Cruising Equipment Co.

Mailing: 6315 Seaview Avenue, Seattle, WA 98107

(206) 782-8100

Offers the ampere-hour+ meter for monitoring the state of battery charge. Sold to Xantrax. Very versatile and powerful SOC instrumentation.

Sevcon, Inc.

Web site: www.sevcon.com

Mailing: 155 Northboro Road, Southborough, MA 01772

(508) 281-5500

European Manufacturers, Converters, and Consultants

This is a small listing of European businesses to get you started.

AVERE European Association for Battery, Hybrid and Fuel Cell Electric Vehicles

Web site: www.avere.org

Mailing: c/o VUB-TW-ETEC, Bd. de la Plaine, 2-BE 1050 Brussels, Belgium

E-mail: avere@vub.ac.be

AVERE is a nonprofit association, founded in 1978 under the aegis of the European Community, as a European network of industrial manufacturers and suppliers for EVs. The association's goal is to promote the use of battery, hybrid and fuel cell EVs.

Electro Vehicles Europe (EVE)

Web site: www.electro-vehicles.eu

Head office: Bergamo, Lombardy, Italy

Conversion garages:

Bergamo, Lombardy, Italy

Neunkirchen, Saarland, Germany

+39-035-0604772

+39-339-5761387

Books, Articles, and Papers

There have been a number of books and thousands of articles and papers written about EVs, both technical and nontechnical. Here are some available related books and manuals and a sampling of a few nontechnical articles that will give you instant expertise in the subject area.

Books

Sherry Boschert, *Well-to-Wheel Emissions: The Cleanest Cars*. Plug In America, Presentation to EVS 23, California, 2007.

T. R. Crompton, *Battery Reference Book*, 2nd ed. Reed Educational and Professional Publishing, 1996.

Tony Foale, *Motorcycle Handling and Chassis Design: The Art and Science*. Tony Foale, 2006.

M. Hackleman, *Design and Build Your Own Electric Vehicles*. Earthmind, 1977.

M. Hackelman, *The New Electric Vehicles: A Clean and Quiet Revolution*. Home Power, 1996.

W. Hamilton, *Electric Automobiles*. McGraw-Hill, 1980.

C. R. Jones, *Convert Your Compact Car to Electric*. Domus Books, 1981.

T. Lucas and F. Ries, *How to Convert to an Electric Car*. Crown Publishers, 1980.

D. F. Marsh, *Electric Vehicles Unplugged*. South Florida EAA, 1991.

E. Marwell, *Battery Book 1: Lead Acid Traction Batteries*. Curtis Instruments, 1981.

S. McCrea and R. Minner, *Why Wait for Detroit?* South Florida EAA, 1992.

Gary Powers, *From Gas to Electric Power: A Conversion Experience*. Longbarn Press, 1997.

S. R. Shackett, *The Complete Book of Electric Vehicles*. Domus Books, 1979.

R. J. Traister, *All About Electric & Hybrid Cars*. Tab Books, 1982.

E. H. Wakefield, *The Consumer's Electric Car*. Ann Arbor Science, 1977.

B. Whitener, *The Electric Car Book*. Love Street Books, 1981.

Manuals

"Battery Technical Manual," Battery Council International, Chicago, 1998, www.batterycouncil.org/.

M. Brown, with S. Prange, "Convert It." Electro Automotive, 1989.

D. Chan and K. Tenure, "Electric Vehicle Purchase Guidelines Manual." EVAA, 1992.

Department of Energy, "Primer on Lead-Acid Storage Batteries." Washington, DC, 1995, http://tis.eh.doe.gov/techstds/standard/hdbk1084/hdbk1084.pdf, www.tpub.com/content/doe/hdbk1084/index.htm.

C. Ellers, "Electric Vehicle Conversion Manual." C. Ellers, 1992.

G. Staff, "Electric Car Conversion Book." Solar Electric Engineering, 1991.

B. Williams, "Guide to Electric Auto Conversion." Williams Enterprises, 1981.

Articles

"Battery and Electric Vehicle Update," *Automotive Engineering*, September 1992, p. 17.

Battery Digest, www.batteriesdigest.com

S. F. Brown, "Chasing Sunraycer across Australia," *Popular Science*, February 1988, p. 64.

R. Cogan, "Electric Cars: The Silence of the Cams," *Motor Trend*, September 1991, p. 71.

L. Frank and D. McCosh, "Power to the People," *Popular Science*, August 1992, p. 103.

——, "Alternate Fuel Follies," *Popular Science*, July 1992, p. 54.

——, "Electric Vehicles Only," *Popular Science*, May 1991, p. 76.

D. H. Freedman, "Batteries Included," *Discover*, March 1992, p. 90.

Chris Longhurst, "Vehicle Basic Maintenance," www.carbibles.com.

R. Krause, "High Energy Batteries," *Popular Science*, February 1993, p. 64.

P. McCready, "Design, Efficiency and the Peacock," *Automotive Engineering*, October 1992, p. 19.

P. S. Meyers, "Reducing Transportation Fuel Consumption," *Automotive Engineering*, September 1992, p. 89.

G. A. Pratt, "EVs: On the Road Again," *Technology Review*, August 1992, p. 50.

"Propulsion Technology: An Overview," *Automotive Engineering*, July 1992, p. 29.

D. C. White et al., "The New Team: Electricity Sources Without Carbon Dioxide," *Technology Review*, January 1992, p. 42.

Publishers

Here are a few companies that specialize in publications of interest to EV converters.

Battery Council International

Mailing: 401 N. Michigan Avenue, Chicago, IL 60611
(312) 644-6610
Publishes battery-related books and articles.

Institute for Electrical and Electronic Engineers (TREE)

IEEE Technical Center
Mailing: Piscataway, NJ 08855
Publishes numerous articles, papers, and proceedings. Expensive, but one of the best sources for recent published technical information on EVs.

Lead Industries Association

Mailing: 292 Madison Avenue, New York, NY 10017
Publishes information on lead recycling.

Seth Leitman

Founder, Green Living Guy
Web site: www.greenlivingguy.com
Author: *Build Your Own Electric Vehicle* and *Build Your Own Plug-in Hybrid*
Consulting Editor: *Green Guru Guides*
Mailing: 100 South Bedford Road, Suite 340, Mt. Kisco, NY 10549
(914) 703-0311

Society of Automotive Engineers (SAE) International

Mailing: 400 Commonwealth Drive, Warrendale, PA 15096-0001

(412) 772-7129

Publishes numerous articles, papers, and proceedings. Also expensive, but the other best source for recent published technical information on EVs.

Newsletters

Here are a few companies that specialize in newsletter-type publications of interest to EV converters.

Electric Grand Prix Corp.

Mailing: 6 Gateway Circle, Rochester, NY 14624

(716) 889-1229

Electric Vehicle Consultants

Mailing: 327 Central Park West, New York, NY 10025

(212) 222-0160

Solar Mind

Mailing: 759 S. State Street, No. 81, Ukiah, CA 95482

(707) 468-0878

Online Industry Publications

These online publications report on industry activity, manufacturer offerings, and local electric drive–related activities.

Advanced Battery Technology

www.7ms.com/abt/index.html

Advanced Fuel Cell Technology

www.7ms.com/fct/index.html

Earthtoys

www.earthtoys.com

A resource for alternative energy and hybrid transportation information and features. In addition to the bimonthly e-magazine, there is also an up-to-date news page, link library, company directory, event calendar, product section, and more.

e-Drive Magazine

www.e-driveonline.com/

Features new products, services, and technologies in motors, drives, controls, power, electronics, actuators, sensors, ICs, capacitors, converters, transformers, instruments, temperature control, packaging, and all related subsystems and components for electrodynamic and electromotive systems.

Electrifying Times

www.electrifyingtimes.com
Provides interesting information on EVs and the industry.

EV World

evworld.com
Houses an online "library" of EV-related reports, articles, and news releases available to the general public. EV owners also can register and share their experiences with others. Visitors can sign up for a weekly EV newsletter. EV World has information about conversions and conversion suppliers and a list of popular EV conversion vehicles (www.evworld.com/archives/hobbyists.html).

Fleets & Fuels

www.fleetsandfuels.com
A biweekly newsletter (distributed online) providing business intelligence on alternative fuel and advanced vehicles technologies encompassing electric drive, natural gas, hydraulic hybrids, propane and alcohol fuels, and biofuels. The newsletter is dedicated to making the AFVs business case to fleets.

Greencar Congress

www.greencarcongress.com

Hybrid & Electric Vehicle Progress

www.hevprogress.com
Formerly Electric Vehicle Progress. Follows new EV products, including prototype vehicles; provides status reports on R&D programs; publishes field test data from demonstration programs conducted around the world; details infrastructure development, charging sites, and new technologies; and includes fleet reports, battery development, and a host of other EV-related news. Published twice a month.

Industrial Utility Vehicle & Mobile Equipment Magazine

www.specialtyvehiclesonline.com/
Dedicated to engineering, technical and management professionals as well as dealers and fleet managers involved in the design, manufacture, service, sales and management of lift trucks, material handling equipment, facility service vehicles and mobile equipment, golf carts, site vehicles, carts, personal mobility vehicles, and other types of special purpose vehicles.

Grassroots Electric Drive Sites

AKOG (Another Kind of Green)
www.reverbrock.org
John Mayer's brand, AKOG (Another Kind of Green) was created from the belief that small steps toward environmental sustainability can effect widespread change when multiplied by a great number of participants.

Coolfuel Roadtrip
www.coolfuelroadtrip.org

The Electric Auto Association
www.eaaev.org
The California-based nonprofit group's site showcases EV technology, has a newsletter, and displays links to EV chapters and owners nationwide.

Northeast Sustainable Energy Association (NESEA)
www.nesea.org
NESEA is a nonprofit membership organization dedicated to promoting responsible energy use for a healthy economy and a healthy environment. NESEA promotes electric drive vehicles (EDs, HEDs, fuel cell EDs) and renewably produced fuels through its annual road rally, the NESEA American Tour de Sol; the U.S. electric vehicle championship; conferences for professionals; and K–12 education that uses sustainable transportation as a theme. NESEA maintains a Web site with a listing of electric cars, buses, and bikes; K–12 educational resources; information on building and energy programs; and a quarterly magazine.

Federal Government Sites

IRS Forms–EV Tax Credits
Qualified EV tax credit forms must accompany any tax returns that are claiming the ownership or purchase of a qualified EV.

Advanced Vehicle Testing Program
http://avt.inel.gov/
Office of Transportation Technologies, U.S. Department of Energy. This Web site is run by the Idaho National Engineering and Environmental Laboratory (INEEL). It offers EV fact sheets, reports, performance summaries, historical data, and a kids' page. Visitors can also request information online.

Alternative Fuels Data Center

www.eere.energy.gov/cleancities/

A comprehensive source of information on alternative fuels. Sections include an interactive map of AFV refueling stations in the United States, listings and descriptions of different alternative fuels and AFV vehicles, online periodicals, and resources and documents on AFV programs. The site is part of the National Renewable Energy Laboratory's (NREL) Web site.

CALSTART/WestStart

www.calstart.org

A California-based nonprofit organization dedicated to "transforming transportation for a better world." Visitors can read daily and archived industry news updates and publications, search EV-related databases, and interact with other EV owners in an online forum.

Center for Transportation and the Environment (CTE)

www.cte.tv

CTE is a Georgia-based coalition of over 65 businesses, universities, and government agencies dedicated to researching and developing advanced transportation technologies. The site includes industry news, studies and projects, a database of products, and a section on EV education.

Energy Information Administration

www.eia.doe.gov

Hawaii Electric Vehicle Demonstration Project

www.htdc.org/hevdp

A consortium dedicated to furthering EV development and sales in Hawaii. The Web site provides visitors with background on the program and lists accomplishments.

International Partnership for the Hydrogen Economy

www.usea.org/iphe.htm

Serves as a mechanism to organize and implement effective, efficient, and focused international research, development, demonstration, and commercial utilization activities related to hydrogen and fuel-cell technologies. It also provides a forum for advancing policies and common codes and standards that can accelerate the cost-effective transition to a global hydrogen economy to enhance energy security and environmental protection.

Mid-Atlantic Regional Consortium for Advanced Vehicles (MARCAV)

www.marcav.ctc.com

A Pennsylvania-based organization that was established to organize industrial efforts to develop enhanced electric drives for military, industrial, and commercial vehicles. Visitors can review a list of MARCAV projects and research specific projects.

Northeast Alternative Vehicle Consortium (NAVC)

navc.org

A Boston-based association of private- and public-sector organizations that works to promote advanced vehicle technologies in the Northeast. Visitors can read about NAVC projects and link to related Internet sites.

NREL Home Page

www.nrel.gov

The National Renewable Energy Laboratory (NREL) has created a Web site detailing research efforts in renewable energies and alternative transportation technologies. Some key areas include hybrid vehicle development, renewable energy research, and battery technology research.

Office of Transportation Technologies EPAct & Fleet Regulations

www.eere.energy.gov/vehiclesandfuels/epact/

Many public and private fleets are subject to AFV acquisition requirements under the Energy Policy Act (EPAct) regulations. These requirements differ for different types of fleets. Visit this site to obtain information on fleet requirements and the ways in which you can comply with the EPAct regulations.

THOMAS

www.congress.gov

Acting under the directive of the leadership of the 104th Congress to make federal legislative information freely available to the Internet public, a Library of Congress team brought the THOMAS World Wide Web system online in January 1995. The THOMAS system allows the general public to search for legislation and information regarding the current and past business of the U.S. Congress.

U.S. Department of Defense Fuel Cell Program

www.dodfuelcell.com

U.S. Department of Transportation Advanced Vehicle Technologies Program

http://scitech.dot.gov/partners/nextsur/avp/avp.html

The homepage includes links to the seven regional members of the Advanced Vehicle Program (AVP).

State and Community-Related EV Sites

California Air Resource Board (CARB)

www.arb.ca.gov

This site provides access to information on a variety of topics about California air quality and emissions. The site has general information on all types of alternative fueled vehicle programs and demonstrations. The CARB's mission is to promote and protect public health, welfare, and ecological resources through the effective and efficient reduction of air pollutants while recognizing and considering the effects on the economy of the state. The CARB's guide to zero and near-zero emission vehicles is available at Driveclean.ca.gov.

California Energy Commission

www.energy.ca.gov

This site gives viewers access to information on a variety of topics about California's energy system. The site dedicates a page to EVs, where it has general information on electric transportation, lists sellers of EDs in California, outlines state and federal government incentives for AFVs, and includes a database of contacts in the electric transportation industry.

Mobile Source Air Pollution Reduction Review Committee (MSRC)

www.msrc-cleanair.org

The MSRC was formed in 1990 by the California legislature. The MSRC Web site offers information on a variety of topics regarding California air quality and programs underway to improve it, including a number of EV-related programs and incentives.

Ohio Fuel Cell Coalition

fuelcellsohio.org

OFCC represents the Ohio fuel cell community to multiple audiences, seeks to expand market access, fosters technological innovation, and advances the competitiveness of the Ohio fuel cell community. OFCC member organizations value their collaborative work in public education, information sharing, and better linking of the academic and industrial communities. OFCC provides thoughtful leadership on issues and policies that affect the worldwide fuel cell industry via advocacy and government relations.

San Bernardino Associated Governments (SANBAG)

www.sanbag.ca.gov

SANBAG is the Council of Governments and Transportation Commission for San Bernardino County. The site has various information about current transportation projects underway in the San Bernardino area, as well as information for commuters. Further, the Web site contains funding alerts for individuals and companies looking to obtain project funding and/or assistance.

General Electric Drive (ED) Information Sites

Many Web sites disseminate information on EDs or report industry news and developments. A few of these, which house specific EV-related information, are provided here.

Advanced Transportation Technology Institute

www.atti-info.org

The Advanced Transportation Technology Institute (ATTI), a nonprofit organization, promotes the design, production, and use of battery-powered electric and hybrid electric vehicles. The organization supports individuals and organizations interested in learning more about electric and hybrid-electric vehicles, particularly electric buses.

Alternative Fuel Vehicle Institute

www.afvi.org/electric.html

AFVI was formed by Leo and Annalloyd Thomason, who each have more than 20 years' experience in the alternative fuels industry. In 1989, following more than 5 years' natural gas vehicle market development work for Southwest Gas Corporation and Lone Star Gas Company, the Thomasons founded Thomason & Associates. The company quickly became a nationally known consulting firm that specialized in the market development and use of alternative transportation fuels, particularly natural gas. In this capacity, they incorporated the California Natural Gas Vehicle Coalition and worked extensively with the California Legislature, the California Air Resources Board, the South Coast Air Quality Management District, and other government agencies to establish policies and programs favorable toward alternative fuels. Thomason & Associates also conducted market research and analyses, developed dozens of alternative fuel vehicle (AFV) business plans, and assisted clients in creating markets for their AFV products and services.

Association for Electric and Hybrid Vehicles

www.asne.nl/

ASNE is the Dutch division of the Association Européenne des Véhicules Electriques Routiers (AVERE), an association founded under the auspices of the European Community. The goal of ASNE is to encourage the easy use of totally or partly (hybrid) EVs and vehicles with other alternative propulsion systems in road traffic.

California Fuel Cell Partnership

www.cafcp.org

Introduced in April 1999 and comprised of the world's largest automakers, energy providers, fuel cell manufacturers, and government agencies, the California Fuel Cell Partnership (CaFCP) evaluates fuel cell vehicles in real-world driving conditions, explores ways to bring fuel cell vehicles to market, and educates the public on the benefits of the technology. The CaFCP primary goals aim to demonstrate vehicle technology by operating and testing the vehicles under real-world conditions in California; demonstrate the viability of alternative fuel infrastructure technology, including hydrogen and methanol stations; explore the path to commercialization, from identifying potential problems to developing solutions; and increase public awareness and enhance opinion about fuel cell electric vehicles, preparing the market for commercialization.

Canadian Environment Industry Association

www.ceia-acie.ca

The Canadian Environment Industry Association (CEIA) is the national voice of the Canadian environment industry. CEIA is a business association that, along with its provincial affiliates, represents the interests of 1,500 companies providing environmental products, technologies, and services.

Fair-PR

www.fair-pr.com/background/about.php

The largest international commercial exhibition on hydrogen and fuel cells at the Hannover Fair in Germany, featuring over 100 companies and research institutions from 30 countries.

Fuel Cell Bus Club

www.fuel-cell-bus-club.com

The Fuel Cell Bus Club consists of the participants in the European fuel cell bus projects who intend to introduce fuel cell transit buses to their fleets and establish a hydrogen refueling infrastructure in their cities.

Fuel Cell Information Center

www.fuelcells.org

Green Drinks USA and International

www.greendrinks.org

Every month people who work in the environmental field meet up at informal sessions known as Green Drinks. These events are very simple and unstructured, but many people have found employment, made friends, developed new ideas, and networked with others in many different fields. It's a great way to meet people in varying fields and also for making new contacts.

Hydrogen Now!

www.hydrogennow.org

The mission of Hydrogen Now! is to educate and motivate the public to seek and use hydrogen and renewable energy technologies for greater energy independence and improved air quality.

National Hydrogen Association

www.hydrogenus.org

The National Hydrogen Association is a membership organization founded by a group of 10 industry, university, research, and small-business members in 1989. Today, the NHA's membership has grown to nearly 70 members, including representatives from the automobile industry; aerospace; federal, state, and local governments; energy providers; and many other industry stakeholders. The NHA serves as a catalyst for information exchange and cooperative projects and provides the setting for mutual support among industry, government, and research/academic organizations.

National Station Car Association
www.stncar.com
Although closed at the end of 2004, the National Station Car Association worked for 10 years to guide the development and testing of the concept of using battery-powered cars for access to and egress from mass-transit stations and to make mass transit a convenient door-to-door service. The NSCA released a report (National Station Car Association History) that gives an overview of the program's history.

Natural Gas Vehicle Coalition
www.ngvc.org
The NGVC is a national organization dedicated to the development of a growing, sustainable, and profitable natural gas vehicle market. The NGVC represents more than 180 natural gas companies; engine, vehicle, and equipment manufacturers; and service providers, as well as environmental groups and government organizations interested in the promotion and use of natural gas as a transportation fuel.

Technology Transition Corporation
www.ttcorp.com
Since 1986, Technology Transition Corporation (TTC) has been creating and managing collaborative efforts to accelerate the commercial use of new technologies. They design and implement strategic initiatives to help emerging technologies move from the research and development environment to profitable and sustainable businesses.

ZEVInfo
www.zevinfo.com
Designed by the California ZEV Education and Outreach Group, which was established under the California Air Resources Board's (CARB) ZEV Program. The basis of the Web site is to serve as a "one-stop shop" for information on electric drive products in California. Moreover, the Web site's goal is to inform the public of the benefits and availability of advanced electric drive technologies, from early deployment and on into the future.

Notes

Chapter 1

1. Bob Brant and Seth Leitman, *Build Your Own Electric Vehicle*, 2nd ed. New York: McGraw-Hill, 2008, p. 2.
2. *Ibid.*
3. *Ibid.*, p. 5.
4. *Ibid.*, p. 9.

Chapter 2

1. U.S. Environmental Protection Agency, www.epa.gov.
2. www.epa.gov/climatechange/emissions/downloads09/07Trends.pdf.
3. www.electric-bikes.com/benefits.html.
4. www.ewhosellelectricmotorcycles.
5. nhtsa.dot.gov/cars/rules/regrEmotorcycle/Emotorcyclealuate/pdf/809662.pdf.
6. U.S. Department of Energy.
7. U.S. Department of Energy, Energy Information Administration.
8. U.S. Department of Energy figures.
9. www.electric-bikes.com/envbenefits.html.
10. www.electric-bikes.com.
11. www.electric-bikes.com/benefits.html.
12. *Ibid.*
13. Basic Petroleum Statistics, Energy Information, U.S. Department of Energy, http://en.wikipedia.org/wiki/Energy_policy_of_the_United_States#_note-PetFact.
14. http://frwebgate.access.gpo.gov/cgi-bin/getdoc.cgi?dbname=2000_register&docid =00-14446-filed.pdf.

Chapter 3

1. A. Girdler, "First Fired, First Forgotten," *Cycle World*, February 1998, pp. 62–70.
2. www.pbs.org/now/shows/223/electric-car-timeline.html and http://en.wikipedia.org/wiki/History_of_electric_motorcycles_and_scooters.
3. www.forkliftparts.co.uk/history.htm.
4. www.econogics.com/ev/evhista.htm.
5. *Ibid.*
6. www.electricmotorbike.org.
7. www.electrifyingtimes.com/bill.html.
8. www.killacycle.com/2007/11/11/7824-168-mph-at-pomona-ahdra-nov-10th.
9. www.A123systems.com.
10. http://evworld.com/article.cfm?storyid=1651.
11. www.vectrix.com/shared/files/Rel-Vectrix percent2007-22-08.pdf.

Chapter 4

1. From *Treehugger.com* and Discovery Communications, LLC.
2. www.treehugger.com/files/2008/11/electric-motorcycles-dirtbikes-7-cool-green.php.
3. *Ibid.*
4. www.zeromotorcycles.com/zero-x-features.php.
5. http://www.treehugger.com/files/2008/11/electric-motorcycles-dirtbikes-7-cool-green.php?page=2.
6. www.electric-bikes.com/motor/ninja.html.
7. www.treehugger.com/files/2008/09/honda-yamaha-electric-motorcycles-50cc- 2010-2011.php.
8. Bob Brant and Seth Leitman, *Build Your Own Electric Vehicle*, 2nd ed. New York: McGraw-Hill, 2008, pp. 81–82.

Chapter 7

1. http://inventors.about.com/library/inventors/blbattery.htm.
2. www.windsun.com/Batteries/Battery_FAQ.htm#Battery%20Charging.
3. www.mpoweruk.com/lithiumS.htm.
4. Frost and Sullivan, "World Starting, Light, and Ignition (SLI) Lead Acid Battery Market," September 7, 2004, and IC Consultants, Ltd., "Lead: The Facts," p. 49, December 2001.
5. U.S. Geological Survey, *Mineral Commodity Summaries.* Washington, DC: USGS, January 2007, and www.batterycouncil.org.
6. Bob Brant and Seth Leitman, *Build Your Own Electric Vehicle*, 2nd ed. New York: McGraw-Hill, 2008, p. 181.
7. www.vonwentzel.net/Battery/00.Glossary/.

8. *Ibid.*
9. U.S. International Trade Commission, "ITC Trade DataWeb," March 2008, http://dataweb.usitc.gov.
10. www.iso.org/iso/iso_catalogue/catalogue_tc/catalogue_detail.htm? csnumber=27117.

Chapter 8

1. www.sparkmuseum.com/motors.htm.
2. *Quarterly Journal of Science* 12:521, 1821.
3. Andrew L. Simon, *Made in Hungary: Hungarian Contributions to Universal Culture.* Simon Publications, 1998, p. 207.
4. "The Dynamo: Current Commutation," *Hawkins Electrical Guide.* New York: Theo Audel & Co., 1917.
5. www.physclips.unsw.edu.au.
6. www.4qd.co.uk/fea/pmm.html
7. Ernest H. Wakefield, *History of the Electric Automobile.* SAE Publications Group, p. 207.
8. http://everything2.com/title/Synchronous percent20speed.
9. www.elec-toolbox.com/Formulas/Motor/mtrform.htm.

Chapter 9

1. www.killacycle.com.
2. Ernest H. Wakefield, *History of the Electric Automobile.* SAE Publications Group, p. 192.
3. www.metricmind.com.
4. www.zapi.co.za.
5. www.navitastechnologies.com.
6. www.alltraxinc.com.
7. www.curtisinst.com.
8. www.brusa.biz.

Chapter 10

1. www.mpoweruk.com/chargers.htm.
2. Bob Brant and Seth Leitman, *Build Your Own Electric Vehicle,* 2nd ed. New York: McGraw-Hill, 2008, pp. 221–223.
3. www.powerdesignersusa.com and www.metricmind.com/bms.htm.

Index

TAB
Green Guru
Guide

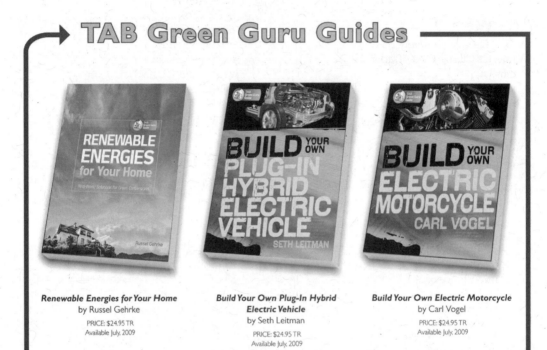

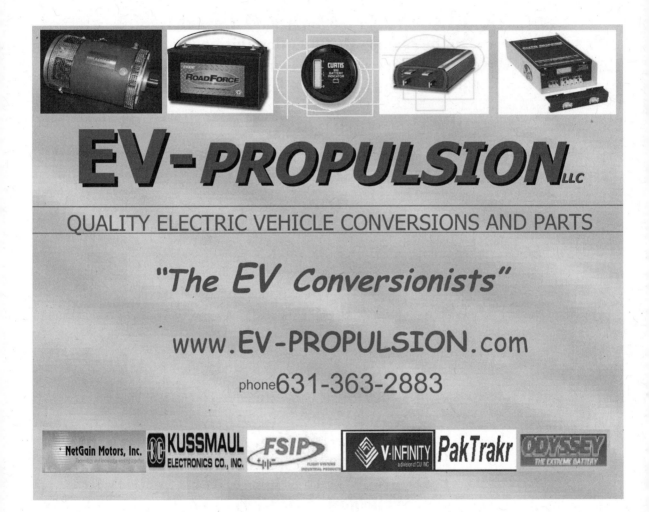

ℕ REVERB

Deeply rooted within the music and environmental communities, Reverb educates and engages musicians and their fans to take action toward a more sustainable future.

Reverb works with artists to minimize the carbon footprint associated with touring by implementing both front stage and backstage greening elements. Some of these backstage components include coordinating biodiesel fueling for tour buses and trucks, setting up extensive recycling programs, providing biodegradable catering products and non-toxic cleaning supplies, and setting the band and crew up with customized water bottles.

Front of stage components are aimed at reaching fans and encouraging them to take action. Informative greening websites let fans know about the green steps their favorite artists are taking and provide resources like online carpooling networks, volunteer opportunities, and more. Reverb's Eco-Village, set up before each concert, allows fans to offset their carbon footprint, sample eco-friendly products, and learn more about actions they can take in their own lives.

With Reverb's help, artists are able to use their voice and set an example to encourage fans to be more mindful of the environment.

- Virtual Eco-Village/Mini-Site
- Facebook
- Myspace
- E-blast content
- Online Outreach
- Carbon Neutral Concerts and Venues
- Biodiesel for Vehicles and Generators
- Waste Reduction
- Biodegradable Catering Products
- Recycling
- Green Bus Supplies and Cleaners
- Energy Efficiency
- Green Contract Rider
- Eco-Friendly Merchandise
- Green Sponsorship
- On Site and On-Line Fan Outreach

For more information: info@reverbrock.og | http://www.reverbrock.org

John Mayer's brand, AKOG (Another Kind of Green) was created from the belief that small steps toward environmental sustainability can effect widespread change when multiplied by a great number of participants.

In fact, through participation in the AKOG program, fans have already offset over 2,200 *tons* of CO_2 pollution, equal to not driving over 4.4 MILLION MILES OF DRIVING!

Join John Mayer in the fight against global warming and take your first step today.

- Carbon offsets to account for CO_2 emissions from venue energy use, trucks and busses, flights and hotels.
- Inviting local and national non-profit groups to be a part of the Reverb Eco-Village to educate and engage fans
- Sustainable supplies such as biodegradable and reusable catering products and local and organic food

In conjunction with Reverb, we will be helping offset each show with wind power, putting together a "village" in the concourse that consists of environmentally and socially minded non-profits and green sponsor types, and most importantly providing cool offset stickers so you can neutralize the pollution from your drive to and from the show

For more information: info@reverbrock.og | http://www.reverbrock.org

To see Carl Vogel's Electric Motorbike in action, and other vehicles powered by wind, vegetable oil, and even FOOD ... you can visit www.coolfuelroadtripstore.com and receive a 10% discount when you buy your COOLFUEL DVDs.

Just enter Vogel on your order for your special discount.